DICKENS THE ENCHANTER

DICKENS
THE ENCHANTER

Peter Conrad

BLOOMSBURY CONTINUUM
LONDON · OXFORD · NEW YORK · NEW DELHI · SYDNEY

BLOOMSBURY CONTINUUM
Bloomsbury Publishing Plc
50 Bedford Square, London, WC1B 3DP, UK
Bloomsbury Publishing Ireland Limited,
29 Earlsfort Terrace, Dublin 2, D02 AY28, Ireland

BLOOMSBURY, BLOOMSBURY CONTINUUM and the Diana logo are trademarks of
Bloomsbury Publishing Plc

First published in Great Britain 2025

Frontispiece image: Dickens at a public reading by flickering gaslight, with some
of his characters in the audience – illustration by Neville Dear © Look and
Learn / Bridgeman Images

For legal purposes the Acknowledgements on pp. 277–8 constitute an extension of this
copyright page

Bloomsbury Publishing Plc does not have any control over, or responsibility for, any third-
party websites referred to or in this book. All internet addresses given in this book were
correct at the time of going to press. The author and publisher regret any inconvenience
caused if addresses have changed or sites have ceased to exist, but can accept no
responsibility for any such changes

A catalogue record for this book is available from the British Library

Library of Congress Cataloguing-in-Publication data has been applied for

ISBN: HB: 978-1-3994-0919-3; eBook: 978-1-3994-0915-5; ePDF: 978-1-3994-0916-2

2 4 6 8 10 9 7 5 3 1

Typeset by Deanta Global Publishing Services, Chennai, India
Printed and bound in Great Britain by CPI Group (UK) Ltd, Croydon CR0 4YY

To find out more about our authors and books visit www.bloomsbury.com
and sign up for our newsletters

For product safety related questions contact productsafety@bloomsbury.com

CONTENTS

Preface: A Visionary Companion

At the conclusion of *The Pickwick Papers*, Dickens arranges happy endings for the Pickwickians, then suffers a tremor of regret. With their future secured, he realises that he must now part from his 'visionary companions of many solitary hours'. This is neither a soft-hearted whimsy nor a knowing meta-fictional wink: the attachment was genuine, and I feel the same way about Dickens. He has accompanied me throughout my life, and his characters have rowdily enlivened the uncountable solitary and silent hours that I have spent reading him.

David Copperfield testifies that, in his unhappy childhood, books represented the 'hope of something beyond that place and time'. So it was for me as a schoolboy in Australia in the early 1960s. Although I was not unhappy, that hope was infused with fear, since Dickens brought an enticing darkness to the bright, bland suburb where I grew up. It was too soon for me to find Dickens funny, because comedy requires knowledge of the world and acceptance of its contradictions; I found him frightening instead. I must have seen David Lean's films of *Oliver Twist* and *Great Expectations* before I read the novels, which may be why my earliest memories of Dickens are starkly monochrome. A pregnant woman hauls herself across a dark moor in a thunderstorm, past bare twitching trees and thorns like barbed wire; a boy runs through a stagnant marsh beneath gibbets with dangling nooses and enters a churchyard where the gravestones tilt on humped mounds, as if the interred bodies were struggling back to the surface. Those opening scenes from the films could not have been more remote from my own surroundings, but that was why they enthralled me. Even dimly and at second hand, I began to understand that art offered new ways to see the world, or glimpses of worlds that were too far away for me to see.

Later, when I read *David Copperfield*, I was taken aback to discover that Dickens had looked back down at our empty continent and found a fictional use for it: it came in handy as a disposal area for characters without a future in England. Emily, disgraced by her rich seducer, is shipped out to Australia to redeem herself in the bush. The shiftless Micawber follows, and in the absence of local talent makes a career as a magistrate in New South Wales. Dickens joked about migrating to my home state of Tasmania, then called Van Diemen's Land and notorious as the harshest of Britain's penal colonies. Exasperated by the prospect of a new Tory government in 1841, he said 'Thank God there is a Van Diemen's-land. That's my comfort.' He wondered whether he would 'make a good settler' and 'force myself to the top of the social milk-pot and live upon the cream', but when one of his characters travels to my birthplace, it is in quest of oblivion, not in pursuit of riches. In *Martin Chuzzlewit* the addled Augustus Moddle flees before his wedding to the shrewish Charity Pecksniff and sends a message saying that when she receives it he 'will be – if not a corpse – on the way to Van Dieman's Land'. Was it the novelist or his distracted character who negligently misspelled the destination? I should have been offended, but even if I had read the book in Tasmania I doubt that I would have resented the slight; in those days I assumed that the other hemisphere was literature's rightful home.

In 1968 I went to Oxford as a Rhodes Scholar and started to see Dickens closer to hand. The university's English Literature course excluded him – in those days it stopped short at 1832, deeming everything after the accession of Queen Victoria to be unacademically modish – but his novels supplied me with prototypes for the dotty social misfits, braying patricians and slyly mock-deferential servants I encountered in my college. During my first northern winter I drifted through a London fog and was at last able to understand the opening of *Bleak House*, where the dense, clammy air becomes a numinous poetic atmosphere. George Orwell said that Dickens is everywhere in the background of English life, taken for granted like Nelson on his column in Trafalgar Square, but by setting him up as a monument, his compatriots obscure his strangeness or weirdness. A handful of London pubs named after Dickens or his characters trade on his reputation for jollity, although The Six Jolly Fellowship Porters in *Our Mutual Friend* – still in business in Limehouse, though now called The Bunch of Grapes – is not as hospitable as you expect: it hides in a warren of back alleys, has a verandah that tilts dropsically towards the river, and ejects customers who can't fit in its cramped bar into a 'dark and draughty passage'. The mystique of the place, to which the drinkers in the passage gullibly subscribe, is an 'enchanting delusion' – a uniquely Dickensian conjunction of magic and mental abnormality that warns us not to think of him as snug or cosy.

Yet in the summer of 1969 Dickens came unexpectedly to my aid on foreign ground, during a road trip around the United States with some ill-assorted acquaintances. On his own American tour in 1842, the worst Dickens had to contend with was overheated rooms, overflowing spittoons, and the crush of over-enthusiastic admirers; my fellow travellers and I had to survive thieves who held our car to ransom in Chicago, a police chief in Wisconsin who ordered us out of town before sunset, a storm in Idaho that washed away our tent, and other almost daily disasters. By the time we reached San Francisco I was pining for bookish Oxford, which led me to buy a copy of *The Pickwick Papers* in a wood-panelled shop in Union Square. I still remember how odd the impromptu choice felt at the time, but on the drive back to New York, as we passed through sulphurous Death Valley and the mind-boggling Grand Canyon, swampy Louisiana and arid, endless Texas, the book kept my spirits up because its harmless mishaps and benevolent mood were so incompatible with the electrically hot and frequently hostile America outside.

This made Dickens my link to a fanciful England, which at least from a distance seemed to be as congenial a place as the cottage in Dulwich to which Pickwick retires when his travels end. I now know that *The Pickwick Papers* had sustained others in deadlier circumstances than mine. A neighbour in London recently told me that when her father left for the war in 1939 his knapsack contained an anthology of sayings by Sam Weller, Pickwick's staunch, canny retainer; according to a hand-inked inscription, the book gave him 'a little bit of England' to keep him company on the battlefield. Sam's anecdotes often end in jocose disaster, but his trench humour got my friend's father through Norway, El-Alamein, Sicily, D-Day and the crossing of the Rhine, and in 1945 he brought his talisman safely home, along with the Croix de Guerre. That somewhat battered family heirloom explains why Dickens is so beloved, valued – in spite of his black moods – as emotional ballast.

Thackeray, Dickens's on-and-off friend, said that *A Christmas Carol* was 'a national benefit', and this was upgraded to a benediction by a woman whose simple response to Dickens, Thackeray reported, was to say 'God bless him!' A nation's culture is an industry as well as a church, and the benefaction touched off a commercial bonanza. G. K. Chesterton wittily linked Dickens to the proprietor of an ever-expanding emporium that began trading in Bayswater during the 1860s: Chesterton called him 'a literary Whiteley, a universal provider'. The magazines Dickens edited, *All the Year Round* and *Household Words*, were indeed department stores that displayed a wide range of literary wares; his characters also became commodities, mass-marketed for domestic consumption. Pickwick lent his name to a penny cigar, and a brand of cocoa received an unlikely endorsement from Mrs Gamp, the gin-soaked nurse in *Martin Chuzzlewit*. In *The Mystery of Edwin Drood*, Dickens compares Mrs Crisparkle and her sister to Dresden china shepherdesses on a mantelpiece. Taking the hint, Royal Doulton's Dickens Ware used the figure of the debilitated Little Nell to decorate a butter dish, set Scrooge's skeletal head on a thimble, and turned the ghost of the defunct miser Marley into a nutcracker.

The merchandising of Dickens reached a terminus at a retail park in what used to be the dockyard in Chatham, where Dickens's father was employed as a naval clerk before the family moved to London. Dickens World opened there in 2007, offering visitors a boat ride through the novelist's nightmares. The itinerary took a detour across a graveyard and ended with a splashing descent into the Thames; along the way, vents puffed out the odour of overcooked cabbage, thought to be an authentically Dickensian fragrance. Warren's Blacking Warehouse appeared as a façade, even though for Dickens – who never forgot the humiliation of the time he spent there as a child labourer – it was hardly a recreational site. In the park's version of the abusive Yorkshire school from *Nicholas Nickleby*, no pupils were starved or beaten; instead, touch-screens administered an elementary quiz on Dickens's life and works. On the way out, The Olde Curiosity Shoppe sold souvenirs, but not enough of them, and after a desperate effort to rebrand itself as a wedding venue, Dickens World closed in 2016, owing a hefty tax bill.

The almost bardic status that Dickens enjoys has made him an easy prey for politicians, who seem unaware that his early stint as a parliamentary reporter left him with a lifelong disdain for their prating kind. At the White House in 1981, Margaret Thatcher flattered Ronald Reagan by quoting Dickens, who found Americans, she said, to be frank, brave, cordial and affectionate. She then applied all those adjectival accolades to Reagan, ignoring the fact that Dickens also describes Americans as loud, crass, venal and bigoted. Then in 1989, when France celebrated the bicentenary of its revolution, Thatcher presented President Mitterrand with a first edition of *A Tale of Two Cities*, presumably as a sarcastic joke. She may have assumed that the novel contains a denunciation of regicide, although in *A Child's History of England* Dickens disparages the crown as 'a stewpan without a handle' and treats a series of kings as divinely authorized wastrels; he even excused himself when Queen Victoria first let it be known that she would be happy to receive him in audience. Far from adhering to the 'Victorian values' upheld by Thatcher, he had a scathing contempt for the society of his time and its political, legal, financial and religious institutions, all of which relied on pomp and circumstance to mask their corruption.

Robbed of this radical outrage, Dickens was enrolled as an honorary Tory during the bicentenary of his birth in 2012, when the culture secretary distributed copies of the novels to his Cabinet colleagues. It was an empty gesture, with no expectation that the books would ever be read. At the end of 2019 the Labour leader Jeremy Corbyn suggested in a lame whimsy that he might slip *A Christmas Carol* into Boris Johnson's stocking to show him 'how nasty Scrooge was'. Not to be outdone, Johnson later trivialised Vladimir Putin's threat to use nuclear weapons in Ukraine by likening it to the tittle-tattle of Joe, the fat boy in *The Pickwick Papers*, who tells a scandalised old lady 'I wants to make your flesh creep.' The allusion merely confirmed the bottomless bathos of Johnson's world view.

Dickens the national treasure has no defence against such appropriation. Up on his pedestal, esteemed as a harmlessly genial comedian, he also forfeits the capacity to captivate and alarm that made him such a dark enchanter. I preferred the reaction of another friend who, far from blessing Dickens, blamed him for upsetting her when she read *A Tale of Two Cities* at school. It was not the guillotine and its industrial assembly line of severed heads that she recoiled from; her bad dreams were provoked by the scene in which an aristocrat's carriage runs down and kills a child in the Paris slums. The 'sickening little jolt' to a wheel of the carriage came as a physical shock to her, as did the victim's reduction to a muddy bundle over which its father howls 'like a wild animal'; the Marquis riding in the carriage is vexed because the noise panics his horses and causes an inconvenient delay – a preview, for my friend, of the world's indifferent cruelty. Although it happened far in the past, it left her with an allergy to Dickens. He would surely have taken her distress as a compliment: introducing *A Christmas Carol*, he said he was sending 'the Ghost of an Idea' to haunt his readers in their homes.

Speaking personally, he haunted me in my home throughout 2020 and much of 2021. Others got through the pandemic by adopting puppies; my solution to the contagious jitters was to re-read Dickens, and I soon found that he knew all about emergencies like ours. In Italy in 1844 he glanced into a pit of bones beneath Vesuvius, evidence of 'a great mortality occasioned by a plague'. Typhus spreads in *Bleak House*; characters in other novels are struck down by malaria or swamp-fever. Infection was so prevalent in Dickens's society that he made it one of his metaphors. 'We human creatures breathe an atmosphere,' he says about the viral credulity of the investors defrauded by

Merdle in *Little Dorrit*; 'the poison is communicable'. More efficiently than the signs that called for social distancing, this sentence echoed in my head whenever I ventured into the street.

In 1796 the physician Edward Jenner devised the remedy for which the word vaccine was coined when he used pus from cowpox blisters to immunise a patient against smallpox; Dickens revered Jenner, and in an assault on the cronyism of parliamentary honours he complained that a 'Vaccination Dukedom' had not been conferred on him. I started my reading months before a vaccine for Covid-19 was available, so I reacted with a twinge when Esther Summerson in *Bleak House* catches what appears to be smallpox and is placed in strict confinement. Her distraught young charge Ada is debarred from the sickroom, but sends in letters twice a day from the other side of the door; Esther kisses and caresses the paper, a substitute for physical endearments that might transmit the disease. Without such effusions, I was grateful to be receiving daily communications from Dickens. He regretted parting from the Pickwickians; I dreaded having to part from him, and I shivered when I found that in *A Tale of Two Cities* he treats 'the awfulness . . . of Death itself' bibliographically: forewarned of completion or closure, he laments 'No more can I turn the leaves of this dear book that I loved, and vainly hope in time to read it all. It was appointed that the book should shut with a spring, for ever and for ever, when I had read but a page.' For me, luckily, there were always more pages to read.

At the start I only wanted the books to quieten my nerves and occupy my idleness, but the diversion soon turned into a compulsion. The novels re-enlivened a locked-down London; they also reinvigorated me, getting my head if not my legs out of the house. Coming and going as I pleased, I could inspect the lair of a taxidermist who also articulates skeletons, a castellated suburban villa with its own little moat, a nouveau-riche household stickily redolent of varnish and French polish, and a hundred other caverns of fantasy. Covent Garden still had its vegetable market, with waggonloads of fragrant hay and dogs dozing beneath them. Pantomimes and circuses remained open in this London, and Aladdin's palace from *The Arabian Nights' Tales* intermittently hovered in the distance. Although Virginia Woolf snootily described Dickens as 'a public thoroughfare trodden dusty by a million feet', I was only too glad to accompany his characters on their treks across a terrain that for me was out of bounds. Kate Nickleby walks from home near the Tower of London to work in the West End, with her mother following in late afternoon to join her on the long trip back; Clennam in *Little Dorrit* goes on a weekend stroll of ten miles to Twickenham; Bill Sikes drags Oliver Twist along to rob a house in Chertsey, eighteen miles away in Surrey. I often hoped that one of these pedestrians might stray onto my turf. Some came close. Three or four characters cross Vauxhall Bridge, less than a mile away from me, and Pickwick has sorties to nearby Camberwell and Brixton. Best of all, in a story published in *Household Words*, Dickens situates the Misses Creebles' Boarding and Day Establishment for Young Ladies near the recently opened cricket ground at Kennington Oval, a few minutes from my front door.

Never mind that Miss Creeble is no more than a surname plucked from the air, conjuring into life a creakily feeble schoolmistress. The non-existence of her establishment proves a point made by Esther in *Bleak House* as the houses in an unfamiliar part of London acquire human shapes and stare at her. 'The unreal things,' she says, 'were more substantial than the real', which is exactly what happens when you are in a Dickens novel, whether as a character or a reader. The Pickwickians are said to be 'visionary' because they were envisioned, created as beings of a new kind rather than being copied from nature; the true visionary is Dickens, whose imagination saves us all from the limitations of what passes for reality.

On Planet Dick

O n the seventh of February 1844, Dickens wrote inviting a friend and his family to dinner that evening. It was his birthday, as he proclaimed with a drum-roll that resonated around the globe. 'On this day two and thirty years ago,' he announced, 'the planet Dick appeared on the horizon. To the great admiration, wonder and delight of all who live, and the unspeakable happiness of mankind in general.'

Finely balancing ostentation and irony, Dickens even at this early stage in his career had the right to such bravado. He appeared on the horizon out of nowhere, a novelty and also a nova, and had been delighting mankind since 1836, when he began to publish *The Posthumous Papers of the Pickwick Club*. By 1841, Americans were said to be waiting at the docks to snatch the latest monthly instalment of *The Old Curiosity Shop* from ships as they arrived from Liverpool – an exaggeration but a plausible one, given the emotional investment of readers everywhere in the fate of the heroine Little Nell, whose decline Dickens so artfully protracted. At the time of his birthday in 1844 *The Life and Adventures of Martin Chuzzlewit* was appearing in serial form. Attuned to his market, Dickens noticed when monthly sales flagged and sent the hero on a diversionary excursion to America; he also slowed down the plot to allow favourite characters a chance to exhibit their quirks. In response to popular demand he went on producing fiction and journalism at an unstoppable speed, and after 1858 he gave lucrative recitals of scenes from his novels on tour in Britain and America. His private life – complicated by a wife he curtly discarded, ten children he had to provide for, and a much younger mistress whose existence he concealed – provided no calming relief from these exertions. Worn out by overwork, he died in 1870 at the age of only fifty-eight.

He left instructions for a quiet funeral near his country home and requested that there should be no public announcement. But mankind in general had an overriding claim on him, and arrangements were hurriedly made to bury him in Westminster Abbey, which signalled instant entry into the national pantheon. G. K. Chesterton later awarded him an even more exalted status. Since his books were to be found 'in every house and hut' on all five continents, Chesterton said that Dickens enjoyed 'the omnipresence of a deity'.

Yet he did more than fill all those shelves and cover all that ground. He was truly entitled to call himself a planet, because he moulded his own eccentric microcosm, an outlandish asteroid that can only be called Dickensian. He might be glancing at this achievement in *A Tale of Two Cities* where, promoting himself to an eyrie high above revolutionary France, he gazes at 'the feeble shining of this earth of ours' and marvels that a 'whole world, with all its greatnesses and littlenesses' can be contained in 'a twinkling star'. That extra-terrestrial perspective suited Dickens: in 1836 the anecdotal snatches of London life in *Sketches by Boz* served, he said, as his 'pilot balloon', and in retrospect he admired his pluck in undertaking 'a perilous voyage in so frail a machine'. In one of the sketches, a party of excited aeronauts lift off from the pleasure gardens at Vauxhall in a hot-air balloon, serenaded by a military band whose blaring gives them reason enough to quit 'that particular spot of earth on which they were stationed'. The first edition had a frontispiece by George Cruikshank in which two men, presumably author and illustrator, wave flags from the balloon's basket as they ascend, while spectators below doff hats and flap handkerchiefs to semaphore the public's unspeakable happiness.

Clouds anticlimactically efface the ground as soon as the balloon gains height, so the passengers miss out on an overview of Planet Dick. Later works by Dickens catalogue the oddities they might have observed on a clearer day. The expected London landmarks appear, although St Paul's Cathedral hollowly booms out a call to faith that no one heeds, the Monument commemorating a fire that incinerated the city seems to be on fire itself, and a rumour circulates that if the piers of London Bridge are removed the river will drain away through the resulting plugholes. Further afield, a town in the industrial north has a river that runs purple and factory chimneys that emit 'serpents of smoke'. Dwellings scattered throughout the land include a beached boat turned upside down, a so-called bower carpeted with sand and sawdust, a derelict mansion that houses 'the spider community', a terrace whose red brick glares 'like the painted face of a savage', and a house that spontaneously emits a rumble of thunder and collapses into 'flying particles of rubbish' and a storm of dust. Humans, animals and plants inbreed there. People often belong to a species with a single member, their bodies lacking symmetry or similitude; increasingly they behave like over-wound machines. Witches and hobgoblins survive from darker ages, and the megalosaurus remains extant.

Dickens created or recreated life on a planetary scale, questioning what a character in one of his stories complacently calls 'the magnificent Order of the vast Universe' – and this pious fellow soon realises his own error when he experiences the mind-bending disorder of a haunted house. On his way to Italy in the summer of 1844, Dickens passed through Lyon and noted that it seemed to have 'tumbled, anyhow, out of the sky', strewn down hills like celestial rubble or madly thrown together with stones plucked out of 'fens and barren places', and overrun by human mites who were 'living, or rather not dying till their time should come'. The cosmic prospect is even more desolate in later novels. As the plot of *A Tale of Two Cities* gets underway, the narrator checks that the 'arch of unmoved and eternal lights' remains intact; he then remembers that light from the remotest constellations never reaches us, which implies that the macrocosm has no concern with the earth as 'a point in space where anything is suffered or done'. The eternal arch suddenly founders in *Our Mutual Friend*. On a stroll beside the Thames, the lawyer Eugene Wrayburn watches the stars kindling at dusk when a blow on the head suddenly knocks him unconscious, which causes the infinite spaces to implode: 'with a dreadful crash, the reflected night turned crooked, flames shot jaggedly across the air, and the moon and stars came bursting from the sky'.

Such catastrophes are to be expected on Planet Dick. The tone of Dickens's dinner invitation echoes the roistering hospitality of the Ghost of Christmas Present in *A Christmas Carol*, published only three months before that birthday. But when Scrooge touches the Ghost's robe the banquet of seasonal treats on which he is enthroned immediately vanishes and the old misanthrope is whirled away on a hectic ride through the air; another phantom deposits him in a church-yard beside his own grave. As readers, we may think we are being welcomed to a feast, but we need to brace both for heady flights and abrupt, doomed crashes.

'Some men,' Dickens concedes at the end of *The Pickwick Papers*, 'like bats or owls, have better eyes for the darkness than for the light'; as for himself, he pretends to possess 'no such optical powers' and says he prefers to look ahead optimistically. The disclaimer was a hearty bluff. Dickens felt at home in the shadows, which is why he patrolled London at night to spy on its secret life. While he basked in the admiration, wonder and delight of mankind, he also took pleasure in provoking nocturnal unease or outright terror.

A Christmas Carol puts this black magic to work immediately: it opens with a sentence of death, enforced in a battery of hammer blows. Dickens announces that 'Marley was dead: to begin with', although that is an end not a beginning; he next cites evidence from the registrar's office to ensure that the old skinflint is truly deceased, and for good measure asserts that he was 'as dead as a door-nail'. Then he worries that this moribund metaphor might not achieve the desired result. He would rather 'regard a coffin-nail as the deadest piece of ironmongery in the trade', but 'the wisdom of our ances-tors is in the simile; and my unhallowed hands shall not disturb it, or the Country's done for'. That protest, as disingenuous as the remark about bats and owls in *The Pickwick Papers*, is actually a back-to-front mission statement. Rather than comforting the country, Dickens aimed to disturb it and upset ancestral wisdom; the hand with which he wrote was hallowed, though not in any officiously clerical way.

Early critics were wary of these assaults on their mental composure. Thackeray, discussing *Oliver Twist* in 1840, said that Dickens made the reader 'his captive', obliged to 'follow him whithersoever he leads'. In this case the reader was led into a seamy urban underworld, and Lord Melbourne, Queen Victoria's first prime minister, warned her that the book would bring her into 'debasing' contact with pickpockets and streetwalkers; to her credit, she read it anyway. Dickens's cheeky or smutty comedy offended Walter Bagehot, who in 1858 reproved him for lacking 'sagacity'. George Henry Lewes went further. In 1872 he claimed that Dickens, though capable of arousing 'the sympathy of masses', had nothing to offer 'the cultivated mind'. Although Lewes hesitated to say that Dickens was insane, he called his imaginings 'abnormal' and likened them to the hallucinations of patients in an asylum.

Dickens might not have been surprised by the diagnosis: he indirectly examines the turbulence of his creative brain in *The Chimes*, the story he wrote for Christmas in 1844. Here the impoverished porter Trotty Veck climbs to the belfry in a church steeple, 'high, high, high, up there', removed, like the day-trippers in the Vauxhall balloon, from 'the earth on which men lived'. He is in a state of suicidal despair, but before he can hurl himself off the tower he succumbs to a 'sleep or swoon', during which reality writhes or wriggles into surrealism. Whereas Planet Dick made a bright new addition to the firmament, now there are only frowning clouds and troubled waters as 'the Sea of Thought . . . gives up its Dead' in an agitated flotsam of images. Goblins 'of all aspects and all shapes' run riot among the bells and overtake the lower world. Positioned beside the beds of sleepers, they invade their dreams or are seen 'flashing awful faces . . . from enchanted mirrors which they carried in their hands'. Among the physical and mental hubbub, 'monsters uncouth and wild, arise in premature, imperfect resurrection; the several parts and shapes of different things are joined and mixed by chance'. This is Dickens's most candid account of the goings-on in his cerebral workshop. The mirrors do not reflect bland normality, and the faces in them belong to monsters like the malevolent dwarf Quilp in *The Old Curiosity Shop*, Miss Havisham the cobwebbed bride in *Great Expectations* or the reptilian Fagin in *Oliver Twist*: Trotty's swoon is indistinguishable from the way Dickens saw reality when he was awake. Rationality and calm will be restored, we are told, as 'the mind resumes its usual form' after Trotty's delirium, because 'every man is every day the casket of this type of the Great Mystery'.

That great mystery is the source of our dreams, although Dickens's capital letters hint at the greater mystery of the world's origins. How did this crazy carnival come to exist? Was it the nightmare of a sardonic creator? Nineteenth-century scientists unriddled what the astronomer John Herschel called the 'mystery of mysteries' by setting geology and zoology to question Genesis. Equally intrepid, Dickens probed a mystery that was psychological and aesthetic. When the casket in *The Chimes* opens, it releases a swarm of 'dwarf phantoms, spirits, elfin creatures'. Trotty clings to a pillar to steady himself, with a 'confused idea that such things were, companioning a host of others that were not'. His 'stunned astonishment' is understandable, but Dickens worked along the entire spectrum from what is to what is not. Imagination endowed him with second sight: he could entice a secret or spectral life out of the most ordinary objects, as when a door knocker in *A Christmas Carol* turns into Marley's livid face and then, in 'a dismal light', becomes 'a bad lobster in a dark cellar'.

Because David Copperfield is born overnight on a Friday, neighbourhood soothsayers prophesy that he will be 'privileged to see ghosts and spirits'. David scoffs at the augury, but Dickens was not so dismissive. In 1859 he consulted William Howitt, a ghost-hunter who wrote a history of the supernatural, asking him to recommend eerie addresses where he would be unable to get through the night 'without sleep molestation', and in *The Haunted House* – a collection of tales to which Dickens contributed later that year – the narrator acts on Howitt's advice. The haunting, however, begins before he arrives at the designated house. On the way there, he shares a railway carriage overnight with a goggle-eyed stranger; in the morning his fellow traveller announces that he spent the hours of darkness in conversation with 17,479 ectoplasmic acquaintances, including Pythagoras, Galileo and John Milton, who confesses that *Paradise Lost* was an 'act of mystification'. The narrator alights at the next station, glad to rejoin 'common humanity' and breathe 'the free air of Heaven'. But is he any saner than the 'Express lunatic' on the train? He turns out to be a writer, accustomed to rising before dawn to do 'a day's work before breakfast'. Early morning, he explains, is 'my most ghostly time' – a phrase that makes his sessions of creativity a communion with the netherworld. Sometimes Dickens's spirits are supernatural visitants; more often the apparitions are metaphors, which tamper with actuality or erase it, like the fog in *Our Mutual Friend* that leaves London 'divided in purpose between being visible and invisible, and so being wholly neither'. On Planet Dick, even the weather can be phantasmal.

Before publishing *The Chimes*, Dickens tested its impact at a reading for a select group of friends. During the performance he noticed the actor William Macready weeping, overcome by compassion for the woebegone Trotty. Writing to his wife Catherine about the occasion, Dickens remarked 'what a thing it is to have Power' – a phrase that is one of his most forthright self-declarations. In readings like this he actually deployed triple powers, as a writer, an actor and a magus: his words created life out of thin air, his performance gave the characters a physical presence, and his almost priestly ministrations made the event as uplifting as a church service because of the charitable fellow-feeling he stirred in the listeners. The painter Daniel Maclise sketched the scene, with some listeners covering their tearful faces and others gazing enraptured into the air. A sun rises behind the planetary head of Dickens and shafts of light crown him like a diadem, so that the gathering is almost a literary Last Supper. Meanwhile the goblins from the belfry glower in the corner, awaiting further orders.

Dickens's wonder-working power of imagination grew ever more imperious, and he came to associate it with the preternatural force of industrial machines. In the editorial introducing his magazine *Household Words* he says that he intends to celebrate the 'stupendous bodies' of steamboats and trains in the hope that the traveller will better appreciate 'the Power that bears him onward'. Locomotion seemed magical to Dickens: whisked from London to Paris in only twelve hours by an express train, he called its engine Compact Enchantress. A similar energy bears us onward as we read him, with metaphors as his means of propulsion. When a steamer on the Thames in *Sketches by Boz* is caught in a gale, the table laid for a picnic shakes with 'a feverish pulse' and 'the pigeon-pies looked as if the birds, whose legs were stuck outside, were trying to get them in': the already dead and cooked pigeons, revivified by fright, scramble to bury themselves again under the pie crust. Dickens's account of a storm at sea on his crossing to America in 1842 begins with a water-jug in his cabin 'plunging and leaping like a lively dolphin'. This metaphor is a lucky charm, since dolphins belong in the ocean and know how to navigate, but then Dickens's shoes spring into the air without being placed on his feet, a mirror nailed to the wall transfers itself to the ceiling, and a door opens in the floor to reveal that 'the state-room is standing on its head'. The ship becomes equine, stumbling through liquid pitfalls 'with broken knees and failing legs'; told that a headwind is to blame for the upsets, Dickens pictures 'a human face on the vessel's prow' battered between its eyes by 'fifteen thousand Samsons in one'. His figures of speech have turned against him, and to stay upright in the capsized room he struggles 'to make any arrangement at all compatible with this novel state of things'.

Adjusting to that novelty requires an effort, because metaphors keep everything in flux. Jarndyce in *Bleak House* says that his bellicose friend Boythorn has the bearing of a soldier and the hands of a blacksmith, but can find 'no simile for his lungs', since when he breathes out to talk, laugh or snore, the beams of the house are supposedly shaken by the air he emits. Dickens himself was only once outsmarted – though not for long – by a reality that had already turned itself into a simile. On his arrival in Venice in 1844 he told his friend and future biographer John Forster 'I never saw the thing before that I should be afraid to describe.' The task took courage, because description always involved altering what he saw. Venice, however, was so extravagantly strange that it defied him. 'Opium couldn't build such a place, and enchantment couldn't shadow it forth in a vision,' he said. 'All that I have heard of it, read of it in truth or fiction, fancied of it, is left thousands of miles behind. You know that I am liable to disappointment in such things from over-expectation, but Venice is above, beyond, out of all reach of coming near, the imagination of a man.' Of course Dickens was far from incapacitated, and in these protestations he gears up to recreate the scene, first citing the drug that gave romantic poets access to an artificial paradise, then setting enchantment and vision to replace dull observation, and almost casually equating truth and fiction. He also accuses himself of over-expectation, the aspiring itch that later motivates Pip in *Great Expectations*. Inevitably he surmounts every obstacle, and in *Pictures from Italy* he fantasticates the city's canals, palaces and underwater prisons until, as he triumphantly announced to Forster, Venice becomes 'a bit of my brain'.

Dickens hailed Christmas as a time when 'all common things become uncommon and enchanted', which is what he hoped for whenever he looked at our customary world. In an essay written in 1850 he converted the religious festival into an interlude of volatile revelry from his beloved *Arabian Nights*: the rocking horse in a nursery lifts its rider into the air 'as the wooden horse did with the Prince of Persia', and dates on the dinner table are a reminder that a merchant in the *Tales* uses one to knock out the eye of a genie's invisible son. But the enchantments are not always so giddy. Dora in *David Copperfield*, inaccessible after her father's death, seems to be locked inside 'a magic circle', its perimeter drawn by 'some grim enchanter'. When Florence's mother dies in *Dombey and Son*, the family home expires as well and the girl is left in a funereally 'enchanted abode', where the clocks either tell no time or strike 'unearthly numbers', the glass pendants of the chandeliers tinkle as if sounding a muted alarm, and dust sheets that muffle the furniture twitch in the 'laggard air' like a 'phantom crowd' of ghosts. Such metaphors allow Dickens to move like a shaman back and forth between life and death, substance and shadow, and he sends some of his characters on similar journeys. Crazed by sexual jealousy and hatred of his rival, Bradley Headstone in *Our Mutual Friend* – it is he who knocks out the star-gazing Eugene Wrayburn – goes through his own existential transition. As he broods about vengeance on the night before his death, the description stealthily mortifies him. With a 'charmed flame', the fire that ought to be warming and revitalising him is said to be 'turning him old'; it makes his face look white and haggard, 'as if it were being overspread with ashes', and even his hair seems to be 'degenerating'. By dawn he is 'this decaying statue', the personification of his surname. Dickens's language has the power to give life and also to take it away.

Henry James said that the house of fiction has 'not one window, but a million', and in each of them stands a novelist 'with a pair of eyes, or at least with a field-glass' focused on 'the human scene'. Pickwick and his friends take to the road to study that human scene, but Dickens increasingly preferred to imagine it. Oliver Twist, left alone in Fagin's den, 'would crouch in the corner of the passage by the street-door, to be as near living people as he could'. But the passers-by remain invisible: do they really exist? The door is locked to stop Oliver escaping; he has an 'observatory' upstairs, but its window is 'nailed down, and dimmed with the rain and smoke of years'. Dickensian windows open inwards onto darkness rather than outwards into the light, and doors cannot protect his characters from a panic they carry around inside themselves. After committing a murder, Jonas in *Martin Chuzzlewit* double-locks the door of a room in which he spends the night, and dreams he has fortified it with iron plates fastened by nails to keep out 'an enemy, a shadow, a phantom' – except that, in another metaphorical siege, the wood crumbles, the nails splinter as flimsily as twigs, and the layer of metal armour curls like paper catching fire.

This trauma is a parable about the insurgency of imagination. In 1851, writing to a doctor who sent him an essay on dreams, Dickens said that after a day spent grappling with a story he sometimes dreamed about trying to 'shut a door that *will* fly open'; on other nights he found himself groping for an exit from 'a series of chambers that appears to have no end'. 'The origin of all fable and Allegory,' he conjectured, 'may be referrable to this class of dreams.' As Little

Nell departs on her wanderings in *The Old Curiosity Shop*, Dickens pictures her 'in a kind of allegory', but hers is no pilgrim's progress. The 'wild grotesque companions' she meets on her travels are living replicas of the monkish or baronial curios in the shop where her grandfather, after 'groping among old churches and tombs', trades in 'strange furniture that might have been designed in dreams'; when she dies, the monsters who have dogged her disperse into the dark city or perhaps change back into arthritically stiff chairs and skeletal fire-irons. The first allegory of all, *Psychomachia* by the Latin poet Prudentius, transcribes a battle for the soul in which a figure called Faith tramples a female demon who represents Paganism, after which there is a service of thanksgiving at the temple where Wisdom is enthroned. In the mind of Dickens the fight rages on, with no assured moral victory at the end.

Dozing on his way through Italy by coach in 1844, Dickens drowsily registered sights that he might have dredged up from 'the incoherent but delightful jumble in my brain'. A castle in Ferrara flushed by the sunrise and the sculpted ogres on a church in Modena were excerpts from 'half-formed dreams'; they appeared 'in full distinctness', then dissolved like transparencies in a magic lantern show. Genoa, where he was then spending one of his continental sojourns, had 'all the inconsistency of a dream, and all the pain and all the pleasure of an extravagant reality!' Marble palaces jutted out from streets that clambered up cliffs and released flights of Cupids from their painted walls, while a steep descent plunged into 'a maze of the vilest squalor' among the slums at the water's edge. The vertiginous city seemed 'so wide awake, and yet so fast asleep', as if Dickens had hypnotised it. Characters in the novels often find themselves in that entranced state. Little Nell, half-awake, watches her grandfather steal money to fund his gambling, tries to convince herself that she has not seen it, admits that 'This dream is too real', and concludes in dismay that 'imagination had all the terrors of reality; nay, it was worse'. The wrongful arrest of Nell's friend Kit happens on the same hazy mental threshold: 'Dream-like as the story was, it was true.'

In 1852, discussing his insomnia in *Household Words*, Dickens occupies the same intermediate zone. As he lies restlessly in bed, one side of his mind fantasises at random while the other, still alert, tries to make sense of those demented frolics. He is, he says, living proof of 'the theory of the Duality of the Brain'. A decade after Dickens's death, Nietzsche derived a metaphysical truth from that duality. 'Without dreams,' he proposed in an aphorism, 'man would have found no occasion to divide the world'; he added that this division was the source of our belief in ghosts and in gods, and it may also be the source of art. Dickens narrowed the gap between dream and reality by assuming the role of sorcerer and casting verbal spells. In *A Child's History of England* he mocks the Druids, who 'pretended to be enchanters, and . . . carried magicians' wands', raising structures like Stonehenge with 'ingenious machines' and then claiming that the work was done 'by magic'. He notes that they also made laws to suit themselves and concludes that 'It is pleasant to think that there are no Druids, *now*, who go on in that way, and pretend to carry Enchanters' Wands and Serpents' Eggs – and of course there is nothing of the kind, anywhere.' This was a jab aimed at the venality of contemporary politicians, yet Dickens himself was also an enchanter, and he occasionally brandished his own version of a wand. As he prepared for the first series of public readings from his novels, he was photographed by Herbert Watkins with his script in his left hand and in the right an ivory-handled paper knife – his baton, which he used not to cut pages but to elicit emotions from his audience. He formally assumed the occult persona in a letter written in December 1857. Here he complained of being harassed by the demands of 'my Art', and in a superstitious joke he reached for an analogy from black magic. 'I am,' he announced, 'the modern embodiment of the old Enchanters, whose Familiars tore them to pieces.'

The familiars he had in mind were an enchanter's bestial attendants, like the cat and toad kept by the witches in *Macbeth*, and they appear throughout his novels, always ready to pounce. The cranky housekeeper Mrs Pipchin in *Dombey and Son* has a cat, and when she sits by the fire between it and little Paul they make up 'a book of necromancy, in three volumes'. Tom Scott in *The Old Curiosity Shop*, jokingly called Quilp's valet, is likened to a toad and summoned with cries of 'you dog'. Bill Sikes in *Oliver Twist* has the cur called Bull's Eye as his fanged guardian, and Dora's lapdog Jip bares its teeth at her fiancé David Copperfield, from whom – in a sly pun – it will not 'hear of the least familiarity'. In *Our Mutual Friend* these domestic helpmates are promoted to cosmographers at the planetary observatory in Greenwich, where 'the Familiars of the Astronomer Royal nightly outwatch the winking stars'. If the astronomers are familiars, their royally appointed superintendent must be a wizard or vizier from *The Arabian Nights*.

The lawyer Grewgious in *The Mystery of Edwin Drood* has a grumpy clerk called Bazzard, 'a mysterious being, possessed of some strange power' over his employer, 'as though he had been called into existence, like a fabulous Familiar, by a magic spell which had failed when required to dismiss him'. Dickens understood the predicament of the comically browbeaten Grewgious: ruled by his imagination, he made his characters responsible for its rampages and presented himself as a hapless victim. In his story 'The Ghost of Art', the narrator encounters a 'terrible Being' on a steamer in bad weather. This 'man, or demon' condenses out of the mist and reels through a succession of attitudes that suggest he might be a king, a saint, 'a powerful monster', or any number of characters from eighteenth-century novels. The narrator, bewildered, asks 'What are you?' The stranger says he is a model, paid a shilling an hour by the painters who hire him. Reappearing in another storm, he shows off a beard he has grown to expand his range of impersonations. He recombs it to pose as Severity or Benevolence, retreats behind it to represent Jealousy, dishevels it to illustrate Despair, tosses it to portray Rage, then dematerialises in a rumble of thunder. The model is ghostly because he exists only as raw material; to escape from that limbo he needs to fasten on a painter – or perhaps a novelist or a dramatist? – who will assign him a specific character. The narrator regards the process as a kind of demonic possession, and he shudders to think that this freak-ish being, who continues to glare at him from the walls of galleries, still 'lures young artists on to their destruction'.

In the letter about the rebellious familiars, Dickens goes on to recall his own recent performances in Wilkie Collins's play *The Frozen Deep*. Cast as an explorer who nobly sacrifices himself on an arctic expedi-tion, he took pride in being able to keep audiences of two thousand rigid and breathless as he expired, while even the stagehands sniffled sympathetically. But the strain, he said, was tantamount to 'rending the very heart out of my body'. His creativity did come to involve self-harm, not only metaphorically. In 1869 a doctor warned Dickens that his impassioned public readings might cause paralysis or apoplexy and diagnosed his giddy spells as 'threatenings of brain-mischief'. By then the mischief-making familiars had seized the initiative: the balance of power changed when Dickens added to the repertory for his tours the frenetic scene from *Oliver Twist* in which Sikes berates the prostitute Nancy for betraying him and savagely kills her. The details in the novel are harrowing enough – Nancy is blinded by blood from the wound on her skull, and her hair sticks to the club with which Sikes fells her; he then spends all night staring at the corpse while his dog paddles in gore – but in a marginal note on his script Dickens directed himself to stir up 'Terror To The End'. His audiences were agreeably terrorised, while he often staggered offstage near to collapse, his pulse racing and his blood pressure dangerously high.

Three months before Dickens's death, his friend Charles Kent witnessed his 'last and grandest reading' of this episode and described it as solemnly as if he were watching Sydney Carton mount the steps to the guillotine in *A Tale of Two Cities*. Advancing from behind a screen, Dickens spoke to Kent 'in a half-whisper' before he crossed to his podium. His confidential aside paraphrased the letter written more than twelve years before, but with a difference. Now, rather than blaming his familiars, the enchanter promised to destroy himself for the admiration, wonder and delight of his public. What Dickens said was 'I shall tear myself to pieces.'

2

In the Family

B y February 1844, Dickens could smilingly assume that his thirty-second birthday was a cue for universal joy. Earlier, the world seemed more inclined to demean or discard him. In 1823, not yet twelve and 'such a little fellow' as he plaintively put it, he was removed from school and sent out to work to help defray the debts of his improvident father. His parents, interned in the Marshalsea prison until they settled with John Dickens's creditors, deposited Charles with a crabby crone who rented rooms to children; from Monday morning to Saturday night he pasted labels onto bottles of shoe polish in a warehouse just off the Strand, storing a small loaf and a piece of cheese in the old woman's cupboard for his suppers. His Sunday treat was to visit his parents in the prison. After a year, a legacy enabled his father to pay off what he owed. Let out of the Marshalsea, he extricated Charles from the blacking factory, though his mother favoured leaving him there.

Shamed and lastingly wounded by his ordeal, Dickens kept it a secret and only disclosed the details in a memoir that he entrusted to John Forster in 1847. His tone in this fragment of autobiography is cheerlessly ironic. 'It is wonderful to me,' he wrote, 'how I could have been so easily cast away at such an age': wonderment here means numb disbelief. He was also a castaway of a peculiar kind, not the victim of a shipwreck far from home like Robinson Crusoe or Walter Gay in *Dombey and Son*, since he had been cast out by those who should have taken care of him. With the same sharp-edged resentment, he described his drudgery as a professional initiation, the start of his 'business life'. His task was to cover the pots with layers of paper, tidy up the edges and then, once they had attained a 'pitch of perfection', apply the printed labels. 'Perfection' was his sour joke about an aesthetic standard; 'pitch' made it sound as if he was already dabbling in black ink. Summing up, he declared that during this period he had 'no advice, no counsel, no encouragement, no consolation, no support, from any one that I can call to mind, so help me God'. His abiding grievance punctuates this enumeration of parental failures, and the concluding oath gives the accusation a legal force.

Fifteen years later he referred in a letter to 'the never-to-be-forgotten misery of that old time' and tried to forget the misery by transferring it to 'a certain ill-clad, ill-fed child' – an indigent, anonymous waif he might have seen in the street, his undersized Doppelgänger. Reversing biological precedence, Wordsworth maintained that 'The child is father of the man' and hoped never to lose the boyhood spirit of 'natural piety' on which his poetry depended. Dickens paraphrased that declaration but dented its glad hope in a *Household Words* account of a childhood outing, when he described an unkempt boy whom he then identified as the 'exceedingly uncomfortable and disreputable father of my present self'.

Dickens retained the fresh and vibrant vision that Charles Baudelaire envied in children, who 'see everything as a novelty' and seem 'always intoxicated', yet his exhilaration was inescapably edged with dread. In one of Wordsworth's poems about his own early years, a boy cups his hands at his mouth and blows 'mimic hootings to the silent owls / That they might answer him'; the hallooing develops into screams of delight which Wordsworth soberly summarises as 'concourse wild / Of jocund din!' Dickens's boys are more likely to be begging or picking pockets than romping through the landscape duetting with birds, and his closest equivalent to those poetic hootings comes in *David Copperfield* when a filthy dealer in used clothes – a 'drunken madman' who is said to have sold himself to the devil – peppers his every utterance to David with the ejaculation 'Goroo' and extends this rasping outburst into 'a sort of tune . . . like a gust of wind'.

For Wordsworth, childhood was a paradise that was lost in time but could be regained in space, and he recovered it on his perambulations through the landscapes in which he grew up. Dickens, however, thought of childhood as a hell that was always liable to return from the old time to ensnare him, even though in space he made conscientious efforts to avoid it: in middle age he still looked the other way when walking past Charing Cross, so as not to see the street running down to the river where the blacking factory was located. Two exchanges in *Dombey and Son* convey his conviction that his childhood, rather than being mislaid, had been stolen from him. Doctor Blimber, headmaster at the school in which the disconsolate Paul has been enrolled, asks a rhetorical question about his ailing pupil: 'Shall we make a man of him?' Paul replies, 'I had rather be a child', but that is not an option. Nor is it for Edith, who cynically marries Paul's father after his first wife dies. 'When was I a child? What childhood did you ever leave to me?' she asks her mother, the raddled coquette Mrs Skewton, who raised her with the sole purpose of beguiling and entrapping a rich man. Her mother 'gave birth,' Edith says, 'to a woman'.

A blithe childhood like Wordsworth's was a luxury, as Dickens recognised when he wrote a pair of sentences that he eventually deleted from the manuscript of *Little Dorrit* because the truth they told was too caustic: 'The poor have no childhood. It must be bought and paid for.' In the absence of anyone to pay, his Christmas story *The Haunted Man and the Ghost's Bargain* shows us the unaccommodated child. A tutelary phantom points to a sleeping boy and calls him 'the last, completest illustration of a human creature', 'abandoned to a worse condition than the beasts', unalleviated by any 'humanising touch'. The child is the phantom when young, and in looking back he echoes Dickens's lament in his memoir. 'No mother's self-denying love, no father's counsel, aided *me*,' he says; he compares himself, as Dickens might have done, to a bird expelled from the nest to scavenge for itself.

Dickens endows the infants in his novels with a desolate foreknowledge of what awaits them. Mr Chillip, the physician who delivers David Copperfield, later has a child of his own, 'a weazen little baby, with a heavy head that it couldn't hold up, and two weak staring eyes, with which it seemed to be always wondering why it had ever been born', and in *Bleak House* Caddy Jellyby's baby is a 'tiny old-faced mite', sadly pensive in its crib. One of the Spirits who visits Scrooge temporises between the first and last ages of man. He is 'a strange figure – like a child; yet not so like a child as like an old man, viewed through some supernatural medium, which gave him the appearance of having receded from the view, and being diminished to a child's proportions'. Dickens has been reproached for not allowing his characters to grow and change; he could hardly do so, because he saw life as circular rather than developmental. Beginning and end conjoin to squeeze the middle. Mrs Skewton, for instance, wears a travelling robe 'embroidered and braided like an old baby's', and Little Nell's grandfather naively falls prey to gamblers because he is a 'grey-haired child'. The emotionally unawakened Sally Brass in *The Old Curiosity Shop* has 'passed her life in a kind of legal childhood'; along the way she manages to produce an illegitimate daughter, who is equally stunted – 'an old-fashioned child', she has apparently been 'at work from her cradle'. A second childhood may perhaps be happier than the first, since at least it will have a definitive terminus. In *A Tale of Two Cities* Sydney Carton asks the elderly banker Lorry if in old age childhood seems remote. Lorry touchingly replies that the closer he gets to the end, the nearer he feels to the beginning: it is 'one of the kind smoothings and preparings of the way'. The sentiment recurs in *The Mystery of Edwin Drood*, where fond recollections of 'nursery time' in Cloisterham have a second coming when those who grew up there reach their 'dying hours'.

In an essay on his frequent visits to the Paris morgue, Dickens speaks of childhood as an 'impressible time': his word imagines an imprint, an indentation that leaves a mark like that of inky type on a blank page, rather than a vivid unfocused sensuous impression. 'An intelligent child's observation,' he says, is remarkable for its 'intensity and accuracy', and – surely unnecessarily – he warns 'some who have the care of children' against taking their young charges on outings to see the bloated corpses fished from the Seine. It is bad enough, he adds, to send children into the dark or to coop them up in a bedroom alone as prey to 'the great fear'; if you treat a child in that way, 'you had better murder it'. When Wordsworth said in *The Prelude* that he 'grew up / Foster'd alike by beauty and by fear', he was thinking of an 'impressive discipline of fear' much milder than the disabling horror experienced by Pip in the graveyard in *Great Expectations* as the convict Magwitch rears up behind the tombstones or by Oliver Twist when he is taken to visit Fagin in the condemned cell. Wordsworthian discipline does not extend to the flogging administered to David Copperfield by his stepfather Murdstone; at worst, Wordsworthian fear is his awed sense that nature silently reproves him when he ravages a tree to feast on its crop of hazelnuts.

Wordsworth's account of his 'seed-time' pays grateful tribute to the green earth as 'the nurse, / The guide, the guardian of my heart, and soul / Of all my moral being'. At the age of six, Dickens had an amoral indoor equivalent in his nurse Mary Weller, who was only thirteen when she was engaged to look after him. He honoured her as a 'female bard' and thought that she must have been descended from 'those terrible old Scalds', the Skalds who recited poems about Norse heroes; despite his later warnings about frightening children, her bardic gift to him was an enjoyable terror. At night, as he claims in *The Uncommercial Traveller*, she told him stories that were 'utterly impossible . . . but none the less alarmingly real' – sagas about a swashbuckling serial killer, or a shipwright who enters into a diabolical pact and as a result is forced to sail in a vessel infested with rats, which nibble their way through the boards and sink it, drowning all hands. Nature nursed Wordsworth 'with something of a Mother's mind', but rather than maternally soothing Dickens, Mary sent him into 'the dark corners we are forced to go back to, against our wills'. He meant the inkier corners of his mind: what may sound like a punishment was also a literary initiation.

He soon learned to play his nurse's game, making macabre jokes about the vulnerability of childhood. In *Sketches by Boz* the misanthropic Nicodemus Dumps 'adored King Herod for his massacre of the innocents, and if he hated one thing more than another, it was a child'. Nicodemus in the Bible is a Pharisee who questions Christ about the notion of spiritual rebirth and objects that no one could re-enter his mother's womb to be born again. The latter-day Nicodemus is taken aback when he is asked to be godfather to his nephew's baby, but he cheers himself up by scanning the newspaper's tally of infant deaths, and when he sees the child at its christening he likens it to 'one of those little carved representations . . . blowing a trumpet on a tombstone!' A passer-by in Dickens's story *Tom Tiddler's Ground* tries to persuade a hermit to abandon his 'unnatural solitude' by telling him about a girl called Miss Kimmeens, who when left alone at school for a few hours curses the other girls and the teachers for deserting her, after which she reflects that although they are away enjoying themselves, 'they would all be dead in a few years. . . . It was a religious comfort to know that.' It is a shocking conclusion, and it so shocks the girl herself that she remorsefully rushes out to make conversation with the first stranger she meets, hoping to be welcomed back into the human community.

Although this is presented to the hermit as a moral admonition, it gives a more illicit glimpse of Dickens's dealings with his fictional creations. At the end of *The Pickwick Papers* he says that 'It is the fate of all authors or chroniclers to create imaginary friends, and lose them in the course of art.' Children, however, do not expect to lose the fantastical playmates they invent; Dickens the novelist knew that he would have to give them up or even kill them off. While at work on *The Old Curiosity Shop* he told Forster that he was 'slowly murdering' Little Nell, yet as he approached the conclusion he represented himself as the victim: 'I am the wretchedest of the wretched. . . . Old wounds bleed afresh when I only think of the way of doing it.' After ceremoniously ushering Paul Dombey out of the world he advised those who mourned the non-existent boy to commiserate with each other; their grief, he said, should be 'of that sort which endears the sharers in it, one to another' – a prescription for group therapy. These were ritual killings, hieratic sacrifices, and despite his protest that the death of Nell would feel like a personal bereavement, Dickens excused himself from having to feel the guilt that overcomes Miss Kimmeens.

Remembering his own 'unmerited degradation' as a child labourer, David Copperfield sees himself as 'an innocent romantic boy, making his imaginative world out of such strange experiences and sordid things!' He survived, he says, by inventing histories that blurred ugly facts in 'a mist of fancy'. The imagination of Dickens was not so innocent or so delicately fanciful. He had a warm-hearted fellow-worker in the blacking factory, an orphan whose name, he told Forster, was Bob Fagin. The boy protected him from their rougher fellows; Dickens later 'took the liberty' – as he put it – of giving Bob's surname to the vicious tutor of under-age criminals in *Oliver Twist*, which hardly repaid the favour. Was he wondering what might have become of his young self if he had fallen among thieves, with the blameless Bob as a different kind of mentor? In 1853, remembering his juvenile vagrancy in central London in an essay entitled 'Gone Astray', he gives in to what might be called his 'nostalgie de la boue' – a phrase coined two years later by the dramatist Émile Augier, one of whose characters remarks that a duck transplanted to a lake to swim with swans will hanker after the mucky pond that was its first home. Dickens recalls being thrust into a low crowd of sailors and other ruffians on an early, unaccompanied trip to the theatre in Whitechapel. He suffered 'no depraving influence' but says he 'often wondered since, how long it would take, by means of such association, to corrupt a child nurtured as I had been, and innocent as I was'. He transferred that tempting thought to the horses at the Dedlock estate in *Bleak House*: bored in wet weather, they 'may even beguile the time by improving (perhaps corrupting) the pony in the loose-box in the corner'. Forster remembers Dickens marvelling over the 'wild visions of prodigies of wickedness' that came to him in a criminal rookery in central London. With such an imagination, there was no need for other corrupters.

The children Dickens describes are often incorrigible reprobates. When the Uncommercial Traveller visits a railway restaurant, the young women behind the counter studiously ignore him, and he expects no better from a surly page, whom he dismisses by saying 'he is a boy, and therefore the natural enemy of Creation'. Can the youth really be such an affront to the universe? In a different mood – not so hungry, thirsty and shaken up after a day of railway travel – Dickens might have admired his unregeneracy. Boys like this are the natural enemies of a world designed by adults for their own convenience, and there are plenty of them in his novels: the Artful Dodger, whose nickname equates crime with art, Joe the fat boy in *The Pickwick Papers*, who eats, sleeps and staunchly refuses to be useful, or the ill-fated Paul Dombey, who when Mrs Pipchin asks 'how do you think you shall like me?', replies 'I don't think I shall like you at all.' With their slick thievery, contented sloth or unedited truth-telling, these boys may break the law or violate agreed codes of conduct, but at heart Dickens belonged in their company, since infantile rebellion was the source of his creative rage.

In another essay, the Uncommercial Traveller revisits Chatham, renamed Dullborough, where Dickens lived from 1817 to 1822 during his father's employment in the naval dockyard. Exploring the town, he bewails the demolition of a coaching office that used to be adorned by an image of a vehicle speeding lucky travellers off to London. It had been replaced by the headquarters of Pickfords – still in the removal business today – which sent its bulky wagons lumbering down the street and caused the houses to shudder. Dickens compares this takeover to the invasion that Napoleon planned but could not execute; in making war on the town, Pickford has 'committed an act of boyslaughter, in running over my Childhood in this rough manner'. Herod reappears here, announced by a word that is calculated to make the reader blink. Manslaughter is a compound that passes unnoticed when we read it, but boyslaughter looks odd, perhaps intentionally: it would be only too easy to insert an apostrophe and turn it into boy's laughter. In that one word Dickens first complains about a virtual infanticide – in effect likening himself to the boy crushed under the aristocrat's carriage in *A Tale of Two Cities* – and then impudently retaliates by making a joke of the accusation.

The double-take indicates how poetically precise his language always is, and how deadly his comedy can be.

———

At the start of *Anna Karenina* Tolstoy proposes that 'All happy families are alike; each unhappy family is unhappy in its own way.' For Dickens, all families are unhappy, and all of them are permutations of his own clan with its stifled grudges and gnawing anxieties about money and social status. As a consequence, his novels do their best to disestablish the unpropitious institution.

He traces the problem back to the first family in Genesis. After quitting Eden, Eve bore Adam two sons, with sibling rivalry as the immediate outcome. As the Bible relates, Cain the farmer envied Abel the shepherd, killed him, and was sent off to wander the earth. Dickens commemorates that primal crime with rhetorical flourishes: Sikes labours under 'the curse of Cain' after his attack on Nancy, and Jonas in *Martin Chuzzlewit* treads in 'the red mire that stained the naked feet of Cain!' when he murders Montague Tigg. Cain expected to be struck down by whoever recognised him; instead the Bible notes that God marked or branded him and declared that any assault on him would be punished sevenfold. The mark of Cain was protective not punitive: did it confer a special distinction or prestige? Dickens might have thought so. In the memoir he gave to Forster he says that, when his parents entered the Marshalsea, 'I (small Cain that I was, except that I had never done harm to any one) was handed over as a lodger to a reduced old lady'; he adds that this woman, 'with a few alterations and embellishments, unconsciously began to sit for Mrs Pipchin in *Dombey*', the boarding-house keeper whom little Paul instinctively dislikes.

Dickens's self-identification as Cain is slipped into a parenthesis, which hardly lessens its oddity. He immediately protests that he was harmless, although by the end of the sentence he admits that more than twenty years later he did imaginary harm to his landlady by turning her into Mrs Pipchin, a desiccated widow from whom the 'waters of gladness and milk of human kindness' have been siphoned off. If he had wanted sympathy, he should have allied himself with Abel, whom he commemorates, suggestively, in the person of the self-destructively generous Abel Magwitch. Instead he chose to be Cain's avatar, taking advantage of the immunity God conferred on the killer. In 1827 Thomas De Quincey declared that Cain, as 'the inventor of murder, and the father of the art', was surely 'a man of first-rate genius'. In a lecture supposedly delivered to a society of 'amateurs and dilettanti in the various modes of bloodshed', De Quincey's claim was an abstruse jest. Dickens took it literally, in art if not in life: while planning future instalments of *Dombey and Son* he informed Forster that 'Paul, I shall slaughter at the end of number five.'

In 1839 Dickens rehoused his vexatious parents in far-off Devon; they did not stay there for long, and his father persisted in begging for hand-outs, sometimes importuning Dickens's publishers. He disposed of his father and mother more permanently in fiction, where they appear as the feckless Micawber in *David Copperfield* and the air-headed Mrs Nickleby. Dickens's younger brother Frederick, a debt-ridden alcoholic, also pleaded for loans and when refused told Charles that he pitied anyone who came 'under your lash'. Frederick got his comeuppance in the figure of Fred Trent, Little Nell's dissolute brother, who is sent to riot abroad before drowning in the Seine and being laid out in the Paris morgue, where no one claims him for burial. Dickens grumbled that he 'never had anything left to me but relations': as his only inheritance, they were a burden not a bequest, and the sudden death of his younger brother Alfred in 1860 added a widow and five children to his list of dependants. 'Smuggled Relations', published in *Household Words* in 1855, is his frankest comment on what he calls 'the fiction . . . of kindred and affinity'. The narrator's wealthy neighbour claims to be an only child; it turns out that he has a father, mother and four sisters 'secreted in lodgings around the corner', who are only permitted to visit him before dawn or after dark. He is ashamed of his family, as upwardly mobile strivers often are, but needs to keep them under surveillance because they are privy to secrets like those Dickens disclosed to Forster.

Novels in the nineteenth century frequently begin with young men leaving home to make their fortunes or young women entering the marriage market. Retreating further into the past, Dickens more often starts with death and/or birth, which are equally wrenching breaches. Oliver Twist's mother dies in childbirth, ejecting him into a society that regards him as one more mouth to be fed at the public expense. David Copperfield recalls his dead mother's face as distinctly as 'any face I may choose to look on in a crowded street', but makes up for her loss with an 'actual remembrance' of the touch of his nurse's forefinger, 'roughened by needlework, like a pocket nutmeg-grater'; despite the grating texture, the homely metaphor carries with it a calming reassurance. Nicholas Nickleby's father dies after being ruined by a bad investment and leaves his family destitute. Mrs Squeers calls Nicholas a 'fondling', by which she means a foundling. The malapropism carries an accusation with it: a fondling is presumably cuddled, caressed and made to feel at home in the world, whereas a foundling in order to be found must previously have been mislaid or deliberately discarded. Nicholas asks Smike if he remembers any kind woman addressing him as her child; he does not, so Nicholas coaxes him to detest the unknown mother who abandoned him. Meanwhile Smike's father, Nicholas's uncle, hunts for the boy, persecutes him from a distance, and initially rejoices when told of his death. Realising too late that Smike was his own illegitimate offspring, he then kills himself in self-disgust.

Fathers, even the one in heaven, are judged by the grief they suffer, not the affection they dispense. Addressing God, a character in *The Haunted Man* says that he is 'so much better than the fathers upon earth!' because 'so much more afflicted by the errors of Thy children!' That may be giving God the benefit of the doubt: the Bible actually does not tell us how afflicted he was by the death of his only begotten son. Earthly fathers as a rule have hardened hearts. For Dombey, paternity means patriarchy, and both are commercial arrangements. When Paul's death deprives him of a male heir, he ignores a daughter who is of no use to the business; at length he becomes a doting grandfather, in a change of heart that happens a generation too late. Two fathers in *Bleak House* are callously detached from their offspring: Caddy Jellyby reports that her father has described his brawling brood as 'wild Indians' and wished they could be 'all tomahawked together', while the fatuous Skimpole rhapsodises about his daughters as muses but can't be bothered to take proper care of them. 'In this family we are all children, and I am the youngest,' he says. Skimpole was a lacerating caricature of the poet Leigh Hunt, and Dickens may have intended a slight when he invited Hunt to a magic show to celebrate his son Charles's sixth birthday in 1843: the guests, he said, would be the boy's friends plus 'children of a larger growth'.

Dickensian fathers may be irresponsible, but his mothers tend to be downright malevolent, like the scaremongering religious bigot Mrs Clennam in *Little Dorrit*. Some see it as their function to teach girls to survive in a mercenary society and profit from it: like Mrs Skewton, they are matriarchal versions of Fagin with his band of boys. Miss Havisham in *Great Expectations* trains Estella, whom she adopts, to avenge her own sexual humiliation by tormenting men. Her relationship with the girl is predatory, and Pip believes that she is 'devouring the beautiful creature she has reared'. In *Our Mutual Friend* Bella Wilfer revises conjugal rules and after her wedding announces that she and her husband will invite her father to join them in 'a partnership of three'. It is almost as if Mr Wilfer, whom she treats as an adorably clueless infant, is to be her first-born. Bella's stiffly supercilious mother, affronted by her exclusion, seems to deny her own 'copartnership in that young lady': for her the family is a contract, but not a binding one. One mother is a little too loving. Mrs Kenwigs in *Nicholas Nickleby* coos over her offspring and says they are 'too beautiful to live', which causes her four apparently doomed daughters to have hysterics.

Martin Chuzzlewit's story begins as he is rejected by the grandfather who raised him. Affecting indifference, he tells Tom Pinch 'I have had no parents these many years', and when Tom commiserates, Martin says that he has no sentimental regrets about two strangers he can scarcely remember. Later in America a tobacco-chewing stranger casually asks him 'how's the unnat'ral old parent?' Mark Tapley is ready to take offence on behalf of Martin's mother, but it is the old country, rightly spurned by its breakaway colonies, that the American has in mind: the Declaration of Independence is a version of Freud's 'family romance', in which children fantasise about breaking free from parental authority. In a happier but hazier outcome, *Sketches by Boz* toys with the urban myth that chimney sweeps were the lost or stolen children of wealthy families, forced to serve a 'probationary term' of sooty slavery; some of them, according to the legend, are reunited with their parents when sent to sweep their chimneys. Boz, supported by Pythagoras, thinks that these tales bestow an 'air of mystery' on the sweeps, and the lucky ones who reassume their proper rank enjoy 'those good effects which animals derive from the doctrine of the transmigration of souls'.

While waiting to metempsychose, Dickens's characters frequently help themselves along by choosing surrogate parents, improvements on those who actually begot them. Betty Higden in *Our Mutual Friend*, giving a home to the orphaned Sloppy, has been 'more than his mother'. Jenny Wren adopts the Jewish moneylender Mr Riah as her honorary godmother, though she later calls him 'my second father' before correcting herself to say he is 'my first, for that matter'; her true father is a drunkard, and Jenny treats him as a naughty child. In *Dombey and Son* Walter Gay views Sol Gills, who is his uncle, as 'the best of fathers'. Esther in *Bleak House* says the same about her guardian, whom she subsequently marries. Esther has a mother – she turns out to be Lady Dedlock's love-child – but she blames herself for her own illegitimacy, feels that when she was born it was 'not intended that I should be then alive', and sees herself as 'the danger and the possible disgrace . . . of a proud family name'. Her mother's ignorance of her existence leaves Esther questioning whether she truly does exist: so far as Lady Dedlock knew, she 'had never . . . breathed – had been buried – had never been endowed with life – had never borne a name'. Those are four ways of saying the same thing, and Esther, jumbling the proper order in her distress, touches on every stage from conception to respiration to christening to burial, with each in turn cancelled out in a sequence of scarring denials or forcible annihilations.

Nurses like Peggotty in *David Copperfield* or Mrs Toodle in *Dombey and Son* replace absent or delinquent mothers, although Dickens warns that those who assume this nurturing role, along with 'matrons, monitors, attendants on sick-beds', sometimes lack the tenderness and the personal hygiene that the work requires. Mrs Bangham, who helps deliver Amy Dorrit in the prison, is gruesome proof of this. As 'charwoman and messenger' she is 'the popular medium of communication with the outer world', and at the same time she seems to be mediumistically in contact with the nether world. While assisting the doctor she lures hundreds of flies into vinegar traps, and when Amy finally emerges, there are so many dead insects afloat in dishes of acid that her 'one little life, hardly stronger than theirs' seems insignificant when set against 'the multitude of lesser deaths'.

Among all this emotional damage, people are orphans almost by default. Discussing theatrical melodramas, Boz grumbles that parents in stage plays are generally obliged to deliver tedious expository speeches about what happened before the curtain rose. To get the show moving, he would 'very much like to see some piece in which all the dramatis personae were orphans', living in the impromptu present without being indebted to the past. Betsey Trotwood is more dubious about this supposed freedom. Her first question to David Copperfield's mother is 'You were an orphan, weren't you?' She takes it for granted, and only asks for confirmation: she sees that this young woman has no idea how to be a mother because she did not have one from whom she could learn. Betsey, childless herself, has strong opinions about maternity, and deplores Mrs Markleham's bad influence on her possibly adulterous daughter Annie Strong. Such parents, she says, seem to think that their return 'for bringing an unfortunate young woman into the world – God bless my soul, as if she asked to be brought, or wanted to come! – is full liberty to worry her out of it again'. We do not volunteer to be born, and if given the choice we might have refused; after our first entrance we are soon set upon by vexations that hustle us towards the exit.

Being an orphan was for Dickens a symbolic state, a synonym for deprivation, with no need for a parent's death. Florence Dombey is said to be 'orphaned' when her father strikes her, and after taking refuge with Captain Cuttle she is able to forget her 'homelessness and orphanage' – an odd use of the term, which makes orphanage a condition to which you mentally assign yourself, not an institution to which you are committed. One of Dombey's friends views a parent's loss as a liberation. When his new wife's mother is immobilised by a stroke, Major Bagstock waggishly tells Dombey that he can look forward to soon being 'an orphan-in-law'. The Marshalsea is likewise 'soon-to-be-orphaned' as Mr Dorrit, its most senior inmate and therefore its honorary father, regains his freedom. After Anthony Chuzzlewit dies, his son Jonas is said to be 'that amiable and worthy orphan': bereavement is a bonus for Jonas, who attempted to hurry up his father's death by poisoning him. It is not a plight to be sentimentalised, and when Skimpole airily says that the orphaned Ada Clare is 'the child of the universe', Jarndyce replies 'The universe makes rather an indifferent parent.' Pancks in *Little Dorrit* regards the foundling Tattycoram as an existential vagrant, adrift in an uncaring world: she is, as he says in a brisk trio of reductions, 'somebody's child – anybody's, nobody's'.

Frustrating efforts to escape from parental inflictions, the convoluted wills that often instigate Dickens's plots expose the burden of heredity. Harmon's misanthropic father in *Our Mutual Friend* specifies that his son can only inherit if he marries a woman he has never met; Bella, the appointed bride, says that she has been bequeathed to an unknown husband 'like a dozen of spoons'. The orphaned Mary Graham takes care of the old, ill and very rich Martin Chuzzlewit but is excluded from his will to ensure that she nurtures no great, greedy expectations while employed by him. The most elaborately manipulative provisions come in the will of Edwin Leeford, the father of illegitimate Oliver Twist and his older half-brother Monks. Half of his wealth is left to the unborn Oliver, on condition that he does not disgrace the family name before he comes of age. The aim is to deter Oliver from following the course of the degenerate Monks; instead the provision goads Monks, with Fagin's help, to devise ways of corrupting Oliver without killing him, which will cause him to be disinherited. Despite this scheme Monks receives a hand-out from the invincibly virtuous Oliver, whose generosity would probably not have pleased their father.

As a family man, Dickens was torn between his responsibility to his ten children and the competing claims of his more abundant imaginary progeny. He could be flippant about the unstoppable succession of new arrivals in his home: after the birth of his third son Francis in 1844 he reported that his wife 'is all right again; and so, they tell me, is the Baby. But I decline (on principle) to look at the latter object.' He complained about the 'inadaptability' of his children, resenting their dependence on him. He was particularly annoyed by the extravagances of his sixth son Henry during his years as a student at Cambridge; two other sons were despatched to Australia, and one more was sent to India. By contrast, Dickens lavished a doting solicitude on his written work. In 1839 he wrote a 'Familiar Epistle from a Parent to a Child', reminding it – although the child was only two years and two months old – of his hard work in caring for it, rejecting anything it could not digest, and ridding it of gross humours. Then he abruptly put the infant up for adoption by announcing 'my child, you have changed hands'. The child in question was *Bentley's Miscellany*, which Dickens had edited for the past two years; resigning, he made way for Harrison Ainsworth. He was even more anxiously fatherly with the manuscript of *Edwin Drood*, and in February 1870 he sent the latest section to the printer with a note saying 'the safety of my precious child is my sole care'.

Micawber, taking stock of the children he has produced but not provided for, refers to himself as 'the Author of their Being'. Dickens made the same connection between authorship and paternity. Although his spendthrift sons and impecunious relatives annoyed him, as a novelist he was an earnest, generous paterfamilias, 'a fond parent to every child of my fancy', and when his novels were reunited in a collected edition in 1869 he insisted that 'no one can ever love that family as dearly as I love them', though he at once singled out *David Copperfield* as his 'favourite child'. In responding to a compliment about *Our Mutual Friend*, he accused himself of being over-indulgent:

his 'inexpressible enjoyment' of anything droll, he said, made him 'pet it as if it were a spoilt child'. Tom Pinch tests such ebullient claims. With low expectations for himself, he is prepared to do without parents or patrons; he tells his sister that he is not 'a character in a book' and does not expect an act of 'poetical justice' to grant him a happy ending. He even suggests that it may be 'a little blasphemous' for people to think of themselves as heroes or heroines. But despite his protests, Tom is a character in a novel, though not the hero; short of allowing him to marry Mary Graham, who is reserved for Martin, Dickens like a godfather does his best to take care of him.

Once at least Dickens's two families collided. In 1850, a few days after the birth of his daughter Dora, he sent his wife a letter from Broadstairs in which he lightly remarked 'I have still Dora to kill.' He specified, surely unnecessarily, that he meant 'the Copperfield Dora', David's child-bride, who is sentenced to death so that the hero can marry the angelic Agnes. Eight months later, the non-fictional Dora suffered convulsions and suddenly died. Dickens's wife was in Malvern undergoing a rest cure; in a letter summoning her home he vowed 'I will not deceive you', but he did just that. To spare her a shock, he said that Dora was very ill and might not recover, and directed his wife's reaction 'if, – *if* – when you come, I should even have to say to you, "our little baby is dead"'. Dropping another desperately clumsy hint, he reminded her of infant mortality rates and warned that 'we can never expect to be exempt, as to our many children, from the afflictions of other parents'. In his novels Dickens happily heightened emotion, but now he tried to suppress it, and with his 'strongest entreaty and injunction' he urged Catherine to retain her composure. Life is accident-prone and appallingly contingent. Fiction helped Dickens to make it bearable, although on this occasion he had to acknowledge the limits of his power.

Birth and death lie at the margins of our experience, stretching our lives between two states that remain unknowable. Dickens is seldom credited with mystical tendencies, but under the cover of comedy his mind often goes on a sortie in that direction.

Mrs Skewton, pretending to soulful refinement, babbles about the elevating influence of music and its 'undeveloped recollections of a previous state of existence – and all that'. She soon loses patience with such ethereality: 'there are so many provoking mysteries, really, that are hidden from us,' she grumbles. She is garbling the theory of pre-existence that Wordsworth expounds in 'Ode: Intimations of Immortality from Recollections of Early Childhood', which suggests that paradise lies behind us not ahead, as a bliss we experienced before birth not a reward for which we might qualify after death. We arrive on earth, the poem says, 'trailing clouds of glory', and still have half-remembered inklings of 'the radiance which was once so bright'. But we are dulled by our education, when 'Shades of the prison-house begin to close / Upon the growing Boy'. For Dickens that incarceration was to be an actual fate: Amy Dorrit is born in the Marshalsea, synonymous with 'the prison of this lower world'. It ages her, and when she passes through its 'little gate' she moves from 'childhood into the care-laden world'; later, when Clennam becomes an inmate of the place, he feels that he is living posthumously, 'removed . . . into another state of existence' where he keeps company with shuffling spectres.

Oliver Twist is improbably unbesmirched by his squalid environment; Dickens takes more care to explain Amy's immunity. He says that what she saw or understood of her soiled surroundings 'lies hidden with many mysteries', and asserts that she was 'inspired' to be better than the rest. He then questions his exalted language and justifies it: 'Inspired? Yes. Shall we speak of the inspiration of a poet or a priest, and not of the heart impelled by love . . .!' Wordsworth and William Blake were romantic poet-priests, and Amy inherits their mission to exalt and transfigure what Dickens calls 'the lowliest way of life', which she does by telling stories in the prison to the disabled and abjectly grateful Maggy. Wordsworth brightens a desecrated world by finding 'splendour in the grass' and 'glory in the flower'; Amy too is almost beatified as she and Clennam leave the prison together. But she cannot redeem the unregenerate city, and the magnificent last sentence of *Little Dorrit*, wearily extending into a survey of the indifferent crowd with its variety of petty vices, suffers a dying fall: 'They went quietly down into the roaring streets, inseparable and blessed; and as they passed along in sunshine and shade, the noisy and the eager, and the arrogant and the froward and the vain, fretted and chafed, and made their usual uproar.' At the end of *Paradise Lost* Milton's Adam and Eve make their 'solitary way' out of Eden into a world that is empty, waiting to be populated by them. Amy and Clennam enter a world that is all too populous, in which they are at once effaced.

According to the painter David Wilkie, Dickens admired Wordsworth's 'We are Seven', in which a little girl with no notion of mortality is badgered by a poet who tries to convince her that two of her seven siblings are dead. She resists, admitting that they are under the earth yet insisting that to her they are still alive; he has to give up, simultaneously vexed by her obstinacy and envious of her serene confidence. Dickens has a more plangently pessimistic version of this naive faith. In her mental haven on the rooftop of a counting house, Jenny Wren in *Our Mutual Friend* enjoys her closeness to the clouds and says that up there 'you feel as if you were dead'. Whereas the girl in 'We are Seven' proclaims the continuity of life, Jenny extols the 'strange good sorrowful happiness' of death, when the anguish of her entrapment in a crippled body will end. Riah visits her in her eyrie, and as he totters back down to the street she cries after him 'Don't be long gone. Come back, and be dead!' Her sharpest critique of the despised usurer Fledgeby is 'But *you* are not dead, you know' and she expels him from her rarified realm by ordering him to 'Get down to life!' Dickens, who accompanies his characters into the world and follows them out of it, explains Fledgeby's clenched, acquisitive nature by filling in his pre-natal history. His father had business dealings with his mother, who married him to pay off a debt. The 'young gentleman' was meanwhile 'waiting in the vast dark ante-chambers of the present world', and when his time came to be born he was 'presented to the Registrar-General'. Nativity is an enrolment, society's classification and certification of us. Judgement Day, it seems, is the date of one's birth. No wonder Jenny prefers an airy, bodiless death.

With glances back at Fledgeby's embryonic waiting room and ahead to mortuaries like the one in Paris, Dickens was at home in a territory that used to be sacred to religion. The subject unexpectedly comes up in *Sketches by Boz* during an investigation of the waterman Bill Boorker's patronymic. Having attained 'a very prominent station in society', he fancily renames himself William Barker, although he can provide no documentary evidence that this is who he is. Rather than exposing him as a fraud, Boz accepts him at his word, since the alternative is to undertake bureaucratic, medical or metaphysical research: 'Mr William Barker was born – but why need we relate where Mr William Barker was born, or when? Why scrutinise the entries in parochial ledgers, or seek to penetrate the Lucinian mysteries of lying-in hospitals? Mr William Barker *was* born, or he had never been. There is a son – there was a father. There is an effect – there was a cause.' This anticipates Esther's sad musing about her mother's ignorance of her: is the self-styled Barker another person who might have 'never been'? David Copperfield uses the same phrase when contemplating the grave of the father who died six months before his birth, which makes David 'a posthumous child'; the recurrence of the idea points to Dickens's tragic sense of how provisional we are, as the chance products of an encounter between two people whom we did not choose as our originators. Perhaps our best hope is to invent ourselves, as Dickens's greatest characters flamboyantly do.

Surprisingly but very significantly, Dickens links our curiosity about where we come from to the Lucinian mysteries, otherwise known as the Eleusinian mysteries – secret religious rites performed in ancient Greece by initiates on the border between life and whatever precedes or succeeds it. In Barker's case those mysteries are obstetric, and although Boz balks at intruding into maternity wards, the Uncommercial Traveller in his reminiscences of Dullborough claims to be almost professionally acquainted with them. He is amazed, he says, that he does not have 'a red and green lamp and a night-bell at my door, for in my very young days I was taken to so many lyings-in that I wonder I escaped becoming a professional martyr to them in after-life'.

His guide on these gynaecological rounds was a child minder whom he calls 'my conductress'. The idea of the conductor had arcane implications for Dickens: it identifies the mythical figure of the psychopomp, the undertaker who like Hermes or the ferryman Charon conducts souls to the next world. On the night before he spontaneously combusts in *Bleak House*, Krook is heard 'humming like the wind, the only song he knows', which is about 'old Charon' taking a drunkard across Lethe – a preparation for his own trip to oblivion. When Little Nell and her grandfather arrive in an industrial town in *The Old Curiosity Shop*, they are lucky to find a labourer – a strangely otherworldly fellow, a worshipper of the blazing furnaces – who serves as their benign 'conductor' through the flames to a place of safety.

The word points to a guided passage between life and death, and in the topography of London it signals an equally fraught movement from one social sector to another. Dickens uses the term in *Nicholas Nickleby* when he mentions that the pretentious Wititterlys live in Cadogan Place, which is said to function scientifically as another kind of conductor: like the moist paper which Benjamin Franklin used instead of lightning rods to trap electricity, the address passes on 'the shock of pride of birth and rank' to remoter regions, but it is also 'the connecting link between the aristocratic pavements of Belgrave Square, and the barbarism of Chelsea', which makes a crossing of Sloane Street as drastic and irreversible as the transit of Lethe. Dickens so prized the word that he chose it to define his position at the magazines he edited. *Household Words* was 'conducted by Charles Dickens'; so was *The Haunted House*, the anthology of stories which he published in his periodical *All the Year Round*. The term mystified his editorial role and made him the guide whose articles about slums and criminal hide-outs led readers into society's areas of darkness, or cajoled them into spending unquiet nights with the ghost-hunters in 'a house that was shunned'.

In Dullborough, the Traveller's conductress takes him to a makeshift domestic morgue where they pay their respects to four or five dead babies, recently delivered 'at a birth' by a 'meritorious woman'. The doleful scene does not stifle the Traveller's humour or restrain his metaphorical audacity. 'By a homely association, which I suspect their complexion to have assisted', the little corpses remind him 'of pigs' feet as they are usually displayed at a neat tripe-shop'. When his young self refuses to donate any of his pocket money to help bury those personified trotters, the scandalised adults tell him to 'dismiss all expectations of going to Heaven'. In his account of the incident, the Traveller implicitly shrugs. If perdition was the price of Dickens's comically warped perspective on biological matters, so be it — and in any case he was glad to be inducted into the overlapping mysteries of birth and death, which he wrote about for the rest of his life.

3

In the Dark

The imagination of Dickens operated in a twilight realm between lucidity and delirium. His characters materialised out of the haunted gloom inside his head, and sometimes stalked him like nocturnal bogeys. As he neared the end of *The Old Curiosity Shop*, he felt that Little Nell was harrying him in dreams. 'All night,' he complained to Forster, 'I have been pursued by the child.' Later, thinking vaguely about what would eventually become *Bleak House*, he sensed 'the first shadows of a new story hovering in a ghostly way about me'. He retrieved characters from that ectoplasmic region, then released them into it again when he had finished with them. At work on the final pages of *David Copperfield*, he explained that 'I seem to be sending some part of myself into the Shadowy World.'

For Dickens's characters, stories are a gateway to dreams. Billeted with Tom Pinch in the house of their employer Pecksniff, Martin Chuzzlewit asks to be read to sleep. When Tom reaches for his precious copy of Shakespeare's plays, Martin says 'He'll do', already yawning. He asks Tom to turn down his vocal volume, but says that the reading should continue even if he falls asleep. 'Don't mind leaving me in the dark,' he adds, stretching out beside the hearth. Though he is soon snoring, Tom perseveres and is so enraptured by the 'living and highly cherished creatures' in the book that he lets the fire go out. After an hour, Martin wakes up and gruffly orders him to call for more coals. Tom, absorbed in his recitation from Shakespeare, also forgets 'to snuff the candle', which means that he fails to trim the charred wick, and Dickens notes that it comes to resemble a mushroom – another overnight growth, sprouting like imagination in the sun's absence.

In the school dormitory in *David Copperfield*, Steerforth begs David to calm him down by reciting bedtime tales as sedatives. Without a library, David relies on his memory of the picaresque plots in the eighteenth-century novels he has read; he is often sleepy but keeps talking so as not to disappoint the wakeful Steerforth. Darkness liberates David, preparing him for his literary vocation: as he says, 'Whatever I had within me that was romantic and dreamy, was encouraged by so much storytelling in the dark.' Listening in, David's loyal friend Traddles serves as 'a sort of chorus', a sample of the populace and a gauge of David's future popularity as a novelist: he howls with mirth at the comic episodes and suffers an 'ague of terror' when a rehashed plot turns more dramatic. David, who mock-modestly refers to his 'simple, earnest manner of narrating', is learning what it means to be Dickens, at once a hired entertainer and a more compelling enchanter. While he is merely a 'plaything' for Steerforth, Traddles is his obedient slave, like the reader who, as Thackeray said, was captivated and potentially led into danger by Dickens. The schoolmaster Mr Creakle, on patrol in the corridor, overhears the raucous enjoyment of Traddles, and he is 'handsomely flogged for disorderly conduct in the bedroom'. David's adverb has the hint of a gratified smirk.

Dickens even volunteered to be a nocturnal terrorist, inciting nightmares as a public service. In 1840 he sent a letter to a government minister offering to write a luridly imaginary account of the sadistic punishments meted out at the Australian penal colony on Norfolk Island, which he promised would deter '*rising* convicts' if placed '*on the pillow of every prisoner in England*'. Fortunately the Commissioners on Criminal Law did not ask him to go ahead with this experiment in mental torture. In the preface to *A Christmas Carol* he archly apologises for the bad dreams his 'Ghostly little book' may induce. When Scrooge's first 'unearthly visitor' appears, Dickens places himself in a territory occupied by phantoms, and situates the reader there as well. The portentous white figure, he says, was as close to Scrooge 'as I am now to you, and I am standing in the spirit at your elbow'. That should induce a shiver: the invisible narrator who whispers in our ear is himself a ghost. The scene is all the more suggestive because the spook's head gives off a vertical beam of light; under its arm it carries a gas extinguisher which serves as a cap, useful for smothering or dulling this cerebral blaze. Dickens may have wished for some such headgear, to dampen down the intensity of his imagination.

The word Dickens uses in describing *A Christmas Carol* had a distinctly uncanny resonance. For him, 'ghostly' meant spiritual, like the German 'geistlich'; 'ghastly' lurked in the vicinity as a synonym. The word reappears with the same frisson in a much later reflection on the storyteller's prerogatives. In 1867 he collaborated with Wilkie Collins on *No Thoroughfare*, a short novel which they adapted as a West End play. Dickens told Collins that he was eager to inflict 'horrors and dangers' on the alpine travellers in the tale, who make a fraught wintry crossing of the Simplon Pass before a final showdown on a precipice. Keen to feel the tingly psychic inklings that he called 'Ghostly interest', he proposed that they should 'force the design up to any powerful climax we please' to 'get a very Avalanche of power out of it, and thunder it down on the readers' heads'. The threat was about supplying audiences with the excitement they craved, but it warned of a rampant violence that Dickens in his final years seemed less able or less willing to restrain.

Stories like those Dickens told need the camouflage of darkness because they involve excursions beyond daylight normality. The Pickwickians, so jolly and mundane, are jolted out of their gregarious world by a series of inset tales that are sometimes literally lunatic. One of these is a soiled and blotted manuscript scribbled by a man with a 'diseased imagination'; Pickwick, having received it from a clergyman as a parting gift, takes out the pages at midnight, when insomnia has made him 'nervous and excited', although the tale is not calculated to soothe him. 'Ho! ho!' screeches the loony, adding 'It's a grand thing to be mad!' 'Old spirits,' he says, goaded him to kill his wife; after committing another murder, he is captured and locked up in chains. The manuscript breaks off as he listens to the shrieks of his fellow inmates and studies a 'pale form' that watches him from a corner of his cell. Pickwick's candle then goes out, so that he, like the madman, is abandoned to the darkness. There is an equally macabre supplement in *Master Humphrey's Clock*, in which quirky or crazy manuscripts are retrieved from the clock-case of the reclusive Master Humphrey. One such tale begins just before the storyteller's execution. 'This is the last night I have to live,' says the author, a child-killer who entertained his friends while sitting on his victim's grave. As he writes his confession, his own grave is being dug, with his name already 'written in the black-book of death'; he concludes by repeating 'I die tomorrow.'

Storytelling can be a mortifying rite: its preterite tense describes contemporaneous actions as if they are happening in the past, perhaps to already moribund actors. Dickens's characters go deeper into that limbo than those of any other novelist. He told Forster that his aim in *Our Mutual Friend* was to enter the consciousness of a man 'feigning to be dead, and *being* dead to all intents and purposes'; he was fascinated by 'the singular view of life' of someone who has stepped out of his allotted existence to become a spectator – or perhaps a novelist by other means? This is the case with Harmon, who allows people to believe he has drowned while he remains alive under another name. Although he says he has 'no clue to the scene of my death', he no longer holds 'a place among the living'. He is not alone. 'I speak of myself as if I had passed from the world,' says the condemned man in *Master Humphrey's Clock*. 'I am dead,' announces a pallid revenant in Dickens's essay on Christmas trees, adding 'I come from another world, but may not disclose its secrets!' In one case, very touchingly, Dickens describes how it might feel to be conducted into the darkness by a narrator who is telling you the end of your own story. As Jo dies in *Bleak House*, he is comforted by a kind doctor. The boy asks about his burial, begs the doctor to visit him in the graveyard, then notices that the shadows are thickening around him. The doctor promises that a light is coming, and coaches him to repeat the faltering phrases of a prayer. 'I hear you, sir,' says Jo, 'in the dark.'

The madman in *The Pickwick Papers* defines Dickens's method when he admits that 'I mix up realities with my dreams.' The mixture reappears in the letter about the enchanters torn apart by their familiars, where Dickens says that 'Realities and Idealities are always comparing themselves before me.'

The comparison did not favour reality, which to Dickens seemed myopic, a symptom of what William Blake called 'single vision'. By official decree, the school pupils in *Hard Times* are ordered 'not to see anywhere, what you don't see in fact', which is why Louisa Gradgrind, oppressed by this prosaic worldview, makes a 'wild escape into something visionary'. Dickens thought of fiction as a similar release into a waking dream, where a secret life – his own, and that of his characters – could be placed on display or acted out. Hence his apologetic correction when he describes the dying Paul Dombey's panoramic overview of the city, the river that bisects it and the countryside beyond. From his sickbed the boy can only imagine this, so Dickens begins by saying that Paul 'pictured to himself' these scenes; he then retracts the verb and emphatically replaces it – 'pictured! he saw'. In *Oliver Twist*, when Brownlow tries to rationalise Nancy's premonitions, she indignantly insists that she is a seer not a fantasist. Her fear, she says, rewrote the book she was reading: death 'came into the print', stamping 'the word "coffin" . . . in large black letters' on every page. Brownlow tells her she imagined it, which she denies, and she adds that a coffin then materialised beside her in the street. That often happens, he points out. '*Real ones*,' she sniffs. 'This was not.'

In an attempt to understand his own gift, Dickens attributed the same frightening clairvoyance to Oliver. In Fagin's den, no longer asleep but not properly awake, he hovers in that intermediary condition when 'a mortal knows just enough of what his mind is doing to form some glimmering conception of its mighty powers, its bounding from earth and spurning time and space, when freed from the irksome restraint of its corporeal associate'. This is one of Dickens's boldest comments on the high-flying, weightless, god-like supremacy of imagination, and it introduces a drowsy glimpse of a forbidden reality: Oliver sees Fagin retrieving his cache of treasure and listens to him exulting in his crimes. In an angry panic Fagin demands 'What have you seen?', and Oliver solemnly gives his word that he was asleep. In a similar episode later in the novel, lapsing out of consciousness at twilight in Mrs Maylie's cottage, he imagines that he is back in Fagin's lair, then starts up to find that Fagin is indeed at the window spying on him. Harry Maylie tells Oliver he must have been dreaming. 'Oh no, indeed, sir,' says Oliver, which both is and is not true. Keats compared imagination to 'Adam's dream – he awoke and found it truth', with Eve lying availably beside him. But Adam had God to gratify his desire; for Dickens, imagination is more like Oliver's dream of Fagin, and it confirms his fear rather than answering his prayer. Dickens goes on to supply an almost medical diagnosis of Oliver's suggestible mental state: 'reality and imagination,' he says, are 'strangely blended', and 'it is an undoubted fact' that the 'visionary scenes' which play out inside our heads while we sleep are 'materially influenced, by the *mere silent presence* of some external object' of which we have 'no waking consciousness'.

Moral scruples remained, despite that earnest pseudo-scientific assertion. Clennam in *Little Dorrit* associates what he thinks of as 'Reality' – an upstanding principle, given a supercilious capital letter – with everything that is 'hard and stern', like his adamantine mother; he is called 'a dreamer' because he inclines towards the gentleness and goodness personified by Amy. Realism soon enough advanced into the harder, sterner, scientifically neutral literary manner that later in the nineteenth century came to be known as naturalism. Émile Zola, the movement's theorist, declared that 'imagination no longer has a function' and debarred any 'waving of the magic wand', the implement so essential to Dickens. Instead Zola called for human beings to be analysed as biological specimens or chemical compounds and 'described without a single lie'. Dickens has a precursor to Zola in the allegorically nameless Physician in *Little Dorrit* who instead of a wand wields a 'plain bright scalpel'. 'Where he was, something real was,' says Dickens, although that reality consists of gore: Physician discovers Merdle dead in a bloodied tub after slashing his jugular vein with a penknife.

Temporising between reality and dream, fiction aims to tell the truth indirectly, by means of what Dickens calls a supposition or a 'supposititious case'. His characters are adept at this kind of fictionalising. Dick Swiveller in *The Old Curiosity Shop* thinks of his meagre single room as an 'indefinite space' of plural apartments in which even the furniture tells white lies: a bedstead, stowed upright during the day, pretends to be a bookcase. Dickens treats Swiveller's domestic folly as a form of religious belief, since 'Implicit faith in the deception was the first article of his creed', to which visitors tactfully subscribe; the novelist protects the 'pleasant fiction' from mockery because we all live by such conceits. Less pleasantly, those deceptions are demolished by the cynical Quilp who, when Swiveller is hired by the corrupt lawyer Sampson Brass, sneers that he will be inducted into 'the beautiful fictions of the law' and 'those charming creations of the poet, John Doe and Richard Roe'. Legal fictions are unproven and may be untrue, while John Doe and Richard Roe are conceptual plaintiffs. *Little Dorrit* punctures other pretences, calling high society and its marriage market a 'fiction to be nursed' by those who profit from the imposture, and exposing the 'genteel fiction' about Mr Dorrit's ancestry that sustains his self-respect. Zola at least grounded fiction in nature; Dickens at his most cheerless saw the world as a palimpsest of flimsy fictions.

Dickens's doubts were relayed back to him by a deaf, dumb and blind patient in a Swiss hospital. The case came to his notice in Lausanne in 1846, during one of several extended stays abroad. Asked at mealtime if he had had a drink, this young man said 'No': it was not true, but like Oliver Twist in the workhouse he wanted more, and he was mildly reproved for lying to obtain a refill. He later dreamed about being bitten by a wild beast, and when he awoke to find this hadn't happened he worried that he had 'told another lie in the night'.

The doctors explained that 'this sort of lie was a harmless one, and was called a dream'. That was not quite an acquittal: fiction remained untrue but not dishonest, so the penalty was waived. Disconcerted by the waywardness of his brain, the young man next asked a metaphysical question, and wondered 'whether dead people ever dreamed while they were lying in the ground'. Dickens, who found this 'curious', was left to ponder the limits of consciousness and the possibility that it might outlive the body that temporarily houses it.

The same uncertainty troubled him in 1844 as he worked on *The Chimes*. The spirits of the bells in the church tower persuade Trotty Veck that he has died after falling from the belfry, and give him a forecast of the miserable future that remains for his despairing daughter and her alcoholic husband. Then the chimes awaken Trotty, who now finds that his family's story has a happy ending after all. But those daylight facts seem to be mere wishful thinking, while the dream induced by the spirits tells an uncomfortable truth. 'Had Trotty dreamed?' Dickens asks. 'Or, are his joys and sorrows, and the actors in them, but a dream; himself a dream; the teller of this tale a dreamer, waking but now?' In a letter to Forster as he raced to complete the tale, he tried to resolve the problem with a paradox. Referring to 'the realities of which dreams are born', he said that he hoped he would be able to answer his own questions by the time he reached the conclusion. In the event he passed the responsibility to his readers, whom he challenged 'to correct, improve, and soften' their own reality.

Dickens usually allows dreams to take precedence over reality, no matter how absurd or incredible they may be. In *Little Dorrit*, Mrs Clennam's servant Affery discovers her husband Jeremiah Flintwinch apparently duplicated. In a secret room, she is stupefied to see one Jeremiah, wide awake, watching the other as he sleeps. The scene is all the stranger because the first Jeremiah then attacks the second, using – appropriately enough – a candle-snuffer as his weapon against himself. What Affery sees is 'not at all like a dream' because it is 'so real in every respect', yet it could not possibly have taken place – although it did: Flintwinch has a hidden twin called Ephraim, with whom he is quarrelling. All the same, Affery might well have been in a medium's trance, since she habitually keeps her apron pulled up over her head as if presiding at a seance. The villain Rigaud salutes her 'genius for dreaming', praises her 'spirituality', and suggests that Flintwinch would make a fortune if he set her up as a fairground oracle, because 'All that she dreams comes true.' Another waking dream occurs in the same novel, when Mrs Tickit sees the runaway Tattycoram in the garden of her adoptive parents. She denies she was asleep, and says she was 'watching with my eyes closed'. Clennam doubts her, but fears she would be hurt by his 'infidel solution of her mystery'. Faith and mystery: the terms, as in Dickens's comments on Dick Swiveller's creed, are borrowed from religion.

Any reality can be redefined as a dream or even as 'a dream within a dream', which is how Dickens classifies the homesick reveries of Martin Chuzzlewit and Mark Tapley. As they fall asleep in New York, 'the shadows of objects afar off . . . take fantastic shapes upon the wall in the dim light of thought without control'. Thoughts that escape from control are liable to take the fantastic shape of nightmares, which Dickens drags into the daylight for inspection. The 'maere' in nightmare is the Old English term for a hobgoblin, not a mare; capitalising on the etymological error, Dickens gave the word a body and changed the horse's sex as he did so. When the malevolently playful dwarf Quilp returns home after being reported dead, his wife faints with a shriek. Having drained a bottle of rum, Quilp locks the door and while 'embracing' the empty flask he hunches his shoulders, crosses his arms and looks at her 'like a dismounted nightmare'. The scene suggests Henry Fuseli's painting *The Nightmare*, in which a bat-eared goblin squats on the chest of an unconscious maiden; behind this gloating troll, the wild-eyed phosphorescent horse on which he may have been riding thrusts its head through the curtains of the bed to ogle the sprawling, filmily night-gowned female dreamer. Has Quilp dismounted in order to mount his abject, insensible wife? Dickens ends the chapter at this point and leaves us to do our own imagining. Equestrian trappings are added to the metaphorical steed in *Pictures from Italy*, where 'in the broad day' Dickens encounters a troop of 'saddled and bridled nightmares' on the Spanish Steps in Rome.

These are not horses but artists' models waiting to be hired, already costumed for sittings as venerable patriarchs, haughty aristocrats or skulking assassins. The characters they portray exist nowhere in 'the habitable globe': perhaps not, although they have a local habitation in Dickens's novels.

Shadows, fantastic shapes in dim light and uncontrolled thoughts are what Dickens works with. *The Battle of Life*, the Christmas story he published in 1846, goes on a descriptive detour to review the shiny pot-lids, kettles and saucepans on display in a country kitchen. These serve as 'a hall of mirrors', but instead of tamely duplicating the appearance of the servant Ben Britain, the curved and burnished surfaces multiply one man into 'so many kinds of men', making him alternately long- or broad-faced, good-looking or hideous. This capacity for transformation is what Dickens found lacking in photography. When Mr Brownlow's housekeeper shows Oliver Twist a painting of the woman who turns out to be his mother, she dismisses the new art, then a very recent invention: Henry Fox Talbot made the first camera negative in 1835, two years before the serialisation of Dickens's novel began. 'The man that invented the machine for taking likenesses,' chortles Mrs Bedwin, 'might have known *that* would never succeed; it's a deal too honest.' Ladies, as she knows, prefer to be flattered, which is why they would rather entrust their faces to painters. At best the camera could produce facsimiles; metaphors obligingly stretch or even supersede our notion of what things look like.

In *The Haunted Man and the Ghost's Bargain*, published for Christmas in 1848, the protagonist Redlaw is haunted by a phantom twin, 'an awful likeness of himself'. This cold, colourless replica is said to have congealed in the surrounding half-light as the result of 'some unreal, unsubstantial process – not to be traced by any human sense'. That could be a bluff: Redlaw is 'a learned man in chemistry', so he surely knows how to coat paper with silver salts to make a self-portrait, and this one may have escaped from the closed chamber of the camera. Whatever its origins, the 'appalling copy of his face' has the marks of Redlaw's festering unhappiness written all over it.

The ghost's bargain offers Redlaw the chance to forget his past, but when he passes this gift on to others he learns that the erasure of early sorrows is a curse not a boon: we should treasure our remembered troubles and setbacks, because they teach us to be compassionate. Was Dickens ruefully reconsidering the way he had obliterated his miserable childhood?

With this moral as a pious distraction, the story had a literally ghostly after-life in 1862, when a dramatic version of *The Haunted Man* was performed at the Royal Polytechnic Institution in Regent Street. Here – in a special effect that came to be known as Pepper's Ghost, a tribute to John Henry Pepper, the chemist who devised it with the help of the engineer Henry Dircks – 'the living man, and the animated image of himself dead' actually came face to face as Dickens prescribed. Light was trained on a figure concealed in a closed pit below the stage, then beamed upwards to reflect an image on a tilted pane of glass inside the proscenium, so the actor playing Redlaw did seem to be sharing the same space with his double. A special effect had made the spectral world visible.

The set-up demonstrated the menace of realism, which confronts us with our ingrown faults and leaves reality unchanged. Oscar Wilde proposed that 'The nineteenth century dislike of realism is the rage of Caliban seeing his own face in the glass.' Dickensian mirrors are more imaginative than the one that grimaces back at Shakespeare's unsightly, self-loathing Caliban. In 'The Ghost in Master B.'s Room', Dickens's contribution to *The Haunted House*, the narrator claims to 'regard with a hushed and solemn fear, the mysteries, between which and this state of existence is interposed the barrier of the great trial and change that fall on all the things that live'; even so, he doubts that the creaky floorboards or slammed doors in the supposedly haunted house are evidence of 'spiritual intercourse'. Then one morning as he shaves, his looking-glass shows him a beardless boy. 'I am fifty,' he reminds himself as he stares at this stranger. The reflection next changes to that of a young man in his mid-twenties. Images of his father and grandfather follow, although he never saw the latter. He has been or will be all of these people, including the skeleton with which he shares his bed the following night: he is looking into 'the old mirror . . . never yet made by human hands' which Dickens muses about in *Our Mutual Friend* – a mirror that remembers, containing time as well as framing space, able almost cinematically to replay every scene it witnessed in the past and also to offer previews of the future. In *Le Rouge et le Noir*, Stendhal defines the novel as a mirror that promenades down a highway, looking now at the sky, now at the mire underfoot. That was too superficial to satisfy Dickens. Fiction was his flight from the real, and from himself.

Because he found it hard to sedate his brain or suspend its activity, Dickens envied those who could happily lapse into unconsciousness. Throughout *Barnaby Rudge*, his novel about the social and political trauma of sectarian riot in eighteenth-century London, he categorises characters by noting how soundly or fitfully they sleep.

The publican John Willet 'sleeps uncommon hard' and snores even if he is wide awake. The privileged Chesters drift through life in a languidly somnolent state: 'do not extend your drowsy influence to the decanter,' says Mr Chester when his son forgets to circulate the port. But Barnaby the Wordsworthian idiot boy suffers from 'phantom-haunted dreams', and Varden the kindly locksmith has to explain that the horrors raging in his head are 'Dreams, Barnaby, dreams'. Varden himself relaxes into a 'dog sleep', jostling his thoughts 'in a kind of mental kaleidoscope'. His wife is 'obliged to go to sleep' after the gormandising plenitude of the inn's kitchen leaves her 'dizzy and bewildered', unable to cope with such mind-bending immensity. Almost indignantly, Lord George Gordon insists 'I have not been sleeping' when his secretary apologises for waking him. It is a remark with subtly sinister implications: open-eyed in the darkness like a sentinel, he later supervises a daylight nightmare as the protestors he has aroused pillage and burn the houses of Catholics. Those civil disturbances interfere with London's circadian rhythm. Because people are afraid to go to bed, 'sleep had hardly been thought of all night', and in the morning the streets are 'haunted rather than frequented'.

Dickens's own nights were equally unquiet. When unable to sleep, he sometimes went for a walk, covering fifteen or twenty miles across the length and breadth of London. These perambulations in the dark, as he told Forster, were 'quite a little mental phenomenon'. In October 1857, agitated after a marital disagreement, he left his house in Bloomsbury at two in the morning and walked thirty miles to his country home in Kent, where he arrived seven hours later. On the way, 'dozing heavily and dreaming constantly', he made up verses and gabbled foreign words as if speaking in tongues: the body strode on automatically while the mind free-associated. As dawn broke, he fancied that he would complete the journey by striding into the sky, climbing up cloud banks that were white mountains as if he were walking out of the lower world and into omniscience. Although the Uncommercial Traveller likens himself to 'a higher sort of police-constable' on the beat during an afternoon expedition that takes him from Covent Garden to Limehouse, Dickens was more of an ambulatory id than a uniformed superego: night allowed him to observe the city after 'all the sober folk had gone to bed'. His walks were exercises in oneirism, and when a patient at a hospital for the insane told him 'Sir, I can frequently fly', Dickens said to himself 'So could I – by night.'

No wonder Dickens found it hard to settle down in bed: his art, he said in his letter when likening himself to an enchanter at the mercy of his familiars, made him 'the most restless of created Beings'. 'My only comfort, is in Motion,' he explained in another letter; elsewhere he changed that to locomotion, which he called his only sport. He joked about emulating Captain Barclay, a fabled athlete who walked a thousand miles in a thousand hours at Newmarket in 1809 and earned a thousand guineas for the accomplishment. Friends predictably quailed when Dickens summoned them to accompany him on 'a hard trot of three hours'. 'Where shall it be – *oh, where* – Hampstead, Greenwich, Windsor?' he badgered Forster when planning one such forced march. 'WHERE??????' He thought of these hikes almost industrially, as valves that released an otherwise dangerous pressure.

'If I couldn't walk fast and far,' he said, 'I should just explode and perish.' He bestowed this peripatetic habit on Betsey Trotwood, who on hearing bad news performs 'pedestrian feats' to walk off her disquiet. Her marathons follow an indoor track that extends to take in 'the bedrooms from wall to wall', and David Copperfield estimates that she covers a hundred miles while working off her concern about the rumoured infidelity of Annie Strong.

Dickens's characters are not blithe Wordsworthian wanderers, since they have to negotiate a crowded city rather than drift across an unpopulated landscape like lonely clouds. Nor do they indulge in the impromptu loitering of the flâneurs or boulevardiers Baudelaire saw in Paris. Their impetus is anxiety. Unable to find his sister Kate when he returns unannounced to London, Nicholas Nickleby paces through Hyde Park at midnight and increases 'his rate of walking as if in the hope of leaving his thoughts behind': is it possible to walk faster than you can think? During his ten-mile outing to Twickenham, Clennam worries all the way across Putney Heath and has so many 'unsettled objects to meditate upon' that he could have gone on walking until he reached Land's End in Cornwall. Bradley Headstone in *Our Mutual Friend* walks to advance his vengeful plotting. He begins before dawn on the border between Kent and Surrey, crosses London from east to west, and has 'outwalked the short day' before he reaches his destination, a weir twenty-five miles upstream on the Thames. When Betty Higden in the same novel loses her home, she prefers vagabondage to life in the workhouse. Although she believes that 'trudging round the country and tiring of myself out, I shall keep the deadness off', in her vagrancy she walks herself into her grave, disproving Dickens's assertion that 'to walk steadily and with a purpose' was a sure way to maintain health and happiness.

Daytime walks may have an athletic value; noctambulism is a more dubious matter. In *Martin Chuzzlewit*, Jonas sneaks out of his house into a blind alley, and under cover of dark leaves London by coach. He sleeps during the ride and dreams that 'it was the Last Day for all the world': Dickensian night often rehearses the apocalypse. After alighting, he walks on for a few miles and hides in a wood throughout the ensuing day. When night returns, he murders Montague Tigg, then walks ten miles to board another coach and at five the next morning lets himself back into the locked room where he has supposedly been sleeping in the 'tumbled bed'. He believes he has gone unobserved, but in the country Dickens warns that nature is wakeful and vigilant: 'its darkness watched no less than its light!', and 'the eye of Night' witnesses his crime. Jonas ends as a guilty wraith, 'his own ghost and phantom . . . at once the haunting spirit and the haunted man'. Dickens's own late-night itineraries acquainted him with what he calls society's 'terrible spectres', 'the embodied spirits of Disease, and Vice, and Famine'. He made expeditions to thieves' kitchens, to the police court at Bow Street, the prison at Newgate, the lock-up for debtors in Southwark and the madhouse of Bethlehem Hospital; along the way he interviewed destitute girls or fallen women who might be eligible for redemption at Urania Cottage in Shepherd's Bush, a benign reformatory which he founded with the wealthy philanthropist Angela Burdett-Coutts.

'Night,' says Master Humphrey as he introduces himself in *The Old Curiosity Shop*, 'is generally my time for walking.' Old and infirm, he prefers the city when it is quieter, although that justification for his habit is questioned later in the novel. 'We have been walking all night,' Nell explains after she and her grandfather are accosted by a gruff boatman. 'A pair of queer travellers to be walking all night,' he comments: one of them is too old, the other too young for that dubious activity. In the hours of darkness, Master Humphrey can console himself for his solitude by 'imagining the sociality and kind-fellowship' inside the warm, lighted houses he passes: sociality and kind-fellowship – unidiomatic terms for emotional states that are alien to him – have to be imagined. A connoisseur of the city at its most shadowy, he enjoys conjecturing about the pursuits of a 'booted exquisite' or an 'expectant pleasure-seeker', Baudelairean decadents whose faces are briefly lit up by street lamps. Later he notices 'unwholesome streams' flowing in the gutters, the residue of overnight debauches. At the end of the novel Sally Brass and her gaunt, lookalike brother Sampson are spotted among the 'archways, dark vaults and cellars' that are London's 'obscene hiding-places' – phrases that point to the city's underworld and to the underside of Dickens's imagination.

Master Humphrey even imagines how it might be to experience the continuing life of the city from underground, like someone 'condemned to lie, dead but conscious, in a noisy churchyard' with 'no hope of rest for centuries to come'. Harmon in *Our Mutual Friend*, having reincarnated himself, both practises and benefits from that posthumous intuition. Lingering beside a churchyard in Limehouse on a wildly stormy night, he likens himself to the occupants of the graves and takes pleasure in 'a sensation not experienced by many mortals': going 'unrecognized among mankind', he is in effect 'a spirit that was once a man'. Anonymous and invisible on his nocturnal rounds, Dickens shared the privileges enjoyed by phantoms.

As Nell and her grandfather quit the curiosity shop, Master Humphrey's morose nocturne gives way to an optimistic aubade. The morning sun purifies places that were 'ugly and distrustful' at night, and has 'shed light even into dreams'. After an account of mice creeping back in safety to their holes in the wall, cats forgetting their prey as they blink in the brightness, and flowers opening their 'gentle eyes', the hymn concludes with what sounds like a commentary on Genesis: 'The light, creation's mind, was everywhere, and all things owned its power', with sickly lamps now 'faint in the full glory of the sun'. That pious effusion is asking to be negated. Light may be creation's mind, but darkness – the resort of unconsciousness and unreason – is the source of creativity.

Missing London during the months he spent living in Switzerland in 1846, Dickens called its streets 'that magic lantern': what he valued was the city's penumbra of illusion and subterfuge, not its industrious daytime bustle. Magic lanterns relied on limelight, created by incandescent lime burnt in gas, so the comparison gave the streets the uncanny aura of Dickens's dreams. It was gaslight that made his midnight ramblings possible, and he enjoyed its victory over old-fashioned oil lanterns. Early in the nineteenth century the fussy glass pots of oil on top of lamp posts gave way to lights fuelled by piped coal gas; Dickens, dramatising the clash between the two systems, made it a matter of life and death. In *Bleak House* the remaining oil lamps hold their ground out of sheer pertinacity: 'with their source of life half frozen', they gasp 'like fiery fish out of water', while 'the bright gas springs up in the streets', bumptiously brilliant. In 'The Lamplighter', a story published in 1838, Tom Grig's uncle disparages gaslights as 'an everlasting succession of glow-worms', and he argues that whales will kill themselves out of spite, enraged at no longer being harpooned so that sperm oil can be extracted from their blubber. Finally, recognising that he is powerless against modernity, he hangs himself from an iron lamp post. 'Gas,' declares the narrator, 'was the death of him.'

When a 'No Gas' faction in Broadstairs objected to the innovation, Dickens joked that officials retaliated by quoting God's initial pronouncement, 'Let there be light', and warning the protestors not to contravene 'the great decree'. But rather than illuminating, warming and healing like the sun, the 'gas looming through the fog' in *Bleak House* only serves to make darkness visible. 'Come, flame of gas,' Dickens commands, calling on it to show passers-by a slum graveyard whose 'poisoned air' exudes a 'witch-ointment'. Attributing emotions and motives to gas, Dickens anticipates the kind of psychological insinuation that we now call gaslighting. The term pays tribute to Patrick Hamilton's play *Gaslight*, first performed in 1938, in which a Victorian husband unsettles the mind of his distraught wife by fiddling with the gas jets in their house, but Dickens, who transfers the blame for upsetting our sense of reality to gas itself, was the first to remark on its hallucinogenic caprices. In *Our Mutual Friend*, the instability of gas makes it as fickle as well as flickery, subject to mood swings and spiritual torments. Lizzie Hexam stares into a fire that suddenly acquires a strange glow. 'That's gas, that is,' her brother explains, 'coming out of a bit of a forest that's been under the mud that was under the water in the days of Noah's Ark.' The primal light here emerges from murky depths, rather than divinely presiding in the sky. Gaslights in shops on a bleary day have a 'haggard and unblest air', aware that they are 'night-creatures that had no business abroad under the sun', and at the premises of Pubsey and Co. there is a 'sobbing gas-light in the counting-house window': it sobs in terror, because the 'burglarious' fog is slinking in through a keyhole, determined to muffle it.

The adder-tongued flames of gas appealed to Dickens because they matched the ignition of ideas that came alight in his head. A mocking metaphor likens the after-dinner stupor of Pickwick, who has been rendered 'somniferous' by wine, to the metabolic cycle of the flame in a gas lamp. At first he exhibits 'an unnatural brilliancy', like gas 'with the wind in the pipe'. Then he grows dim, but flares up once more 'to enlighten for a moment'. After that he subsides, and emits only 'an uncertain, staggering sort of light'. Finally he goes out altogether, and Dickens leaves him snoring. In his essay on night walks, the Uncommercial Traveller refers to 'the conscious gas', and observes that it 'began to grow pale with the knowledge that daylight was coming': like a vampire, it dreads sunrise. The same protest against dawn recurs the morning after Krook's death in *Bleak House* when the lamp-lighter, 'like an executioner to a despotic king, strikes off the little heads of fire that have aspired to lessen the darkness. Thus the day cometh, whether or no.' The humour in the metaphor is deadly: the return of light ought to be purgative or progressive, which is why the flames are said to be nobly aspirational, agents of what the liberal nineteenth century thought of as the march of mind. But the man with the hooked pole is extinguishing lamps rather than firing them up, and his trade is blackened by association with the axeman on whom despots rely. Decapitating the lamps, he protects the mental chiaroscuro that was Dickens's creative source. Although the day inevitably comes – or cometh, as the parody of biblical diction puts it – the novelist is already looking forward to dusk.

At the start of the twentieth century, the young heir in Conan Doyle's *The Hound of the Baskervilles* scans the dim avenue of yew trees where his predecessor died of fright and announces his intention to install a row of electric lamps, 'with a thousand-candlepower Swan and Edison right here in front of the hall doors'. This brash novelty would not have pleased Dickens. Before his last reading tours, he designed a lighting bridge to hang above the podium on which he placed his scripts – a baldachin of pipes, like an up-to-date version of the ceremonial canopies that hover over altars or thrones. A maroon panel at the top concealed gas jets and their tin reflectors; at the sides, extra gas outlets behind green shades surrounded his head with an eerie nimbus. As Dickens walked onstage, the gas on the rig was turned up, and it beckoned him out from the obscure realm where he did his imagining into a glow that was not day but an artificial night.

4

Cabbalistic Words

In 1859 Dickens fancifully recalled a childhood outing to a bazaar in Soho, during which he made his first attempt to officiate as an enchanter. He says that he coveted a harlequin's wand as a New Year's gift; in retrospect he calls it 'this talisman', a word that in its Arabian or Greek origins refers to an amulet used in esoteric rites. In remembering – or, more likely, inventing – the incident, he tried out the implement on the bossy minder who accompanied him, hoping that it would turn her 'into anything agreeable', but she remained unregenerate, which persuaded him of 'the wand's total incapacity'. Eventually he settled on another way of imposing his will. He exchanged the ineffectual stick for a pen, and used language to charm or change obdurate reality.

Words for Dickens did more than describe a world that already exists. They were magic spells; they even possessed an abstruse and mystical power that looked beyond the appearance of things and spurned intelligibility. The New Testament makes the Word a synonym for God and sets Logos to sponsor logical order; Dickens preferred an inspired illogic. In *Great Expectations* Magwitch asks Pip to read to him, specifying that it must be in a foreign language. He doesn't mind not understanding the recitation, and drinks in the glamorous sound without being vexed by meaning, as if he were at the opera. Dickens revelled in such entrancing obscurantism. When reflecting on language he often referred to the Kabbalah, the Jewish oral tradition that brought to light the recondite wisdom enshrined in scripture, and in doing so he aligned his own writing – sometimes ironically, sometimes not – with Holy Writ.

He advertised the affinity in 1849 when he performed a magic act at a children's party on the Isle of Wight: on that occasion he adopted the persona of the conjurer Rhia Rhama Rhoos, who claimed – in the spelling Dickens preferred – to have been 'educated cabalistically in the Orange Groves of Salamanca'. Clemency in the Christmas story *The Battle of Life*, learning to write, seems to occupy the same territory. Prayerfully positioned with elbows on the table and head low on an outstretched arm, she undertakes 'the formation of certain cabalistic characters, which required a deal of ink'. Equally solemn, a notary in *The Old Curiosity Shop* repeats some 'cabalistic words' which admit an articled clerk to the firm. In *Household Words* in 1851 Dickens reported that the railway network had introduced 'a code of cabalistic signs in use all over the country', challenging harried travellers to make sense of its abbreviations. The term demonstrates its true potency in *Nicholas Nickleby* when Newman Noggs gains entry to a closed room by 'merely uttering the monosyllable "Noggs", as if it were some cabalistic word, at sound of which bolts would fly back and doors open'. The trick works onomatopoeically: spoken out loud, Noggs's odd surname verbalises the noise that a knock on the door would have made. Another word releases a wish-fulfilling force as Martin Chuzzlewit and Mark Tapley return to England from America. They rejoice to catch sight of 'the old churches, roofs, and darkened chimney stacks of Home' and do not even mind returning in penury, because 'it was home'. Dickens then uses the emotive noun a third time and marvels at its charismatic power as if calling up a genie. 'Though home is a name, a word,' he says, 'it is a strong one; stronger than magician ever spoke, or spirit answered to, in strongest conjuration.' A fiercer potential is uncorked when a word threatens what Dickens calls 'verbal smifligation'. In *Nicholas Nickleby* the pugnacious Mr Pyke threatens to smifligate a harmless old man, which leads Mrs Nickleby, who has no 'previous acquaintance with the etymology of the word', to fear bloodshed. In fact the word is nonsensical bluster, but that does not weaken its ominous effect.

The Kabbalah's hermetic lore connects it with a cabal of another kind. In *A Child's History of England* Dickens slides sideways from theological riddles to political conspiracies when he mentions the alphabetical cabal of King Charles II's ministers – Clifford, Arlington, Buckingham, Ashley and Lauderdale – whose initials became an acronym for their seditious plotting. Dickens's language often has its own clandestine agenda. Like the romantic poets, he uses words to suggest a correspondence between outer and inner, nature and supernature, with metaphor as a way of tentatively reaching across the gap. 'To what shall I compare it?' asks Keats in a poem about sleep, admitting that it is 'beyond thought'. 'What thou art we know not,' Shelley says of the high-flying skylark; wondering 'What is most like thee?' he goes on to compare it to a glow-worm, a rose and 'a Poet hidden / In the light of thought'. Venice presented a similar challenge to Dickens. 'No waking words,' he says in *Pictures from Italy*, could match it; he uses dreaming words instead. He assumes that the cloisters and galleries he glides past must be 'the work of fairy hands', and glances at arcades that are 'garlands of hoarfrost or gossamer'. In a dungeon he touches a 'guilty door – low-browed and stealthy', which opened only to carry out the bagged bodies of dead prisoners. Later he recalls 'this Dream of mine' and wonders if the unnamed and unreal city still floats on the water: his Venice is the combined handiwork of fairies and demons.

Verbal sorcery like this dents the stable mental architecture that language is supposed to uphold. *Bleak House* mocks lawyers who bang their heads against obstructive 'walls of words' and a preacher who piles up 'verbose flights of stairs' that lead nowhere. Gradgrind in *Hard Times* expects education to 'form the minds of reasoning animals', but the school in *Dombey and Son* shows what that means: Dr Blimber's young pupils are harassed all day by 'stony-hearted verbs, savage noun-substantives, inflexible syntactic passages' and haunted at night when 'ghosts of exercises . . . appeared to them in their dreams'. Boz, writing about his schooldays, likens full stops to punitive pinpricks and associates them with the hard knuckles of the old woman who rapped his head to drum in her teachings. Dickens resisted this punitive regime by making up rules of his own. At school he invented a private lingo and gabbled in a kind of pig Latin. Later he established his literary identity by adopting a garbled word as his pseudonym. His youngest brother Augustus was nicknamed Moses, which if uttered through the nose came out as Boses and when shortened turned into Boz, less a name than an infantile noise. In 1837 an American reviewer of *Sketches by Boz* called Dickens a vulgar buffoon because he had disowned 'a name derived from his ancestors, and another conferred by his sponsors in baptism'. But the provocation was deliberate: it demonstrated that words begin as sounds, which are not necessarily articulate. Dickens was creating language all over again.

During his time as a child labourer he frequented a coffee room advertised by lettering on a window pane, and he later remembered the place whenever he saw a similar inscription from inside and read it backwards as MOOR-EEFFOC. Mirror writing presented him with an epiphany, demonstrating that the world can suddenly become exotic if words encrypt things rather than simply denoting them. Jo the crossing sweeper in *Bleak House* is unable to read the London street signs or identify the shops. He lacks 'the least idea of all that language' and sees only 'mysterious symbols': would the city be drearily demystified if he understood its commercial insignia? The illiterate scavenger Krook collects waste paper and is fascinated by the unintelligible writing on it, which he laboriously copies. He forms the signs singly and erases one before starting the next so that they never consolidate into words; he also arranges them back to front, 'beginning at the ends and bottoms of the letters'. In his view these graphic puzzles are hieroglyphs, encoding truths that are beyond his comprehension.

Mispronounced or misspelled, words blurt out new meanings. When Pickwick is sued for breach of promise by his landlady Mrs Bardell, who imagines that he has proposed to her, Sam Weller's father Tony suggests that he needs an 'alleybi'. Innocuous when spoken, the word when printed opens up an intriguing byway, an alley down which Pickwick might escape. Tony gets entangled in legal and financial terminology after his wife dies, but the words he muddles lighten his cares. Explaining his distraction, he tells Sam 'I was in a referee' – not a pensive reverie but an attempt to arbitrate opposed claims, as in a sporting match. Then he discovers a will that appoints him as his wife's 'sole eggzekiter'. His word makes execution eggy and edible, with a kite attached as a symbol of aerial frolics. When he contemplates an investment, a dropped consonant converts the funds – a worryingly unstable stock market – into 'the funs', where a return in the form of amusement is guaranteed. Eventually he cashes in the bequest and proposes an adjournment to 'hordit the accounts'. There is no question of hoarding because he is so open-handed, and the audit proves to be a euphemism for taking a drink.

Dickens was thrilled by the fluent excess of language and had no patience with concision. Ralph Nickleby, exasperated by his sister-in-law's prattling, says that 'An absence of business habits in this family leads, apparently, to a great waste of words', which is enough to mark him as a cold-hearted enemy of life. Bulging lists are Dickens's protest against this parsimony, celebrating the plenitude of commodities and of the words attached to them. At the legal stationer's establishment in *Bleak House* he enumerates the varieties of paper and parchment for sale, together with stamps, quills, pens, pencils, ink, inkstands, pocket-books, almanacs and diaries – 'in short, articles too numerous to mention', though they are all meticulously mentioned. Another shop in *The Chimes*, 'quite crammed and choked' with goods, is said to be 'voracious' like a shark's maw, but it is Dickens the omnivore who devotes an entire paragraph to a gorged survey of the food-stuffs, kitchen utensils and other 'petty merchandise' on display. Love is repetitious for the same reason. 'My little, little child! My little child!' says Bob Cratchit as he grieves for Tiny Tim in *A Christmas Carol*. Tilly Slowboy, the mentally sluggish nurse in *The Cricket on the Hearth*, rocks a baby while burbling gibberish, with 'all the nouns changed into the plural number': it is her way of fondly maximising the comfort she is employed to provide.

Attempts to regiment or regulate these proliferating words are doomed to fail. David Copperfield's headmaster Dr Strong is compiling a Greek dictionary, a weary chore which he never completes. 'What a necessary work! The meaning of words!' says his mother-in-law, adding that without Samuel Johnson's English dictionary we might be 'calling an Italian-iron, a bedstead'. Johnson's definitions pre-empted such a muddle, but Dickens would have been quite capable of making a crimping iron metamorphose into a bed frame. The young David instinctively improves on Dr Strong's pedantry. Informed that the rusty scholar is 'engaged in looking out for Greek roots', he assumes that this is 'a botanical furor' rather than a search for the inorganic 'roots of words'; his metaphor is not mistaken, because words for Dickens were vital growths. At the school attended by Paul Dombey, the Lexicon – as Dickens calls it – stays open, but only because it is 'so dropsical from constant reference, that it won't shut, and yawns as if it really could not bear to be so bothered'. The words that spill from that gaping mouth cast off the dictionary's discipline, and Logos gives way to a wickedly lively logomania.

Dickens feasted on words, like the Marshalsea official he remembered who, when toasting the monarch, would give a 'luscious roll' to the phrase as if it was 'delicious to taste'. More indigestibly, a single word, charged with emotion, obstructs the speech of Trotty Veck in *The Chimes*. Thinking aloud about his daughter Meg, he can't get beyond 'my darling M – e-' as 'the final letter swelled in his throat, to the size of the whole alphabet'. He is glutted or glottally stopped by language itself. But the words that swell and fatten so ripely are products of artifice, first pieced together by children when they experiment with combining letters. Dickens, a maker rather than merely a user of language, was fascinated by these early efforts. Once he quizzed a boy he met in Dublin about his vocabulary. The lad admitted to knowing a few 'wureds of one sillibil', though he had not learned to write; when Dickens asked whether he could 'cipher', he replied 'I can make a nought, which is not asy, being roond.' Stalled at zero, he had all the same designed a circle, which stood for nothing but could potentially contain everything.

During his American tour in 1842, Dickens became interested in the education of two blind patients in Boston. The boy whose case he summarised began to write by making descriptive squiggles that stood for things he could not see, then replaced them with purely arbitrary marks, as we all do after learning the alphabet. The other patient suffered extra disabilities, which made her triumph over them all the more valiant. She was unable to see, hear or speak, had no sense of smell and almost none of taste, and was effectively incarcerated in her own body. Her instructor Dr Samuel Howe taught her through touch, her 'one outward sense'. He developed a 'manual alphabet', proceeding from objects that could be handled to letters that were fitted together to demarcate those three-dimensional things; he then equipped her with a 'set of metal types' and a board into which she could slot them. She toiled alone, correcting her errors and amassing a vocabulary that could not be voiced, until – in a moment of overjoyed excitement – she began 'swiftly telegraphing' with her tiny fingers as she embraced an unseen friend. Dr Howe's journals retell the story almost allegorically to celebrate 'the power of mind in forcing matter to its purpose'.

Dickens made up his own version of Dr Howe's therapy, then comically sabotaged it. In a story written for Christmas in 1865, the travelling auctioneer Doctor Marigold adopts a mute called Sophy. He aims to make her literate, acquires 'large alphabets in a box, all the letters separate on bits of bone', and delivers the first lesson on their way to Windsor. He spells out the name of the place, gives Sophy the letters for CART while also chalking them on their conveyance, and hangs the inscription DOCTOR MARIGOLD on his waistcoat. Sophy assumes that he is the cart, which she also mistakes for 'the abode of royalty'. She can be forgiven: in Dickens's perpetually metamorphosing world, a cart, a castle and a man are only too likely to change places.

In his *Child's History*, Dickens commends King Alfred for learning to read, but explains that the king was attracted by the 'beautiful bright letters, richly painted' in an illuminated manuscript; when the narrative reaches the Reformation, he notes that Protestant iconoclasts rid churches of 'the images which the people had gradually come to worship' and enforced the authority of scripture. Dickens, no puritan in linguistic matters, reverses that ban and encourages words to effloresce into images. Hence his account of Mr Dorrit's courtly correspondence, which turns verbal flummery into a visual fantasia: his affectations recall the flourishes added by writing-masters to copy-books, in which titles that ought to be simple ciphers 'diverge into swans, eagles, griffins, and other calligraphic recreations, and . . . capital letters go out of their minds and bodies into ecstasies of pen and ink'. Mr Dorrit's circumlocutions are insane but ecstatic, and Dickens cannot help admiring this extravagance. He is not shy about uncovering secondary sexual characteristics in written words. Jobling in *Bleak House* guesses that a specimen of handwriting is female because it 'slopes a good deal' and 'the end of the letter "n"' is 'long and hasty'. In *Edwin Drood* the contents of Mrs Crisparkle's dining-room cupboard have binary labels: the jars of pickles are identified in sober business-like capitals, whereas the jams, 'of a less masculine temperament . . . announced themselves in feminine calligraphy' with frills and curlicues. The orphaned Pip in *Great Expectations* never knew his dead parents, so he pictures them as the personification of the weathered inscriptions on their tombstones: he assumes that his father had a square, stout, chiselled body, and pictures his mother with freckles like the discoloured rock. After a blow on the head leaves Pip's sister Mrs Joe unable to speak, she can only communicate by drawing on a slate. As she traces a T, Pip runs through a mental glossary 'from tar to toast and tub' but can't complete her thought; then he realises the mark is not a letter but a hammer, anthropomorphic shorthand for Joe and the sign of the forge where he works. 'It's *him*!' cries Biddy.

Dickens's characters can be eloquent even when silent, communicating with their whole bodies. In Naples, he marvelled at the beggars whose vocabulary of gestures articulated 'a copious language' with five fingers rather than one tongue. Tony Weller more economically conveys his detestation of the temperance preacher Reverend Stiggins in a 'perfect alphabet of winks'. After a deranged neighbour woos Mrs Nickleby by tossing marrows and other produce over the wall into her garden, Nicholas disqualifies this attempt at courtship by ruling that 'there is no language of vegetables which converts a cucumber into a formal declaration of attachment' – but perhaps there ought to be, since the mad Ophelia is allowed her language of flowers, with rosemary signifying remembrance. The flirtatious Mrs Nickleby compliments the lunatic's blather by saying that it sounds 'very like a musical glass', an instrument that when moistened and rubbed gives off slithery vibrations that words cannot paraphrase: Donizetti used a glass harmonica to transcribe the heroine's mad mental divagations in his opera *Lucia di Lammermoor*. Still more abstrusely, the retired mariner Captain Cuttle in *Dombey and Son* gesticulates with an arm that ends in a hook, 'like those Chinese sages who are said in their conferences to write certain learned words in the air that are wholly impossible of pronunciation'.

Other characters come alive when Dickens notices the odd ways in which spoken words emerge from their mouths. Fanny's violently plosive enunciation of 'Pauper!' in *Little Dorrit* is like the firing of a pistol. The governess Mrs General has a less aggressive use for the same consonant: she recommends that her female charges should train themselves to be pouty by repeating the litany of 'Papa, potatoes, poultry, prunes, and prism' because the alliterating consonant gives 'a pretty form to the lips'. The landlady Mrs Billickin in *Edwin Drood* aspirates aspirationally, imagining that this sounds refined. 'I am as well,' she announces, 'as I hever ham.' Offended when the schoolmistress Miss Twinkleton slights her for lacking 'accurate information', Mrs Billickin declares that 'my informiation, Miss Twinkleton, were my own experience'. The extra syllable is slipped in, Dickens notes, 'for the sake of emphasis at once polite and powerful', just as a crony of the aristocratic rakes in *Nicholas Nickleby* ends every sentence with 'hey?' – a hiccup that gives him the chance to display his gleaming teeth in an almost canine show of menace.

Dolly Varden in *Barnaby Rudge* orders her servant Miggs to 'hold her tongue directly', a phrase that mimes the disabling of language. In response, Miggs uses her tongue like a flag, flaunting her superiority with a fancy grammatical inflection: '"*Which*, was you pleased to observe, Miss Varden?" said Miggs, with a strong emphasis on the irrelative pronoun.' Cockneys supposedly pronounced v as w because some of them had no upper teeth with which to touch their lower lip: the phonetic flaw trips up Miggs, an ill-favoured spinster who disdains 'earthly wanities' and says she wouldn't stoop to use feminine wiles, 'not if I was Wenis'.

Dickens was equally happy to transcribe wordless noise. He onomatopoeically records the 'Whirr-r-r-r-r-r-r' of a grindstone or the silvery 'tink, tink, tink, tink, tink' of a locksmith's workshop. Public conveyances add to the din, sometimes unspeakably: delayed by Miss La Creevy's fuss and bustle, an omnibus in *Nicholas Nickleby* 'swore so dreadfully, that it was quite awful to hear it'. In Genoa, Dickens enjoyed the sneezy pronunciation of 'Batcheetcha', the name of the local saint Giovanni Battista, though he was less pleased by the incessant 'dingle, dingle, dingle' of church bells. The Uncommercial Traveller admires the virtuosity of a fairground ventriloquist who rasps and barks like a child with whooping cough, reproduces a bee's infuriated buzzing, and performs a symphonic solo in which the instrumentalists are farmyard animals.

To verbalise was never enough: Dickens wanted people to vocalise as well. Hence the detailed account he gives of Oliver Twist's nativity. The infant first breathes, sneezes, then discovers 'that very useful appendage, a voice' and emits a loud cry, which is 'proof of the free and proper action of his lungs'. Our vocal cords are an internal organ not an external attachment like a limb, but Dickens chooses to call Oliver's voice an appendage because at this stage it is his only means of projecting himself into the world. Mrs Gamp gets it right in one of her anecdotes. She remembers Mrs Harris's husband suffering a fit after being shown their first child, and confides that 'to ease her mind' Mrs Harris was told that 'his owls was organs': the poor man's howling was attributed to a barrel organ churning out tunes in the street. In the *Child's History*, the ownerless voices that direct Joan of Arc are villains. An ecclesiastical pedant asks Joan 'What language do your Voices speak?', to which she pertly replies 'A pleasanter language than yours.' This is thought to be the right answer, proving that she takes her orders from heaven. But then the voices multiply, which makes them suspect: 'the Voices had become (very like ordinary voices in perplexed times) contradictory and confused', so that Joan 'lost credit every day'. The orphan Sloppy in *Our Mutual Friend* has it easier, and is praised by his protector Betty Higden for his dramatic recitations from the newspaper. 'He do the Police in different voices,' she says in awe. In *The Haunted Man and the Ghost's Bargain* a young paper-seller keeps his wares fresh by varying a single vowel at intervals throughout the day. He starts by shouting that he has the morning paper for sale, after which, maintaining the correct 'grammatical succession', he changes to 'pepper', 'pipper' and 'popper' before he concludes by calling out 'Eve-ning Pup-per!' A cry in the street, listened to by Dickens, becomes an aria.

Magwitch, ordering Pip to repeat his name when they meet in the graveyard, wants the boy to be vociferous. 'Give it mouth!' he says – a command that recurs in *Barnaby Rudge*, where the hangman Mr Dennis coaches condemned prisoners to make final statements that will resonate from the scaffold. 'That's my maxim. Give it mouth,' he says. 'I've heerd . . . a eloquence on them boards – you know what boards I mean – and have heerd a degree of mouth given to them speeches, that they was as clear as a bell, and as good as a play.' The degrees of mouth resound polyphonically throughout Dickens's novels, and in the port of Marseille at the start of *Little Dorrit* the sailors and traders are 'descendants from all the builders of Babel'. In Genesis the skyscraping tower of Babel is toppled by God, who punishes men for their conceit by making them speak a babble of mutually unintelligible idioms. For Dickens, however, the jabbering plethora was a creative bonus rather than a curse.

Mr Boffin in *Our Mutual Friend* hires Silas Wegg to read Gibbon's *Decline and Fall of the Roman Empire* to him because, as he says, he is too old for 'alphabeds': instead of the dreary predict-ability of alpha followed by beta, he makes the stiff, upright letters relax into a comforting couch. Negotiating terms, Wegg warns that he charges extra to recite verse because of its mental strain, but his mangled pronunciation adds a zany poetry to his every utterance. Offered a slice of veal and ham pie, he responds by accepting a 'weal and hammer', which sounds both diseased and punitive – a proper snack for this gnarled, knotty man. He and Boffin confer new vernacular identities on the characters in Gibbon's chronicle by marring their names. Belisarius becomes the thuggish 'Bully Sawyers', the Greek chronicler Polybius is recon-ceived as the Roman virgin 'Polly Beeious', and Vittelius, briefly enthroned as emperor, emerges as 'Vittle-us', paraphrasing Oliver Twist's request for more. A mispronunciation by Sissy Jupe in *Hard Times* is equally pointed. 'Statistics', which the schoolmas-ter M'Choakumchild prates about, emerges from Sissy's mouth as 'stutterings'. An example follows, tallying the percentage of maritime travellers who drown at sea: to a statistician, people are numbers, as uselessly repetitious as stuttered consonants. The stumbling of another speaker touchingly summarises a small trag-edy. As Jo in *Bleak House* lies dying, he thanks the attendants who cluster around him for making him 'more cumfbler'. The conso-nants bump into each other almost unpronounceably, perhaps because Jo has no breath left for intervening vowels or for extra syllables: this is a word he has not tried to say before, because comfort is something he has never previously felt.

Even a speech defect like the asthmatic wheezing of the circus owner Sleary in *Hard Times* can become a kind of poetic diction. 'Thith ith a bad piethe of bithnith, thith ith,' Sleary laments; in a peroration he announces 'My latht wordth to you ith thith', and then with heroic persistence goes on to outline 'the philothophy of the thubject'. When Sleary admits 'My voithe ith a little huthky, Thquire,' Dickens comments that he has 'a voice (if it can be called so) like the efforts of a broken old pair of bellows'. Despite this slur, the metaphor reinflates his lungs: bellows were used in smelting or welding iron because their blasts of air increased combustion. Sleary's breath may be thick and slurred, but the man is a megaphone.

Writers have their own challenges to contend with. Confronted by 'very large, staring Roman capitals' in a placard, Boz remembers his bewilderment at school when he was 'first initiated in the mysteries of the alphabet'. The initiation and the mystery hint once again at the Kabbalah. David Copperfield, less intimidated, warms to 'the fat black letters in the primer' and has a particular fondness for 'the easy good-nature of O and Q and S'. Writing starts as drawing, so how could he not enjoy forming a circle and adding a tail to it, or tracing the convolutions of a serpent?

Letters became Dickens's childhood playmates, although some proved to be gamier than others. He was fond of A, as he says in his essay on Christmas trees, because it could stand for 'a good many things', whereas X and Z were less versatile. Miss Mowcher, the manicurist in *David Copperfield*, has an aristocratic Russian customer whose name has 'got all the letters in it, higgledy-piggledy'; she calls him 'Prince Alphabet turned topsy-turvy', taking a truly Dickensian delight in jumbling the sequence. Only a bureaucrat would proceed straight ahead from A to Z. The beadle in *Oliver Twist* therefore decides in advance on names for the foundlings he has to register: he calls Oliver's predecessor Swubble, then comes Twist, to be followed by Unwin, and next – merging the consonants that cockneys interchange – by Vilkins; when he reaches Z he will start all over again. 'You're quite a literary character, sir!' simpers the matron of the baby farm, though Bumble is at best dully literal-minded. A clerk in an unfrequented lawyer's office in *Our Mutual Friend* devises a similar system, arranging non-existent clients in an alphabetical queue by calling them Aggs, Baggs, Caggs, Daggs, or Alley, Balley, Calley, Dalley, and so forth. The whimsy affords Young Blight the 'fiction of an occupation', and in making the names rhyme he exhibits a rudimentary lyrical flair. Dickens shares his linguistic bravura with his characters, for whom the alphabet is a set of building blocks that enables them to construct a personal world and people it with their creations.

In Carlyle's *Sartor Resartus*, the German sage Teufelsdröckh pays an exalted but unorthodox tribute to 'The WORD', which he says empowers 'man, thereby divine, [to] create as by a *Fiat*'. We have inherited Adam's task in Eden, which was 'giving names to natural Appearances', and Teufelsdröckh suggests that science and poetry are both 'no other . . . than a right *Naming*'. With fewer theological rumblings, Dickens also saw naming as a creative summons, a command like Carlyle's 'Awake, arise! Speak forth what is in thee.' As he described the inception of *The Pickwick Papers*, a word served as the vital spark that created a character. 'I thought of Mr Pickwick,' he said, 'and wrote the first number.' The name's inane rhyme probably appealed to him, although he did not think it up himself: it was borrowed from the owner of a coach that travelled to and from Bath. Sam Weller spots that very coach and complains that the company has purloined his master's name, with Moses cheekily added as a prefix – a private joke that asserts Dickens's proprietorial rights. Sam then protests against the plagiarism and grumbles that it adds insult to injury, 'as the parrot said ven they not only took him from his native land, but made him talk the English langwidge arterwards'. The bird, loquacious and multilingual, adds its own protest about its re-education by the colonists who took it captive, even if Sam's chunky 'langwidge' is hardly the idiom of imperial conquest.

'Magnus is my name,' says the puffed-up Peter Magnus as he introduces himself to Pickwick. 'It's rather a good name, I think, sir?' This is mere pomposity; to be named by Dickens, however, certifies that a character is truly 'sui generis' – self-generated and therefore identifiable only by a neologism. Mrs Nickleby dispenses that grace on Dickens's behalf when she drops the names of former suitors called Tipslark and Smifser and alludes to her friends the Dibabses or the illustrious Peltiroguses. The medical authority Sir Tumley Snuffin does not need to appear in the novel, because his name speaks, or huffs and puffs in portly smugness, on his behalf. Before settling on Chuzzlewit as the surname for the titular family, Dickens reeled through a range of unwieldy compound words – including Chuzzlewig, Chuzzleboy, Chuzzletoe, Sweezleback, Sweezlewag and Sweezleden – that denominate a buzzing squadron of mismatched freaks. Naming of this kind is a primitive and magical practice, willing a character to personify a word. In *A Child's History* Dickens admires the Saxon habit of calling people Horse, Bear, Wolf or Hound, and he often gives the people in his novels animal avatars: Badger and Guppy in *Bleak House*, Bantam in *Pickwick*, Chick in *Dombey and Son*. When his history reaches the reign of William II, Dickens looks sideways to the royal favourite Ralph, 'nicknamed – for almost every famous person had a nickname in those rough days – Flambard, or the Firebrand'. At once this fellow seems to ignite: the rough days do justice to ruffians. In *American Notes* Dickens inspects treaties that native chieftains signed with 'drawings of the creatures or weapons they were called after' – Great Turtle, Buffalo, War Hatchet – and comments sadly on the difference between their 'feeble and tremulous' signatures and the manual power they possessed when drawing a bow or firing a rifle. Literacy for them entails a loss of power.

Patronymics enroll us in a collective as offshoots of a genetic type. Dickens, however, expects his characters to be exceptional: Nicholas is not really a Nickleby, nor Martin a Chuzzlewit, because they share no characteristics with their mercenary relatives. Betsey Trotwood marvels that 'any human being has gone into a Christian church, and got herself named Peggotty', which prompts David Copperfield's mother to point out that 'It's her surname' and was not of her choosing. Actually it sounds like a fond demotic nickname: Margaret may have been shortened to Meg and given a different vowel, then changed by a playful rhyme to Peg or Peggy, leaving Dickens to insert an extra syllable as he verbally conjures up this endearing woman. Luckily the narrator of *Great Expectations* cannot pronounce his given name – though why ever did his parents call him Philip Pirrip? – and as a result he becomes Pip, which defines him as a seedling and announces that his growth will be the subject of the novel. His friend Wemmick, sending him a message, comically confuses his official identity with the familiar version and adds a title left over from the chivalrous past: he addresses the missive to Philip Pip, Esquire.

When Tom Pinch in *Martin Chuzzlewit* visits the pretentious suburban household where his sister is employed, the footman asks 'Hany neem?', aspirating one vowel and distorting another to convey his contempt for this 'nameless and obscure individual'. Tom says he is Ruth's brother, at which the footman drawls 'Mother?' It's a valuable lesson: snobbery is an exercise in nominalism, underscored by a mannered accent. The haughty Mrs Sparsit in *Hard Times* emphasises her lineage by saying that she is 'a Powler', though strangers puzzle over what a powler might be – 'a business, or a political party, or a profession of faith'? Mr and Mrs Meagles in *Little Dorrit* take pains when naming Tattycoram, the foundling they adopt. The child starts out as 'Harriet Beadle – an arbitrary name, of course', but the reminiscence of Bumble's profession in *Oliver Twist* is an ill omen. Hoping that 'a playful name might . . . have a softening and affectionate kind of effect', they shorten Harriet to Hattey and subsequently change that to Tatty; to this they add the surname of the 'blessed creature' who established the London Foundling Hospital, the philanthropist Thomas Coram. It serves as the secular equivalent of a saint's name, and ultimately, following a long setback when Tattycoram succumbs to a malevolent influence, the benediction works.

Jo in *Bleak House* is unaware that his name is a meagre colloquial contraction, and with 'no father, no mother, no friends' he 'don't know that everybody has two names. Never heerd of sich a think.' His ignorance is indignant, not pitiable: Jo, by not being Joe, remains irreplaceably himself. Any further editing, however, would reduce a life to a minimal initial. After Merdle's disgrace in *Little Dorrit* he is downgraded to a pecuniary symbol: school pupils 'who were in the large text and the letter M' are 'set the copy "Merdle, Millions."' Except in Merdle's case, Dickens resists this ignominy. The narrator in 'The Ghost in Master B.'s Room' is obliged to sleep in a room once occupied by the defunct Master B., about whom he knows nothing. He wonders whether the former occupant was called Benjamin, Bartholomew, Bill or – assuming he was born in a leap year – Bissextile; he goes on to muse that he might have had Brains, liked Books, been good at Boxing and 'in his Buoyant Boyhood Bathed from a Bathing-Machine at Bognor, Bangor, Bournemouth, Brighton or Broadstairs like a Bounding Billiard Ball'. Outfacing the ghost he expects to encounter, he makes the inert abbreviated capital bounce into alliterative and athletic life.

In *Martin Chuzzlewit* a person becomes a predicate. 'If there's a Werb alive,' declares the eternally resourceful Mark Tapley, 'I'm it.' Mark knows that a verb signifies 'to be, to do, or to suffer', and on his travels with Martin he is 'always a-bein', sometimes a-doin', and continually a-sufferin''. Pancks, the assiduous rent-collector in *Little Dorrit*, is also a figment of grammar, forever 'conjugating the Imperative Mood Present Tense of the verb To keep always at it'. Who, by contrast, would choose to be a noun, stolid and inert like the staircase of pious truisms or the wall of legal jargon in *Bleak House*? And adjectives describe secondary characteristics, which can be easily blanked out: on one of Dickens's journalistic tours of the criminal underworld, a villain who has been roused from his bed says he won't 'have no adjective police and adjective strangers in my adjective premises!' Such expletives are nothing but bombast, as when Bumble in *Oliver Twist* declares that 'of all the artful and designing orphans that ever I see, Oliver, you are one of the most bare-facedest', giving vent – as Dickens says, emphasising the beadle's windy vacuity – to 'this compound adjective'. Mark Tapley rightly chooses to be a verb, which makes language rise up from the page: in him the word becomes flesh, though not quite as the Bible intended.

Because language is an obstreperous vital sign, Dickens tried to save it from dying into the respectable silence of literature. Inspecting a town – possibly Newbury in Berkshire – that quietly languished when the railway bypassed it, the Uncommercial Traveller observes a building sign that announces

L   Y INS T   .

Before the rest of the inscription fell off, it advertised the local Literary Institution; now it might be apologising that it is 'Lamentably Insolvent'. The problem, the Traveller says, is that the doomed institutional letters were too ambitiously addressed to eternity.

Print has a fatal fixity. Scrooge, aghast when he is shown his own grave, begs to be allowed to 'sponge away the writing on this stone!', though water will not efface the predestining numerals. Stephen Blackpool, trapped in a miserable marriage in *Hard Times*, dreams that an accusing beam of light picks out a line from the tablet of the Ten Commandments and beams the words through the church. No longer printed or engraved, the threatening decree resounds 'as if there were voices in the fiery letters'. Perhaps he was reading Blake's *The Marriage of Heaven and Hell* at bedtime. There, on his trip to hell, Blake sees a printing press at work oppressively regulating and standardising human experience; the heavenly alternative is Blake's pictorial illumination of his verses, which makes words germinate and flower. In *Martin Chuzzlewit* Mrs Gamp inadvertently paraphrases Blake's anathema when she gapes at the swaggering of the undersized servant boy Benjamin Bailey. 'All the wickedness of the world,' she says, 'is Print to him.' 'Print and paper!' snorts Jeddler in *The Battle of Life*, rebuking his daughter when she cries as she reads about the tribulations of a fictional heroine who consists of 'rags and ink' rather than flesh and blood.

How can those dead letters be vivified? Although God is the Word, St Paul warned against taking divine utterances literally, and separated 'the letter that kills' from 'the life-giving spirit'. Dickens, for whom writing was close to a religion, often returns to that distinction with his own unspiritual intent. At the end of *Oliver Twist*, Mr Brownlow asks Monks, Oliver's villainous half-brother, about an explanatory document that their father addressed to Oliver's mother. 'What of the letter?' demands Brownlow. Monks nonchalantly defines it as 'A sheet of paper crossed and crossed again': the letter is cross-hatched, with a diagonal layer of writing to save space, but the difficulty of reading it matches the snarled motives of the writer, who wanted both to confess his adultery and to obscure it. 'The will,' Brownlow dryly remarks about the dead man's testament, 'was in the same spirit as the letter.' *The Old Curiosity Shop* answers back on behalf of the letter. Kit wallows in inky blotches while learning to write, but makes better progress when relying on physical instinct with his girlfriend Barbara: 'she was the book' and her desire to be kissed was 'as plain as print'.

When Dickens visited Niagara Falls, a place he called enchanted ground, he asked himself 'what voices spoke from out of the thundering water'. At the precipice he said he felt close to the Creator, so the hubbub might have been the amplified word of God. But the deafening sound was inarticulate and the voluminous water hurled itself into an abyss, leaving only a 'tremendous ghost of spray and mist' in the air. He remembered this spectacle on Valentine's Day in 1850 when he toured the postal sorting office in London. Here he pictured the impassioned missives swirling across the room as 'a Niagara of language' – a dry cataract, but one in which the voices, amorous rather than furiously thundery, sent endearments to their addressees rather than being doomed to expire in a rocky gulf. At Niagara the crushing weight of water dissolves into clammy air; in the rooms at St Martin's-le-Grand, the cascade leaves 'not a drop behind', as every letter buoyantly sails on to arrive at its destination later that day. As a sequel, fifteen minutes before the deadline for posting newspapers without a fee, Dickens watches a linguistic downpour: it begins with 'just drizzling newspapers' and is soon followed by 'the first black fringe of a thunder-cloud' of newsprint, after which a harder storm 'rained, hailed, snowed, newspapers'. Although his aim is to report on 'the system of stamping, sorting, and arranging' mail, he allows this linguistic flux to overwhelm the routine of classification and distribution, and nature's self-destructive torrent condenses into a maelstrom of wild, whirling words.

Dickens's own writing was an exuberant release of energy, yet he knew that the activity could have a more urgent or desperate motive. In his cell at the Bastille in *A Tale of Two Cities* Dr Manette uses a 'rusty iron point' to write the story of his persecution, scraping soot and charcoal from the chimney and mixing it with his blood to make ink. At once a deprived cave-dweller and a crafty engineer, he manufactures the tools he needs, produces a 'written paper' that contains his 'last recorded words' and hides it in a cavity he has scraped out inside a chimney. This is Manette's testimonial: perhaps no one will ever read it, but it testifies to the fact that he was once alive.

Amid the uproar of the London docks, the Uncommercial Traveller happens upon a scene of rapt concentration. The deck of an emigrant ship could be Dr Manette's prison cell in the open air and multiplied almost to infinity, as groups of Mormons bound for Utah kneel, crouch or lie in every available space, preparing farewell letters to those they have left behind. One old man dictates to an amanuensis, who periodically removes his thick fur cap 'for the ventilation of his brain' and stares at his customer, whom he views as 'a man of many mysteries'. In this still, silent tableau, Dickens might be looking at his divided self in the act of composition. The fantasist in him guided the hand of the more alertly rational writer, equipped with the same valve in his head to discharge excess excitement. Although the Traveller marvels at 'the power of self-abstraction' the writers display, Dickens could not match their self-contained calm and did not want to. Even in the solitude of his study he was performing as if for the benefit of an audience, and the utensils he identifies on the migrant ship – 'pens and inkstands in action', together with sheafs of paper – were deployed as theatrical props.

In another essay, the Traveller remarks that a craft such as chair-mending is best transacted in front of lookers-on, who encourage the worker by admiring his skill; on behalf of his fellow writers, he regrets that 'no one looks at us while we plait and weave these words'. The metaphor is chosen with Dickens's usual care. A text, like a textile, is intricately woven from separate strands, which is why the shamefaced letter Winkle writes to his father in *The Pickwick Papers* is said to consist of 'four closely-written sides of extra superfine wire-wove penitence'. Weavers, using needles or sitting at their looms, need deft and dexterous fingers, and Dickens's pen shared those skills. Its capacities were all the more impressive in view of its lowly origins: the Traveller, exploring a scruffy neighbourhood near Waterloo, casts a rueful glance at a moulting hen 'afflicted with a paucity of feather and visibility of quill, that gives her the appearance of a bundle of office pens'.

Energised by Dickens, pens do more than tentatively dip into inkwells. Fanny Squeers uses hers as a pretext for flirting with Nicholas Nickleby: she tells him it needs mending, and he carves her a new nib. In *Bleak House* journalists reporting on Krook's spontaneous combustion scribble with 'ravenous little pens on tissue-paper'. The hacks are hungry for the sensational story, and their implements seem equally famished. Beyond the chore of forming words, ink has a free-flowing life of its own, so that Kit, during his lessons with Little Nell, begins 'to daub himself with ink up to the very roots of his hair'. A repressed schoolmistress in *Our Mutual Friend* has to be more cautious, because 'if her faithful slate had had the latent qualities of sympathetic paper, and its pencil those of invisible ink', the dry arithmetical sums she writes up would flame with unpedantic desire. Sympathetic paper entices the writer to confide in it, but because the ink is invisible, prim Miss Peecher stays spotless. The characters in *The Battle of Life*, by contrast, have a keen physical appetite for the black liquid. Snitchley the lawyer requests 'a mouthful of ink' so signatures can be added to a legal document, and Clemency, 'having once tasted ink . . . became thirsty in that regard', like a tiger 'after tasting another sort of fluid'. The affinity with blood is creepily enforced in *Little Dorrit*, where Merdle borrows a tortoiseshell handled penknife for an unspecified purpose. 'I'll undertake not to ink it,' he reassures its owner; it is retrieved after his suicide in a bath, 'soiled, but not with ink'.

In *Somebody's Luggage*, first published in 1862 in Dickens's journal *All the Year Round*, the output of ink becomes pathological. Here the head waiter at a London hotel takes possession of some abandoned bags which contain smeary manuscripts scrawled in 'a dreadful bad hand'. The departed guest was an obsessive writer, who once called for a fresh pen and paper five times in a single morning, after which he retired to bed where he 'immolated those materials' and left a stain on the pillowcase. Stuffed into his boots and hat, folded into the whalebones of his umbrella, mixed with his shaving kit, the besmirched pages replace his absent body. He seems to have suffered a symbolic decapitation, the most Dickensian of fates: 'He had put no Heading to any of his writings. Alas! Was he likely to have a Heading without a Head, and where was *his* Head when he took such things into it?' The waiter tries to sell the screeds, which to his surprise are accepted for publication by *All the Year Round*. Then the writer himself unexpectedly returns, and the waiter hands him the proofs sent back from the journal. 'I am in print!' the writer cries; savouring the precious word, he elongates it to 'Per-rint'. He orders the waiter to fill the inkstands and bring new pens, and sits up all night correcting the pages. But his scratches and superimpositions make them unreadable, and when he returns them the disgusted printer throws them into the fire.

Dickens was amused to hear about a medium in Philadelphia, another 'appalling author' who alleged that the pencil exerted an iron grip on her and did its writing automatically. 'Is this Insanity?' she reportedly asked; in his essay on spiritualism Dickens remarked 'we rather think it is'. He might have been wondering about his own headlong impetuosity. Near the end of *A Christmas Carol*, the manuscript shows his pen running away with him, as it did in the zigzagging flourishes it added beneath his signature in letters. After the last of the phantoms shrinks and dwindles into Scrooge's bedpost, the pen forms no more words, and the rest of the page is filled with three wheeling curlicues that might have been traced by the harlequin's wand that Dickens tried out in Soho. These loops take the nib spiralling to the bottom, and during its descent it spits ink in a black spray – perhaps a hint that the bedpost may not after all be safely inanimate. Language originates in an ebullient chaos, which it purports to rationalise; now it returns there, imploding into a blot.

5

The Great Creator

Dickens, having made and managed a planet of his own, felt entitled to question more orthodox accounts of creation. He found
it hard to believe that the universe had a divine overseer, as he implies
in a letter to Forster about the metaphysical gropings of a patient at
the Blind Institution in Lausanne. This was the young man – born
deaf and dumb, then blinded by an accident in childhood – who had
been reproved for telling a harmless lie, which his minders blamed 'on
nature's prompting (the devil's of course)'. Dickens remarks that the
earnest fellow 'knows of God, as of Thought enthroned somewhere'
– but was his knowledge only an agnostic projection? The throne's
location in the sensory darkness remains unclear, and the enthroned
thinker seems not to have noticed the ordure and iniquity Dickens
saw all around him. When a character in *Tom Tiddler's Ground* rhapsodises about 'GOD's working world and its wholesomeness, both
moral and physical', Dickens nudges us to remember the drudgery
of an overworked society and London's unwholesome slums. *Hard
Times* accuses the industrial regime of Coketown of repressing our
need for relaxation and enjoyment, and predicts that these fanciful
cravings will persist 'until the laws of the Creation [are] repealed'.
That phrase hints at Dickens's ambition, which was at once meta-
physically bold and endearingly humane: he set his novels to relitigate
creation and to regenerate the weary world.

To start the process, *Martin Chuzzlewit* almost casually disestablishes
the biblical creator. The pompous architect Pecksniff is described
as 'that Great Abstraction', like the merely conceptual First Cause

extolled by Enlightenment philosophers; Pecksniff, however, is not so much abstracted as absent, too listless to qualify as a prime mover. He sets his pupils to mimic the workmanship of God's world by pointlessly sketching elevations of Salisbury Cathedral or piling bricks into the shape of St Peter's in Rome and St Sophia in Constantinople. Does God, like Pecksniff himself, expect us to spend our lives praising him and erecting monuments to his glory? Tom Pinch's devotion to his sanctimonious master counts as an article of religious faith, and his abrupt dismissal leaves a hole in the sky. 'There was no Pecksniff,' Tom tells himself, 'there never had been a Pecksniff.' Shocked into recognising 'the unreality of Pecksniff', he at first finds it hard 'to say his prayers without him': to whom should those obsequious utterances be addressed? But he soon recovers, falls asleep, and dreams of the old imposter 'as he Never Was'. He then sets off for London, and as the coach that carries him to freedom speeds through Salisbury, Dickens notes that it noisily 'defied the Cathedral', whose precincts are meant to be reverently hushed and unhurried. This defiance or deviation is extended in later novels. When Clennam in *Little Dorrit* returns from abroad, he winces at the church bells that browbeat Londoners on Sunday and spoil their day of rest by ordering them to worship a God who approves of their sweated toil. The more privileged can afford to ignore that summons: for them, faith is a lazy, ritualised fashion, defined in *Bleak House* as religious dandyism, and Lady Dedlock, installed in a shrine by her fawning admirers, is said to be 'an exhausted deity'. By the mid-nineteenth century, God had succumbed to the same enervation as this bored high-society goddess; a Nietzschean act of deicide was hardly necessary.

Ironically enough, Dickens himself was first condemned and then acclaimed for usurping powers that were no longer wielded from on high. The accusation of self-deifying conceit came in 1858 after his separation from his wife Catherine, whom he unjustly reviled as an unfit mother. He first partitioned their bedroom and then ejected her from his house, even keeping their children away from her. Hoping to fend off a scandal, he sent an account of his 'domestic trouble' to the newspapers and printed it on the front page of *Household Words*.

In this self-vindication he let his covenant with his readers take precedence over his marriage vows, declaring that he had entered into 'my present relations with my Public' twenty-three years earlier and had been 'as faithful . . . as they have been to me'. He went on to invoke the 'sacredly private nature' of the case he had chosen to publicise, lied by calling the breach amicable, fulminated against the rumours about his infatuation with young Ellen Ternan, and accused the gossips of foully bearing false witness 'before Heaven and earth'.

Outraged by such self-righteousness, the satirist Percival Leigh said that he expected Dickens would next 'proclaim himself to be God Almighty', and Shirley Brooks, the editor of *Punch*, vowed to become an atheist if that happened. Then in 1880, ten years after Dickens's death, the poet Edward FitzGerald used the same epithet to honour him as a universal paterfamilias. Dickens, FitzGerald said, had been 'inspired to Create like a little God Almighty'. A god of might is a patriarchal autocrat, but FitzGerald's capitalised verb paid tribute to Dickens's unstoppably prolific output. Piety inserted the adjective, although Dickens's achievement was hardly little: his books contain well over a thousand distinctly individualised characters, including Barnaby Rudge, a village idiot who is viewed as the 'despised and slighted work' of 'the Great Creator of mankind'. The 'Infinite Benevolence' recommended in 'the Everlasting Book' is not extended to him; Dickens makes up for God's negligence by eavesdropping on Barnaby's lyrical inner life.

Virginia Woolf called Dickens 'a born creator' and added that he was 'prodigious in his fecundity', a sniffy remark that applied alike to his fifteen novels and his ten children. Creation for him was a biological as well as an aesthetic affair, and he often unashamedly said so. When Mark Tapley leaves home in *Martin Chuzzlewit*, he calculates that he won't be missed because the abundant village children will replenish the place, along with the likely progeny of 'the terrier-bitch from over the way'. As a sequel to the dog's serial litters, Magna Mater herself waddles into view later in the novel when Mrs Gamp tallies the childbirths at which she has tipsily presided and claims the offspring as her own: 'The families I've had, if it was all knowd, and credit done where credit's doo, would take a week to chris'en at Saint Polge's fontin!' The cathedral font flows with milk in *Dombey and Son*. A wet nurse is hired to suckle motherless Paul along with her own brood, and the busybody Miss Tox loosely refers to the all-suc-couring bosom of Polly Toodle as 'one common fountain'. The God of Genesis fashions mankind without recourse to a sexual partner and later begets an only son asexually; the village dog, Mrs Gamp and Polly Toodle together suggest that the biblical account has omitted half of the truth.

Dickens pointed to a contradiction that for him was psychologi-cal as much as metaphysical. He personified nature as 'our mighty mother', yet insisted that as 'creatures of one common origin' we owe a 'duty to the Father of one family'. Duty is what the tycoon Dombey expects from the son and daughter he bullies. One parent is supposed to nourish us, while the other regulates our conduct. Dickens, however, had been allocated a mother deficient in nurturing instincts and a father too weak to be authoritative: how could he believe that the nuclear family had a celestial prototype? To complicate matters, during his lifetime God's monopoly faltered and pagan replacements began to fill up the newly empty sky. Dickens explored that polyglot pantheon, and he also looked back at the sacrilege of Mary Shelley's Frankenstein, the scientist who competes with God by redesigning mankind. The motive for these speculative forays was not a quest for faith: Dickens the demiurge was examining his supernatural competitors and testing himself against them.

At the start of *Sartor Resartus*, Carlyle complains that in the utilitarian nineteenth century 'the Creation of a World is little more mysterious than the cooking of a dumpling'. To Dickens, the creation of a world remained as mysterious as his own superabundant creativity, and in trying to understand it he tiptoed into prohibited terrain.

In *Tom Tiddler's Ground* the schoolmistress Euphemia Pupford lectures her female pupils on the creation stories of 'the misguided heathens', censoring the more salacious tales. Cupid is never mentioned; when she describes how 'Minerva sprang, perfectly-formed, from the brain of Jupiter', Miss Pupford seems to imply 'So I myself came into the world.' Inspector Bucket in *Bleak House*, fascinated by Lady Dedlock, likens her to 'Venus rising from the ocean', though that image is also bowdlerised: according to myth, the love goddess was born from the spermatic foam of the waves on which she rides in Botticelli's painting. Dickens recoiled from what he called the 'uninteresting condition' of his more or less continuously pregnant wife but he laughed at the fable of an immaculate conception. While living in Genoa in 1844, he noticed a rotting fresco that portrayed a Madonna 'with a mildewed glory round her head, holding nothing in an undiscernible lap with invisible arms'. Mould on the halo, an empty womb, a saviour who dissolves into thin air: so much for sacred virginity and parthenogenesis.

During his Italian sojourn, however, Dickens received a nocturnal visit from the same Madonna, whom he welcomed because in this manifestation she resembled a precious personal muse. In a dream he was approached by a figure in 'blue drapery', a match for the Virgin Mary as painted by Raphael. He addressed her as 'Dear' – at which she recoiled, aghast at his 'gross nature' – because, although he saw no face, he took her to be the spirit of his wife's teenage sister Mary Hogarth, who had died suddenly in his house seven years earlier. Dickens grieved obsessively for his sister-in-law and even wanted to be buried with her; she was the model for two of his homespun angels, Rose in *Oliver Twist* and Agnes in *David Copperfield*. Paraphrasing the question his characters often ask about their over-vivid imaginings, he wondered whether he should regard this beatific version of Mary as 'a dream or an actual Vision'. Perhaps this was his venture into theogony, demonstrating that man creates gods (or goddesses) rather than vice versa.

He asked the apparition 'What is the True religion?', guessing that she would recommend Catholicism, and with 'heavenly tenderness' she agreed that it would suit him best. Although he ignored her advice and never stopped denouncing 'the Romish Church' as a curse on humanity, he continued to debate the question he put to her. Canon Crisparkle in *The Mystery of Edwin Drood* tells an evangelical bigot that he will neither 'bow down to a false god' nor 'deny the true God!', but Dickens doubted that any creed possessed an exclusive right to the truth. During his conversation with the ghostly Mary, he begged for some proof that she was a real presence, not a fantasy. 'Form a wish,' said the spirit, echoing the genie's invitation to Aladdin in the *Arabian Nights' Tales*. This suggests that religion like art exists to answer our prayers, which makes it quite literally an exercise in magical thinking. Alternatively it is the capacity to compel belief, regardless of its right to do so. Magwitch in *Great Expectations* carries round with him 'a greasy little black Testament', probably pocketed in a courtroom during his criminal career, and he brandishes it when making Pip and others swear irreligious oaths of fealty. God's register of rules has become a sorcerer's implement, all the more effective when used, as Pip says, like 'a sort of legal spell or charm'.

Dickens catalogues a variety of strange gods, all of whom are fictitious. To begin with, *The Pickwick Papers* glances at the tutelary spirits of pre-Christian Britain. On his trip to Bath, Mr Pickwick reads about Prince Bladud, who in a latter-day Ovidian metamorphosis was transformed into the spring that made the spa town's fortune. Disappointed in love, Bladud wept for his lost lady and wished that his tears might flow forever. Immediately the ground gaped open, an abyss ingested him, and a new source of water gushed up in his place. As Dickens comments, 'The heathen deities . . . used occasionally to take people at their words', although the instant gratification of Bladud's wishes proves 'extremely awkward' for him. Foreign idols have startling walk-ons. In *The Pickwick Papers* a pagan spirit from *The Arabian Nights* is charged with protecting a Christian sanctuary: Holyrood in Edinburgh is 'guarded day and night' by the crag known as Arthur's Seat, which towers above it 'surly and dark, like some gruff genius', a geological version of the tutelary djinni who emerges from Aladdin's lamp. After Mercy Pecksniff's betrothal in *Martin Chuzzlewit*, her rejected suitor Moddle announces that 'the car of Juggernaut had crushed him', and when Mercy's acid-visaged sister Charity snaps him up he is tempted to act out a 'private little Juggernaut' by lunging into the road so that passing vehicles can run over him. The juggernaut was a wagon that carried an image of a Hindu god; ardent believers were supposedly encouraged to sacrifice themselves under its wheels. A religion that commends meek human kindness is here overturned, leaving Moddle as a martyr to his own ill-tempered Krishna. The British Museum, established on its Bloomsbury site in the 1850s, housed a convocation of savage gods from outposts like Assyria or Polynesia. Joining Inspector Field of Scotland Yard for a night-time round of low-life catacombs in central London, Dickens notes that before their rendezvous his guide has been on patrol in the galleries of the museum: as its 'guardian genius', he keeps a wary eye on 'cat-faced Egyptian Giants', 'the Parrot Gods of the South Sea Islands' and 'other traces of an elder world'. In *Edwin Drood* the lawyer Grewgious suddenly acquires a bizarre religious aura when he is likened to 'the carved image of some queer Joss or other'. Joss, remotely derived from 'deus', is pidgin English for a votive figure in a Chinese shrine, so the stiffly upright Grewgious has a puzzling affinity with a Chinese addict in the East End opium den who in his drugged stupor 'convulsively wrestles with one of his many Gods or Devils'.

The financier Merdle in *Little Dorrit* is a temporary god, an 'object of worship' to credulous investors, having surely been made from something other than 'the commonest clay' – perhaps from excrement, with which Merdle is all but synonymous. A New Testament rule about virtuous poverty is relaxed for him: despite his riches he has 'already entered into the kingdom of Heaven', or has been welcomed into 'good society', which amounts to the same thing. Merdle's cult also brings him close to the parrot gods in their jungly hide-out at the museum, and the believers he bankrupts are likened to a deluded native bowing before 'some log or reptile' that is 'the Deity of his benighted soul'. Merdle's wife, tired of London, says she fancies a life among 'the Savages in the Tropical seas'; as if already there, she keeps a screeching parrot in her salon. Imagining that migration, she recalls a poem she once read, 'something about Lo the poor Indians whose something mind!' She is garbling a couplet from Alexander Pope's *Essay on Man*:

Lo! the poor Indian, whose untutor'd mind
Sees GOD in clouds, or hears him in the wind.

Pope rebuked the untutored mind, but this pantheism appealed to romantic poets: in *The Prelude* Wordsworth is guided back to his childhood Eden by a little wandering cloud, and Shelley heard the west wind as a trumpet prophesying radical change.

The Indian in Pope's poem is ignorant of 'proud Science' and is happy just 'to be'. In the mid-nineteenth century, science grew even prouder: the geologist Charles Lyell estimated the true age of the earth and examined the elemental forces that shaped its evolution and doomed it to slow decay. Those undivine energies make themselves felt throughout *Little Dorrit*. Marseille, where many of the characters are detained in quarantine at the start of the novel, is blistered by the 'universal stare' of the meridional sun, while Calais is assailed by 'the undermining and besieging sea'. As Mr Dorrit and his family cross the Swiss Alps on their grand tour, the monastery at the St Bernard Pass is suffocated and then effaced by cloud, 'as if the whole rugged edifice were filled with nothing else, and would collapse as soon as it emptied itself'. In *The Prelude*, the craggy heights and plummeting depths of the Alps offer Wordsworth a preview of apocalypse when, as the Bible predicts, nature will be absorbed into eternity. The landscape described by Dickens in 1856, only six years after Wordsworth's poem was published, has a merely negative sublimity. Here God is vaporous or vapid, anything but almighty.

Reducing God to 'a literary term, in short', Matthew Arnold recommended that the Bible should be read as literature, with poetry separated from dogma. Instead of accepting this secular compromise, Dickens produced his own version of the grand scriptural narrative.

He thought that the Bible disagreed with itself, but the schism between the stern prohibitions of the Old Testament and the redemptive gospel of the New matched a disparity in his own motives. In the Old Testament, God like an omniscient storyteller foreordains fates and imposes penalties. Dickens sometimes does the same, and in *Dombey and Son* he rains down 'social retributions' by sending the 'Destroying Angel' from Exodus to spread disease in the slums. With its gentler code of love and forgiveness, the New Testament envisages a roseate happy ending for us all. This is anticipated at the end of *Martin Chuzzlewit* when, as Tom Pinch plays the organ, Dickens imagines the music enveloping both him and his sister and wafting them straight to heaven. Each part of the biblical diptych harbours a mystery that Dickens saw as a preserve of imagination, not a divine prerogative – in the Old Testament, a world that is created out of nothing, and in the New a second life that arises from or conquers death.

The London pea-souper with which *Bleak House* begins is more than a weather report. Whereas God in Genesis separates day from night, sky from earth, water from dry land, Dickens mixes them up, and the command 'Let there be light' is nullified in a city bogged down in mud and muffled by fog. Mud and fog were the raw material of his own creation, first merged in 1837 when he invented the backward town of Mudfog – another parody of Chatham – and transcribed the muddled, foggy-brained proceedings of its municipal Society for the Advancement of Everything; later in *Great Expectations* a convict describes the Thames estuary, where Dickens grew up, as a mishmash of 'swamp, mist, and mudbank'. *Bleak House* uses the same ingredients to query the events of the first seven days as recounted in Genesis. The primal dawn is indefinitely delayed, questioning 'if this day ever broke', and in the sodden streets it is 'as if the waters had but newly retired from the face of the earth'. A metaphor blots out our energising star when Dickens suggests that snowflakes of soot have 'gone into mourning . . . for the death of the sun'. The Lord Chancellor, who presides over a legal system that stultifies society, possesses only a 'foggy glory', a tarnished aureole like the mildewed halo of the Genoese Virgin. As fog condenses in the Essex marshes and creeps from the river through the London docks, this revision of the Old Testament skips ahead from Genesis to Exodus: Dickens is tracking an Egyptian plague. In the rank slum of Tom-all-Alone's, a thick, formless gloom spreads after sunset, the moon's cold beams show up a warren that is a grazing ground for 'the blackest nightmare in the infernal stables', and darkness 'propagates infection and contagion' by disseminating typhus. Having blackened the Bible, Dickens jeers at Britain's slogan about the sun never setting on its dominions. Better, he says, that the sun should never rise on 'so vile a wonder' as this slum.

Characters elsewhere amend scripture to suit their own monetary interests or prudish scruples. In *The Chimes* the smug parliamentarian Sir Joseph Bowley replaces our supposed maker with a new financial potentate when, in a slip of the tongue, he mentions 'a matter of deep moment between a man and his – and his banker'. Bowley then paraphrases God's command that his creatures should 'Go forth and multiply', but with a crucial difference. After listening to the pleas of the impoverished Trotty Veck, he tells him to 'Go forth erect into the cheerful morning air, and – stop there.' Like Thomas Robert Malthus, the Victorian theorist of austerity and population control, Bowley believes that the working class is already too eager to reproduce, which is why he does not complete the quotation; in case the injunction to stay erect sends the wrong message, he specifies that Trotty should 'exercise your self-denial'. The God of Genesis also rethinks his original scheme, and having created the first human beings he dooms them to mortality after they fail the moral test he has set them. Dickens several times cites the conclusion of *Paradise Lost*, when Adam and Eve confront their mortal future outside the garden:

The world was all before them, where to choose
Their place of rest, and Providence their guide.

As Nicholas Nickleby thinks about defecting from the Yorkshire school where he is employed he reflects that 'The world is before me, after all', and Pip in *Great Expectations* sees that 'the world lay spread before me' as he travels to London. But whereas Milton's Adam and Eve leave Eden 'with wandering steps and slow', Nicholas and Pip are buoyant not downcast. Novels call the Bible's moralising bluff: life becomes more interesting when people escape from the garden and take to the open road.

After a few generations, the Bible's easily infuriated God turns against his creation and sends a flood to wipe out the human race, although he orders Noah to prepare a vessel to preserve representatives of all species until the waters recede. Dickens loved the story of the Ark, and saw it as a model for his own creative generosity: when a theatre was being rigged up in his house in Tavistock Square for performances of Wilkie Collins's *The Frozen Deep*, he happily likened the din and disarray to the busy carpentry of Noah. The rainbow in Genesis announces a reprieve for mankind, but the Bible's last books disclose God's ultimate plan for an all-consuming apocalypse. The mad Miss Flite in *Bleak House* is eager for this finale, and predicts that the day when the Lord Chancellor delivers his judgement in the Jarndyce case will be the actual Day of Judgement. Dickens, accustomed to dispensing fictional justice at the end of his novels, also kept this universal conclusion in mind. In Geneva in 1846 he visited the dungeons at the Château de Chillon, where Catholic heretics and Jews were viciously tortured during the religious wars of the sixteenth century. 'Good God,' he exclaimed after studying a charred stake and the trapdoor through which bodies were dropped into the lake, 'the greatest mystery in all the earth, to me, is how or why the world was tolerated by its Creator through the good old times, and wasn't dashed to fragments.'

Dickens condemns Mrs Clennam in *Little Dorrit* for getting the Genesis story back to front. As if 'sheathed in brass', with a face carved from granite, she has raised her son Arthur in 'a creed too darkly audacious', which replaces 'the making of man in the image of his Creator' with 'the making of the Creator in the image of erring man'. Later the charge is repeated more forcefully, with an allusion to the moment when God infuses Adam with independent life: Mrs Clennam is said to have 'reversed the order of Creation, and breathed her own breath into a clay image of her Creator'. That may be perverse, but Dickens himself makes erring men whose prosthetic limbs, single eyes and manifold tics show them to be genetically Dickensian, not lineal descendants of Adam and Eve. Arthur resists his mother's rigour and vows 'to judge not, and in humility to be merciful, and have hope and charity'. Those are impeccable Christian values, but Dickens had a different creed, dictated by his own dark audacity.

Dickens called the New Testament the greatest of all books, and he paid tribute to it when he wrote *The Life of Our Lord* during the late 1840s. He read this aloud to his children every Christmas, but insisted that the manuscript should not be copied or taken out of the house; it did not appear in print until 1934, after the widow of his last surviving child put the matter to a vote within the family. Dickens's precautions are telling: his reverence for Christ – 'so good, so kind, so gentle, and so sorry for all people who did wrong' – was the pretext for another self-revealing reinterpretation of Holy Writ, which reaches a conclusion that is not explicitly religious.

Miracles vouched for Christ's pedigree, which did not deter Dickens from hinting that the Bible's episodes of supernatural intervention might be contrivances or artful dodges. In *A Christmas Carol* he recalls Aaron's transformation of his staff into a wriggling serpent when the face of the dead Marley 'like the ancient Prophet's rod . . . swallowed up' all the painted tiles in Scrooge's fireplace: here a miracle is downgraded to a metaphor. In *The Battle of Life*, another Christmas story, a daughter whom the staunch rationalist Dr Jeddler has given up as lost reappears as if from the dead. Her disappearance was a benign deception, a plot; nevertheless the doctor abandons his Voltairean philosophy and concedes that miracles can happen. 'It is a world of sacred mysteries,' he says, 'and its Creator only knows what lies beneath the surface of His lightest image!' But the mysteries might be profane, and the creator with his light imagery could be playing games of make-believe, as Dickens did when he performed conjuring tricks at parties. In his *Child's History* he enjoys the miraculous stunts of the sanctified priest Dunstan, who wins a doctrinal argument by projecting his own voice into a crucifix on the wall and booby-traps some floorboards to make them give way on cue and send his enemies plummeting into a pit.

Even Christ's miracles are treated as a show of virtuosity. God, as Dickens puts it in *The Life of Our Lord*, enabled Christ 'to do many wonderful and solemn things' in order to persuade sceptics, and 'many people . . . hearing that he cured the sick, did begin to believe in him'. The wording is tactfully ambiguous: were they taken in by rumours or propaganda? When Christ raises the dead Lazarus, Dickens emphasises the sensational nature of the feat, which he calls 'awful and affecting'. While writing his life of Christ he was at work on *David Copperfield*, in which the young David's mother unwisely tells him about Lazarus; the boy is so upset that he has to be shown the undisturbed churchyard beneath his bedroom window, where his father lies quietly buried. To David, the fact of death is less terrifying than a story that imagines the revival of a corpse, which suggests that religion may rely for its survival on our fearful credulity.

The Life says that Christ worked his wonders with 'God's leave and assistance'. Artists need no such permission. In 1862 Dickens travelled to Paris to see the celebrated mezzo-soprano Pauline Viardot in Gluck's opera *Orphée*. Here music, more emotionally persuasive than words, allows Orpheus to calm the Furies with his singing and to descend into the underworld, where he wins a reprieve for the dead Eurydice. The novelist Turgenev spotted Dickens weeping in the audience, overcome by what he had seen and heard: Viardot had made him believe in Orphic powers that were prophetic as well as lyrical, able to challenge the edicts of nature. Viardot's husband took him backstage to meet her, and the next day Dickens wrote apologising for his emotional state and burbling that nothing could be 'more magnificent, more true, more beautiful, more profound!' than her performance. He had witnessed an un-Christian miracle, this time without niggling irony.

Regarding Christ's parentage, the most Dickens will say in the *Life* is that by changing water into wine or multiplying loaves and fishes he showed himself to be 'not a common man'. The slightly grudging phrase coincides with the doctrine of the Unitarians, who rejected the Trinity and did not see Christ as God's son and heir. Dickens late in life attended services at a Unitarian chapel near his London home, and he too preferred to think of Christ as a model of altruism and compassion rather than a saviour. Dostoevsky regarded Pickwick as a worldly Christ, sublime but also silly, possessing lovable human foibles that Christ lacks. Starting as a holy fool, suffering mishaps and embarrassments, Pickwick grows into an exemplar of Christian forgiveness when he pardons the trickster Jingle, whose plots repeatedly trip him up; with the members of the Pickwick Club as apostles and Sam Weller as his truest disciple, this Christ needs no cross.

G. K. Chesterton believed that Christmas turns people every-where into 'psychological Christians', but for Dickens the celebration of Christ's birth was almost an alibi: his version of the festivity is close to a saturnalia, and the Ghost of Christmas Present appears to Scrooge as a kind of Bacchus, enthroned on a cornucopia of food. Dickens defined the holiday as a time of 'beatified enjoyment', although beatitude does not usually involve such over-indulgence. In 1850 his essay 'A Christmas Tree' ponders other origins when it describes the indoor tree as 'that pretty German toy', brought to England by Queen Victoria's Teutonic consort. A toy or a heathen totem, carried over from wintry northern forests? The elderly man who reminisces here says that in his boyhood he identified Christmas with the enchantments of 'the bright Arabian Nights' and eagerly awaited 'the necromancy, that will make the earth shake'. Rapidly advancing from Christmas to Easter, he repeats the phrase when the sun darkens as Christ expires, 'with the earth beginning to shake'. He may be inviting us to choose between the marvels in the Arabian tales and the more wrathful theology of the Bible, or Dickens could have been thinking of his own unholy talents. For his conjuring act in 1849, he jokily called Rhia Rhama Rhoos an 'Unparalleled Necromancer', pretending that he had access to the secrets of the grave and was able to raise the dead – a warning that such sorcery could be ghoulish as well as playful.

In 1835, looking for journalistic work, Dickens sent a business card to an editor that advertised his capacity to dig up stories and startle them into life. On it he introduced himself as

CHARLES DICKENS, Resurrectionist,
In search of a subject.

The card alluded to the gruesome nocturnal trade of so-called 'resurrection men', also known as bodysnatchers, who in earlier days robbed graves to supply medical students with cadavers for dissection. Jerry Cruncher in *A Tale of Two Cities* supplements his wages as a porter with this second job; having reformed, he ends as a gravedigger. Whether unearthing corpses or putting them to bed, Jerry is at home in a novel whose characters shuttle to and fro between life and death. A coffin Jerry unearths in St Pancras cemetery turns out to be empty because the spy whose body it is meant to contain is already back on duty in Paris, while a shrewd French aristocrat escapes from the revolutionaries by announcing his own death and treating himself to 'a grand mock-funeral'. *A Tale of Two Cities* begins as Dr Manette is 'recalled to life' after being imprisoned in the Bastille for eighteen years, and it ends with Sydney Carton steeling himself for his expiatory sacrifice at the guillotine by repeating Christ's words to Martha, 'I am the resurrection and the life.' An irreligious resurrection occurs in *The Old Curiosity Shop* when Nell and her grandfather disembark at a wharf in the industrial Midlands: they are bewildered by the fiery violence of this new world, 'as if they had lived a thousand years before, and were raised from the dead and placed there by a miracle'.

Elsewhere Dickens stretches the meaning of this revivification. He was amused by the practice of dyeing or inking ragged clothes to 'revive' them, which awarded a new lease of life to the shabby-genteel wearer; another mock-resurrection occurs in an essay about a Wapping warehouse, where he learns that would-be suicides dragged from the Thames are dumped in a hot bath to be 'restored'. 'I dunno about restored,' says a sallow youth who assists in these rebirths. 'For some occult reason,' Dickens notes, he 'very much objected to that word' – perhaps because it actually is an occult business and, like David Copperfield after he learns about Lazarus, he prefers death to be final.

In *Bleak House*, when Inspector Bucket arrests the haughty French maid Hortense for the murder of Lawyer Tulkinghorn, they have a coded exchange about the same subject. We might be eavesdropping on another dialogue between two voices inside Dickens, as creator and killer or moralist and malefactor compare notes. Hortense compliments Bucket for his cleverness in trapping her, and says – in a phrase that is unidiomatic but apt – that he is 'very spiritual'. She means that Bucket does his snooping with ghostly invisibility; as it happens, investigating Hortense is for him a more carnal pursuit, analogous with the loves of the lascivious classical gods, and he arrests her by 'enfolding and pervading her like a cloud, and hovering away with her as if he were a homely Jupiter and she the object of his affections'. As they snarl back and forth, she calls him, interchangeably, an angel and a devil – heaven's avenger and also a diabolical co-conspirator who solves crimes because he can imagine committing them. In return he addresses her intimately as 'my dear' and 'darling'. Returning to the lore of the New Testament, she then taunts Bucket. 'Can you restore him back to life?' she demands, referring to the man she has killed. Bucket replies 'Not exactly', which is hardly an outright denial.

At the very end of his life, Dickens was reproved for having trivialised the agony of the crucified Christ. In *Edwin Drood* Canon Crisparkle's doting mother takes him off to be dosed in her medicinal herb-closet; as he trots behind her, Dickens likens Crisparkle to a lamb led unresistingly to the slaughter. This suggests that his mother is consuming him with her fussy coddling, but the simile has a hint of sacrilege. In June 1870 a civil servant called John Makeham wrote to Dickens complaining that he had belittled 'the sufferings of our Saviour', who is identified in scriptural allegories as the paschal lamb put to death on Good Friday. In a huffy reply, Dickens testified to his 'veneration for the life and lessons of Our Saviour', and claimed that he had merely employed a 'much abused social figure of speech'. But in context the phrase is anything but a cliché: Dickens – who once made the startling claim that the Montmartre abattoir was 'infinitely purer and cleaner . . . than the Cathedral of Notre Dame' – calls Crisparkle a type of 'the highly-popular lamb', which reminds us that the sacrificial beast is a delectable treat for springtime dinners. Luckily Makeham did not notice that at the end of the paragraph Dickens contrasts Crisparkle's purifying dips in the Cloisterham weir with Lady Macbeth's vain efforts to cleanse her bloody hands. Redemption and absolution are set against an abiding guilt that will not be purged by 'all the seas that roll'.

Dickens assured Makeham that no 'reasonable reader' would think he had treated scripture flippantly – but surely a reader of his novels, like the man himself, has to be an irrationalist, ready for metaphorical and metaphysical twists and turns? In any case this was Dickens's last word on Christianity. A few hours after writing the letter he was felled by a stroke, and he remained unconscious until he died the next day.

Dickens toyed with an alternative theory of creation, more agreeable to him than that in the Bible. The classical account of our world's origins in chaos – like the 'dense formless jumble' of Coketown in *Hard Times*, where 'sheets of cross light . . . showed nothing but masses of darkness' – better suited the muddy, foggy beginnings of Planet Dick, and Dickens was especially intrigued by a Greek myth that describes a creator who challenges the gods and proceeds, like an artist, by trial and error.

In 1844 in Milan he spent an evening at La Scala, hearing an opera whose title he did not record. The ballet that followed left more of an impression: it was *The Creatures of Prometheus*, choreographed by Salvatore Viganò to a score by Beethoven. Dickens had already mentioned the music in *Sketches by Boz*, where the overture is played by a thumping piano and a few scratchy strings to introduce a farcical amateur performance of *Othello* at a house in Clapham. In *Pictures from Italy* he abbreviates the title to *Prometheus*; Boz translates it as *The Men of Prometheus*, although the German word is 'Geschöpfe', meaning creatures, which is what Dickens often called the beings he created, not all of whom are conventionally human. Prometheus, a Titan at war with the Olympian gods, was a hero for the romantics – a political revolutionary in Shelley's lyrical drama *Prometheus Unbound*, and in Mary Shelley's *Frankenstein*, which is subtitled *The Modern Prometheus*, a scientist who flouts religious taboos; Carlyle called him 'the Poet and inspired Maker' who 'can shape new Symbols'. What he shapes are manikins, which he sculpts from the mud of a riverbed. This act of creation is not instantly perfect like that in Eden. The creatures fashioned by Prometheus look lumpy and sluggish, so he steals fire from the hearth of Zeus to quicken them mentally. He is punished for this outrage by being chained to a rock as an eagle gnaws his liver, which repairs itself nightly so that the torture can be endlessly repeated. Myths undergo perpetual revision, and Dickens amused himself by rewriting this one. First, in a short story published in 1838, the men responsible for street lighting in London dignify their occupation by maintaining that 'the history of Prometheus himself is but a pleasant fable, whereof the true hero is a lamplighter'. Then *Barnaby Rudge* warps the Titan's agony into comedy when the treacherous apprentice Sim Tappertit is misled by delusions of glory that, 'like the liver of Prometheus, grew as they were fed upon'. Sim rallies the anti-Catholic rioters, and in the scrum loses the two shapely legs that are his pride and joy. In a typically Dickensian comeuppance, he is fitted with wooden replacements and subserviently goes to work as a bootblack.

The ballet stops before Prometheus is punished because its concern is the choreographic training of his creatures: the rudimentary beings are mentally awakened when they hear the flute, harp and cello played by the gods, and they finally show off their newly graceful state by dancing in the presence of Apollo. Dickens forgot about the minuet that leads them to Parnassus; what moved him was their 'weary, miserable, listless, moping life' before they acquire a soul. Claiming that he 'never saw anything more effective', he made the 'pantomimic action' more amply and lustily Dickensian. He claimed that there were 'some hundred or two' dancers on stage, which expanded the corps de ballet into an urban crowd, and he elaborated a plot of his own when he claimed that he saw them succumb to 'sordid passions and desires'. He also marvelled that the idea of 'our mortal race' before its elevation or refinement could be expressed 'without the aid of speech' – a compliment to the dancers but also an aside about his own creative methods, since his characters owe their unrefined liveliness to their verbal vagaries.

In the ballet Prometheus begins with two inert neoclassical statues, which he endows with motion. The original myth is murkier: there Prometheus kneads wet earth. Dickens derived his people from the same squelching protoplasm, as he often acknowledged. Among the docks in *Our Mutual Friend*, for instance, 'the accumulated scum of humanity seemed to be washed from higher grounds, like so much moral sewage'. Foraging through a 'mud-desert' in the Stepney slums, the Uncommercial Traveller stumbles across an amorphous brown bundle with a sick woman – called a 'craythur' by an Irish bystander – slumped on it; her associates are labourers who have somehow 'come into existence, and . . . propagate their wretched race'. They are prole-tarian creatures of Prometheus, deemed unworthy of the sacred fire, like Barnaby Rudge in whom the soul's 'noblest powers are wanting'. Pecksniff joins them in the mire when he is disgraced. Ejected from the heights, he has no hope of being salvaged by Prometheus. 'Legions of Titans,' Dickens declares, 'couldn't have got him out of the mud.'

The Promethean myth is even present between the lines in 'A Plated Article', written for *Household Words* in 1852 by Dickens and his colleague W. H. Wills. Here one of the plates turned out by a pottery in Staffordshire describes its own birth and says that it sprang from 'heaps of lumps of clay', fortified by minerals from 'hills of flint'. After this, the Titan's manual work is replaced by machines: the moist earth is burnt in kilns and then 'laid under the four iron feet of a demon slave' whose insanely violent 'stamping fits' flatten it. Having endured such pangs, the speaking plate expresses its sympathy for samples that shrink unequally when they emerge from the flames and have to be discarded. Two human equivalents to this 'misshapen birth' are named, intrinsically Dickensian characters although he did not create them. One is the hunchbacked bell-ringer Quasimodo from Victor Hugo's *Notre-Dame de Paris*, whose name defines him as half-made, not properly shaped. The other is Sarah Biffin, an artist who was born in 1794 with no arms but taught herself to paint using a brush gripped between her teeth or pinned to her sleeve. Dickens chose not to be impressed by her astonishing ingenuity and instead emphasised her deformity. One of the dummy books with which he stocked his library had the title *Miss Biffin on Deportment* on its spine; likewise Merdle, as hollow as the promises of enrichment he makes to investors, is said to have 'not much more appearance of arms in his sleeves than if he had been the twin brother of Miss Biffin'. Questioning the perfectionism of Prometheus, Dickens finds the irregular rejects in Staffordshire more interesting than the lookalike generic crockery.

The modern Prometheus in *Frankenstein* begins, like Dickens, as a resurrectionist. Researching the secrets of life, he uses exhumed corpses to assemble a malformed figure whose clumsy bulk he jolts back to life. Instead of a divine spark, the animating agent is presumably electricity or galvanism, both of which Frankenstein studies. But the creature's ugliness disgusts him and he balks at its demand for a sexual mate; it retaliates by killing his loved ones. When Frankenstein dies in despair, the monster regrets its own 'demoniacal design' and sentences itself to extermination. The parable preoccupied and even troubled Dickens, for reasons suggested by the quotation from *Paradise Lost* that Mary Shelley chose as an epigraph. After the Fall, Milton's Adam upbraids the creator who made him fallible and then punished him for going astray:

> Did I request thee, Maker, from my clay
> To mould me man? Did I solicit thee
> From darkness to promote me?

This could be the protest of a child demanding why he was born to parents who resent his existence, as Dickens's father and mother seemed to do; the same words might be spoken by a literary character as he remonstrates with the author who extracts fictional people from the darkness inside himself and subjects them to gratuitous trials and torments in his stories.

Whether he was the accuser or the accused, Dickens edged around Shelley's novel, alluding to it without ever naming it. Frankenstein dabbles in 'the unhallowed damps of the grave' and collects bones from charnel-houses and dissecting rooms, horrified by his 'secret toil'. Less squeamish, the medical student Bob Sawyer in *The Pickwick Papers* works up an appetite while he conducts gruesome anatomical experiments using choice cuts of cadavers bought on the black market. 'I wouldn't mind a brain,' he says, but he doesn't have the budget for 'a whole head'; luckily, arms are affordable. In *Martin Chuzzlewit* Dickens twists Frankenstein's blasphemous project into crazy comedy when the barber Poll Sweedlepipe grieves over the apparently deceased Benjamin Bailey, the stunted but boisterously puffed-up servant boy who fancies himself a man of the world. Frankenstein is deliberately vague about the 'instruments of life' that 'infuse a spark of being into the lifeless thing' he has pieced together. Poll knows about more up-to-date equipment, but despairs of its reviving the lad. 'If you was to crowd all the steam-engines and electric fluids that ever was, into this shop,' he raves, 'and set 'em every one to work their hardest, they couldn't square the account.' As it turns out, the prodigy needs no scientific help and later bounces back to life, resurrected by Dickens's fictional whim.

Dickens draws closer to *Frankenstein* in *The Haunted Man and the Ghost's Bargain*. Here the scientist Redlaw enters into an agreement with his own evil spirit, which offers to relieve him of his remembered sorrows. He corrupts others by passing on to them his gift of forgetfulness; finally repentant, he says 'I am only so much less base than the wretches whom I make so, that in the moment of their transformation I can hate them.' The phrasing is tortured because Dickens was grappling with the same problem that causes Frankenstein to recoil from the monster: did characters like Fagin or Dombey expose something hateful in him? A moral is finally drawn from Redlaw's change of heart, but what truly attracts Dickens is the chance to describe his laboratory, installed in a mouldy crypt sunken below 'the upper world', like a subterranean equivalent of the attic that Frankenstein calls 'my workshop of filthy creation'. During Redlaw's experiments, 'spectral shapes' cavort on the walls, projected by firelight. Actually these are reflections from glass tubes containing chemicals, and they shudder as if in alarm because Redlaw knows how 'to uncombine them, and to give their component parts to fire and vapour'. In an attempt at reassurance, he paraphrases Lavoisier's law about the conservation of matter and insists that such chemical reactions do not diminish the world's solidity. 'No step or atom in the wondrous structure could be lost,' he says, 'without a blank being made in the great universe.' But Redlaw is speaking 'from the darkness of my mind', and art has no obligation to uphold Lavoisier's rule. Although mass may be safe, alchemical mutations occur: Redlaw's 'impious thoughts' come out to play in a swarm of ghostly chimerae and the shadows in his den 'fantastically mocked the shapes of household objects'. As the fog that blots out London in *Bleak House* demonstrates, Dickens had no qualms about making a blank in the universe.

Frankenstein is cited in *Great Expectations*, though obliquely, for fear of giving too much away. When Magwitch sneaks back from New South Wales, Pip has to shelter his uncouth benefactor. Pip reads to him as Magwitch requests, and while doing so he thinks about another unnamed book, whose plot matches his own predicament: 'The imaginary student pursued by the misshapen creature he had impiously made, was not more wretched than I, pursued by the creature who had made me, and recoiling from him with a stronger repulsion, the more he admired me and the fonder he was of me.' This is an elliptical synopsis of Mary Shelley's novel, in which Pip first assumes the role of maker, implicitly aligning himself with Dickens who specialised in making misshapen creatures; the admission of impiety conceals an outburst of brazen creative pride. Then, as Pip admits to being wretched, the sentence swivels. Now the two roles are remorsefully re-allocated, and Magwitch becomes Frankenstein. It is he who made Pip, by spending money not by performing surgery or channelling electrical or galvanic currents, since his bequests allowed the disadvantaged boy to recreate himself as a gentleman. Pip, rejecting his honorary parent with snobbish disgust, becomes the moral monster. Frankenstein and the being he creates are connected by their mutual loathing, but what makes the relationship in *Great Expectations* so painful is the admiration and fondness that Magwitch one-sidedly and self-destructively exhibits towards the ungrateful Pip.

The Promethean myth gave Dickens an answer to the question about true religion that he asked in his dream: it identified the artist as God's rival – capable of altering nature as Redlaw does in his laboratory and as Dickens did in concocting his metaphors, ultimately able to manufacture life. Assuming responsibility as a creator, Dickens commiserated with the shuffling humanoids he saw in the Beethoven ballet and allowed them to remain idiosyncratic, independent and potentially disobedient. This pointed to another outcome of the story: what if Prometheus were menaced not by the eagle but by one of the men who are his handiwork, as Frankenstein is by the monster and as Dickens was when Sikes or Fagin invaded his body at his public readings? That is the prospect Pip anticipates when he turns Mary Shelley's plot back to front and envisages an enchanter pursued by his vengeful familiar. Rather than a dispute that sets a rebellious artist against the deity, the imbroglio in *Great Expectations* is uniquely Dickensian – a battle to the death between creator and creature.

6

Devilkins

In 1856, in a backward glance at his journalistic career, Dickens said that when starting out he exerted himself 'with a celestial or diabolical energy'. Angels are seldom so frantic: ambitious agitation better suits demons, and Dickens once chuckled that he had 'a strong spice of the devil' in him. This lent an infernal zest to his writing. While at work on *Barnaby Rudge* he felt himself joining forces with the anti-Papist rioters of 1780 as they rampaged through London. 'I have just burnt into Newgate,' he informed Forster, accompanying the mob as it stormed the prison and let out the internees. He next announced that he had 'burnt down Lord Mansfield's' – the Bloomsbury house belonging to the Lord Chief Justice – and boasted of having 'played the very devil'.

Dickens's imagination was initially aroused by his nurse's hilariously grisly bedtime tales about the serial-killing cannibal Captain Murderer, 'the first diabolical character who intruded himself on my peaceful youth'. The Captain had many successors, all of whom were made welcome. In later life a pet raven Dickens kept in his menagerie spoke for him almost ventriloquistically when it cackled 'I'm a devil, I'm a devil', and he even nicknamed a shower that he designed for his house The Demon because of its invigorating force. Free to sound mildly risqué in a foreign language, he mused about the 'diableries de Paris' before travelling there with Wilkie Collins. He thought he spotted the devil in the cathedral at Lyon as a sacristan showed him the workings of a prized astronomical clock. On cue an automated figurine of the Virgin Mary appeared on the clockface, at her prayers in a tiny chapel; then an 'ill-looking puppet' flopped down from a pigeon-hole and at once retreated, violently banging his little door. 'Aha! The Evil Spirit,' said Dickens, assuming the figure had been affronted by the sight of the chaste maiden; the sacristan explained that it was actually the Archangel Gabriel, come to announce Mary's pregnancy. Dickens shrugged off his sacrilege as 'a small mistake'.

In a more sombre mood he admitted to having periodic 'outbursts of causeless rage and demoniacal gloom'. These were seldom on display in his daily life; instead he passed them on to characters like Nicholas Nickleby, who warns Squeers of the consequences 'if you do raise the devil within me', then grabs the sadistic schoolmaster's cane and lashes him with it. In *Little Dorrit* the same ferocity causes an enormous dog called Lion to rear at Blandois, ready to tear him apart. 'What devil have you conjured into the dog?' demands its owner. Lion, however, is right to be mistrustful and is soon afterwards poisoned by Blandois.

Although Dickens was more inclined to raise devils than to cast them out, he often alluded to an exorcism in St Mark's Gospel, where a deranged man begs Christ to relieve him from an impure spirit that has taken up residence inside him. Christ begins by asking the spirit what it is called; it replies in both the singular and plural, saying 'My name is Legion, for we are many.' Extracted from its victim, it gives proof of its multiplicity by swarming into the Gadarene swine, which career into the sea and drown. Dickens frequently quoted the spirit's teasing rejoinder, edging the retort into a variety of unexpected contexts. He fumed about the legion of talentless writers who bedevilled him with unsolicited manuscripts, and on his trip to Lyon he grumbled that all the steep, narrow, scorching streets were named Legion. Suffering from a hangover after Christmas, he complained in a *Household Words* article that his head reeled under assault from a 'vast Legion' of black shapes like tadpoles, just as indigestion makes Scrooge feel that he is being 'persecuted by a legion of goblins, all' – as he pointedly specifies – 'of my own creation'. Edith in *Dombey and Son* walks out on her husband and then spurns Carker, who expects to become her lover. Astonished and frustrated, he asks what devil possesses her, to which she coolly replies 'Their name is Legion.'

For Dickens, the plurality of which the spirit boasts was not a threat; instead it advertised the eerie abundance of his vocabulary. His novels run through a prolific legion of names, pseudonyms and nicknames for the devils who make mischief in them. Jingle in *The Pickwick Papers* plays a trick worthy of 'the Prince of Darkness' when he mischievously romances a spinster aunt, and at a fair in *The Old Curiosity Shop* Mr Punch bludgeons 'the enemy of mankind', not out of righteousness but to extract coins from the rural crowd. When Jo in *Bleak House* yawns while being catechised, he is denounced as 'a limb of the arch-fiend'; the workhouse superintendents likewise believe that Oliver Twist emerged 'direct from the manufactory of the very Devil himself', which suggests that the inferno is an industrial enterprise, a Satanic mill that mass-produces illegitimate brats. Sikes calls Fagin 'the old 'un', another of the devil's honorific titles, which changes to 'the Old Gentleman' in *The Cricket on the Hearth*. 'Old Scratch' and 'Old Boguey' are mentioned elsewhere. In *Little Dorrit*, Flintwinch calls Blandois 'Mr Beelzebub' and Clennam's pious mother 'a female Lucifer', while Mrs Clennam herself believes that 'Satan entered into Frederick Dorrit.' The hapless Lammle in *Our Mutual Friend*, duped when he marries in the hope of financial gain, spends his honeymoon 'with a drooping tail' that befits a member of 'the Mephistopheles family'. The aristocrat dubbed Monseigneur in *A Tale of Two Cities* is said to have recited the Lord's Prayer backwards, among 'other potent spells for compelling the Evil One'.

The legion expands to include a recruit from the Kabbalah: a saturnine French traveller on a train reminds Dickens of Zamiel, chief of the gnostic angels of destruction, who goes to ground as the demon huntsman of the Germanic forests in Weber's opera *Der Freischütz*. Appropriately enough, Dickens's own name became a diabolical euphemism, and when people in more genteel days exclaimed 'What

the dickens!' or declared that something had scared the dickens out
of them, the phrase saved them from having to say 'devilkins', which
refers to infernal imps, like horned and cloven-hoofed versions of
Fagin's juvenile gang.

Analysing Dombey's pride, Dickens in a telling phrase says
that this vice is 'as hard a master as the Devil in dark fables'. He
found a prototype for his own dark fables in Alain-René LeSage's
licentious satire *Le Diable boiteux*, published in 1707. Here the
crippled demon Asmodeus, trapped in a glass phial by an astrologer, offers his services to the student Cleophas who has set him
free. Asmodeus peels off the protective roofs of houses as if they
were pie crusts and invites Cleophas to study the indiscreet or
shameful antics of the people within. Dickens envied that act of
exposure, and in *Dombey and Son* he wishes that a spirit with 'a
more potent and benignant hand' than that of 'the lame demon
in the tale' would remove such layers of concealment to 'show a
Christian people what dark shapes issue from amidst their homes'.
Asmodeus additionally endows Cleophas with second sight,
enabling him to see the blanched shadows of the deceased. Dickens
had no need of this gift: his metaphors were a kind of extra-sen-
sory vision. After Merdle borrows Fanny Dorrit's penknife she
watches him depart with 'waters of vexation' in her eyes, so that
the jerky figure she sees through her tears appears 'to leap, and
waltz, and gyrate, as if he were possessed of several Devils' – a
dance of death that is nimble and jubilant, because Merdle slips
out of life and leaves those he has defrauded to suffer the consequences of his crimes.

Baudelaire claimed that comedy is a symptom of 'the Satanic
in man', with laughter as a 'monstrous phenomenon'. Some
Dickensian humour is jovial, befitting a genial god. The Dulwich
wedding at the end of *The Pickwick Papers* is an occasion of
'unmixed happiness', with Pickwick shedding tears 'in the full-
ness of his joy'. But this mirth can turn sulphurous. Elsewhere in
Pickwick, goblins with 'a perpetual smile on their faces' abduct the
misanthropic sexton Gabriel Grub while he digs a grave. Their

evil mirth is a recurrent Dickensian mood. As lightning flashes, Montague Tigg – a swindler whose ferociously shaggy moustache is 'the regular Satanic sort of thing' – thinks he sees Jonas Chuzzlewit raise a bottle to smash his head, wishfully killing him in 'diabolical fun'. After murdering Nancy in *Oliver Twist*, Sikes encounters a raucous pedlar, an 'antic fellow' who among other potions has cleansing fluid for sale. He advertises its virtues in a rhythmic chant as he recommends it to Sikes: it will purge 'Wine-stains, fruit-stains, beer-stains, water-stains, paint-stains, pitch-stains, mud-stains, blood-stains!' In a comment on the incident, G. K. Chesterton, otherwise so staunchly Catholic, gazed into the inferno of Dickens's imagination and declared that the rhyming refrain of 'mud-stains, blood-stains!' was 'one of the highest moments of his hellish art'.

When Pickwick returns in *Master Humphrey's Clock*, he regales the old fogeys in the storytelling club with a tale about witchcraft during the reign of James I. His preamble cites the king's dissertation on *Daemonologie*, in which he condemned 'these detestable slaves of the Devil, the Witches or enchanters' and called for them 'most severely to be punished'. Pickwick notes that, as a result of His Most Gracious Majesty's anathema, harmless old women throughout the realm were 'most graciously hanged, drowned, or roasted'. Loyal citizens in Windsor even 'boiled a witch on the king's birthday and sent a bottle of the broth to court', accompanied by a loyal address; the monarch rapidly regifted the offering to the Archbishop of Canterbury. The story Pickwick goes on to tell concerns a well-fed, self-satisfied exorcist called John Podgers, who claims to treat people 'taken forcible possession of by the Devil'. This trickster relies on the king's vendetta to rid himself of a rheumatic housekeeper. He denounces her as a witch, sees her burned at the stake, and is knighted for his 'service to the state'.

Such sour irony about the iniquities of royalty, religion and employment law is hardly characteristic of the good-natured Pickwick: it comes directly from Dickens, and its purpose is to reverse the edict of the king, whose tract sought to render God-fearing people 'proof against unholy spells'. Dickens, who had his own agenda, set out to demonise the land all over again.

———

In *Paradise Lost* Milton coined a word to denominate the assembly of devils, who debate their assault on heaven in a purpose-built gilded temple: their 'high capital' is called Pandemonium, a place to accommodate all the demons. The term later became a synonym for havoc and uproar, but in both senses it suits Dickens.

Hell for him could be other people – an incensed mass of 'ten thousand incoherences' like that which storms the Bastille in *A Tale of Two Cities* – but he also identified pandemonic locations in nature. During a downpour at Glencoe in Scotland in 1841 he saw foaming cataracts 'tearing like devils across the path'. On his moonlit ascent of Vesuvius in 1845, his clothes and those of his guides were scorched and blackened on the crater by 'the Hell of boiling fire below'. 'You never saw such devils', he wrote to his friend Thomas Mitton, a comment he deleted when describing the expedition in *Pictures from Italy*. On the way from London to Portsmouth, Nicholas Nickleby and Smike pass around the rim of the Devil's Punch Bowl, an eroded crevasse in Surrey. Nicholas recites a local legend about a murder victim whose blood seeped into the hollow; perhaps he did not know that the devil was supposedly responsible for the excavation – annoyed by all the churches in the area, he planned to dig a trench to the English Channel and flood the entire God-fearing region.

Angry torrents, spitting lava and subversive earthworks were atmospheric extras. The devil with whom Dickens allied himself was primarily an imaginative impetus, at once a surrogate artistic creator and a creation of the superstitious popular mind. He took his cue from works by two fellow novelists – Defoe's *Political History of the Devil*, published in 1726, and the *Letters on Demonology and Witchcraft* addressed by Walter Scott to his friend James Lockhart in 1830. Scott's treatise on popular superstitions is cited in *Sketches by Boz*, where a shabby-genteel man who spends the day lounging around Drury Lane is compared to one of the phantoms evoked by what Scott calls 'the credulity of our ancestors'. Dickens read Defoe's satire while writing *Oliver Twist*, and its sardonic tone influenced his account of the criminal underworld and its sleazy dealings. Extolling the 'craft and artifice' of the devil, Defoe compares Satan to 'one of our Newgate thieves', and the devil described in the *Political History* is as irrepressible as the Artful Dodger, who turns his trial into a roistering performance, taunts the magistrate, and when locked up goes on embellishing his 'glorious reputation'. Even an act of petty theft in the novel has a diabolical sponsor, thanks to a sideways glance at *Paradise Lost*. The woman responsible for the infant Oliver purloins the allowance for his care, 'thereby finding in the lowest depth a deeper still': the phrase echoes the lament of Milton's Satan, who claims that 'in the lowest deep a lower deep' gapes open to devour him, except that the venal Mrs Mann suffers no such anguish.

Defoe calls the devil 'the calumniator and deceiver, that is, the misrepresenter' – a metaphor man, who 'puts false colours, and then manages the eye to see them with an imperfect view, raising clouds and fogs to intercept our sight', which is exactly what the fog does in *Bleak House*. We humans, Defoe contends, are devilish enough on our own, so we can give up pretending to be corrupted by a cosmic malefactor armed with a pitchfork. Instead Satan becomes 'the master of an opera or a comedy', who assigns his human converts 'parts to act' without requiring them to attend 'a rehearsal in his presence'. In Paris in 1861 Dickens saw just such a stagey devil in Gounod's opera *Faust*, where Méphistophélès, the functionary summoned from hell by Faust, preens in his debonair contemporary costume, boasts of being 'un vrai gentilhomme', and offers to serve as a sexual procurer in exchange for Faust's soul. A similarly worldly demon has a walk-on in *The Pickwick Papers* when Sam Weller tells his master that a visitor 'wants you partickler; and no one else'll do, as the devil's private secretary said ven he fetched avay Doctor Faustus'.

Defoe's satire and Scott's treatise lurk behind two of Dickens's strangest comic characters, the fire-breathing ogre Quilp in *The Old Curiosity Shop* and Mrs Gamp, the garrulous alcoholic nurse in *Martin*

Chuzzlewit. Quilp is called a fiend, an imp, an evil spirit and an evil genius, as well as a devil and a 'familiar demon'; taunting a chained dog, he performs a jubilant, jeering 'demon-dance'. He presides over his household with inflamed eyes and a cigar permanently alight, and in his waterfront den he has a naval figurehead salvaged from a ship that resembles an effigy set up by a religious cult. This is the 'goblin or hideous idol whom the dwarf worshipped', though in his devotions he gleefully mutilates the sacred totem, scarifying it with a red-hot poker, driving nails into its nose and puncturing its eyeballs with forks. These 'outrages and insults' are blasphemous, and the bland wooden smile on the figure's wounded face goads Quilp to fresh attacks.

Milton's Satan defies God on principle, begrudging his loss of political status after Christ's promotion, and his disguise as a slick, wily snake in Eden suits his intellectual guile. Quilp is a grubbier domestic pest, likened to a fly and a bluebottle but also to an unclassifiably omnivorous monster: as he chews eggshells or the heads and tails of prawns while gnawing his fork and spoon until they bend out of shape, lookers-on 'doubt if he really were a human creature'. The devils in *Paradise Lost* invent gunpowder during their war against Christ's heavenly army, mining for dark materials and firing these subterranean deposits of ore through 'hollow engines' in a cannonade. On a smaller scale Quilp manages to be explosive without such exertions, and when he rubs his dirt-encrusted hands together he seems to be 'manufacturing . . . little charges for popguns'. Those ballistic pellets are another by-product of Blake's Satanic mills, which toil everywhere in Dickens's novels: when Carker is run over by the express train in *Dombey and Son* a 'fiery devil' whirls his mutilated remains on 'a jagged mill', and Little Nell and her grandfather are taken through a steel mill in the Midlands, where workers scuttle about 'like demons among the flame and smoke' in an underworld of hot black iron. Fuelled by cigars, feasting on metal, using his hands as artillery, Quilp is a devil for the industrial age.

Walter Scott assumed that 'the increasing civilization of all well-instructed countries' had sent the devil into retreat, but he admitted that 'the powers of the Magi' were still active in cultures he regarded as backward. His examples include the elfin people of Nordic folklore – dwarfs or duergar, 'spirits of a coarser sort, more laborious vocation, and more malignant temper', skilled in mining or smelting metals: a later example is Mime the dwarfish smith in Richard Wagner's operatic epic *Der Ring des Nibelungen*. Scott also notes that kobolds or hobgoblins had a habit of 'carrying off children, and breeding them as beings of their race', and this, although Dickens never says so, might be Quilp's creepy motive for stalking Nell. Alberich, the malignant demon king in Wagner's tetralogy, begets a son with a human bride; Nell's demise saves her. Other scattered comments in Scott's *Letters on Demonology and Witchcraft* add up into a preliminary sketch of Quilp. His yelping and screeching ape the 'tricks and fits of mimicry' and 'contortions, strange sounds and other extravagances' which Scott records as symptoms of demonic possession. At home Quilp reigns as 'the small lord of creation'; Scott says that in folktales the Foul Fiend insists on being addressed as Lord, requires 'ceremonious attention from his votaries' and – anticipating what Nicholas calls the 'dastardly cruelties' of Squeers at Dotheboys Hall – behaves like a schoolmaster who enjoys beating his pupils. There is a further premonition in Scott's comment on the biblical episode in which Saul, assisted by the witch of Endor, raises the dead prophet Samuel. Scott reads the incident as evidence of 'juggling . . . between mortals and spirits of lesser note' and likens the witch to the optical illusions in the phantasmagoria, a playground for apparitions whose shadows were cast onto screens by magic lanterns. Quilp resembles the spooks in these shows as he glares at Nell's friend Kit, dwindling in size and then bulbously swelling as he steps back and then returns to glare from close quarters 'like a head in a phantasmagoria'.

The witch consulted by Saul has many avatars in Dickens's novels. In *Dombey and Son* the malevolent rag dealer known as Good Mrs Brown interrogates Rob the Grinder while howling imprecations and reciting spells as she paces around him in a circle that is her zone of conjuring, exactly four feet in diameter. In *Little Dorrit*, Affery's nocturnal patrolling of Mrs Clennam's house is a 'witch excursion', perhaps a kind of somnambulism since she wanders in 'the witch-region of sleep', and Mr F.'s crabby aunt briefly resembles 'a malignant Chinese enchantress engaged in the performance of unholy rites' as she fumes and curses while bent over a steaming teapot. All these beldames are the weird sisters of Mrs Gamp. Hired as a nurse for the new-born and the dying, she is another Dickensian conductress, a psychopomp who – a little roughly, since she is usually fuelled by gin – ushers her patients into the world and out of it.

Defoe says that the devil recruits 'ugly, deformed, spiteful, malicious old women' as his helpers. That makes Mrs Gamp a natural candidate, although it is her bearded, gruff-voiced colleague Betsey Prig who emits a 'diabolical laugh' during the quarrel that ends their friendship. Betsey's unforgivable offence is to doubt the existence of Mrs Harris, the confidante whose pronouncements are quoted verbatim by Mrs Gamp, generally as an excuse to repeat the fulsome compliments her friend pays her. No one has ever seen Mrs Harris; she remains 'a fearful mystery', and is widely held to be 'a phantom of Mrs Gamp's brain' – a projection, like the 'Goblin slides for magic-lanterns' produced by the child-hating toy merchant Tackleton in *The Cricket on the Hearth*, 'whereon the powers of Darkness were depicted as a sort of supernatural shell-fish, with human faces'. Dickens describes the conversations Mrs Gamp relays as 'visionary dialogues', and Mrs Harris could be one of the characters he too conjured up, to whom he wistfully referred as his 'visionary companions'. After their disagreement, Mrs Gamp denounces Betsey's 'Bragian words', orders her out, and settles down to doze with a watchman's greatcoat tied round her neck, the sleeves appearing to embrace her 'so that she became two people'. The phrase entices us to imagine an ungainly sexual interlude, although we are actually spying on an act of creation. Mrs Gamp the midwife, who is 'heard to murmur "Mrs Harris" in her sleep', has engendered and delivered a literary character: at this point she is a deputy for Dickens when he thought of Pickwick or dreamed up Quilp.

Mrs Gamp is awoken by the noise of her clogs falling off, followed by the clatter of her tumbling umbrella, which leads Dickens to liken her disturbed nap to 'the fabled slumbers of Friar Bacon'. That enigmatic comment is his clue to her commerce with the nether-world. Roger Bacon was a thirteenth-century Franciscan friar, an Aristotelian philosopher whose dabbling in alchemy and esoteric lore caused him to be nicknamed Doctor Mirabilis. Bacon's grandest feat of wizardry was reputedly his sculpting of a brass head that could speak, relaying information from the afterlife. Urban folklore kept alive the story of this automaton, and in the *Political History* Defoe claims that in London during the 1665 plague an image of the oracular head advertised the establishments of 'pretenders . . . to the black art'. In 1594 Robert Greene wrote a play about the 'frolic friar' Bacon, who has 'dived into hell', paid visits to 'the darkest palaces of fiends', and practised 'cabalism' in his 'secret cell' at an Oxford college called Brazen-nose. Whether she knows it or not, Mrs Gamp's mispronounced adjective 'Bragian' – which she applies to the brassy upstart Benjamin Bailey as well as to Betsey Prig – learnedly puns on Bacon's brazen head and on Brasenose College, which took its name from a door knocker made of brass or bronze. Waiting for the brass head to speak, Bacon in Greene's play keeps watch at night for weeks on end. Eventually he nods off – hence Dickens's reference to his fabled slumbers – and it is then that the head utters three vacuous slogans about time, after which a gigantic fist gripping a hammer descends from above and shatters it. Chastened, Bacon vows to spend the rest of his life making amends for having misused God's sacred name.

In Dickens's revision of the parable, Mrs Gamp's woozy catnap is a creative reverie, with Mrs Harris taking the place of Bacon's metallic head. No censorious mallet intervenes, but Mrs Gamp's invention is dangerously put to the test when the novel's plot is finally disentangled in Jonas Chuzzlewit's house. Interrogated about her doddering patient Mr Chuffey, Mrs Gamp says that another woman is currently looking after him; asked to identify her deputy, she gasps and groans before managing to say 'Her name is Harris.' When Jonas demands that she physically produce what she calls 't'other person', her voice is reduced to 'a quavering croak' and she is seen to 'labour under a complication of internal disorders' that might be the birth pangs of the character she harbours within her: will she be able to duplicate herself, as Dickens did at his public readings when he impersonated Mrs Gamp and all those other characters? Almost as a favour to a fellow artist, he rescues her by reporting that 'the other person was already seen' – but this newcomer is the elder Martin Chuzzlewit, who arrives to accuse Jonas and fortuitously pushes Mrs Gamp aside as he enters. Unlike Greene's penitent Bacon, she soon recovers.

The narrator can protect Mrs Gamp because he is all-seeing, all-knowing and conveniently invisible. Dickens had plans for a journal called *The Shadow* in which he intended, he told Forster, to 'loom as a fanciful thing all over London', 'cognisant of everything', like 'a sort of previously unthought-of Power going about'. This oversight might have seemed godlike, but Dickens traced it back to a different source, again invoking *Le Diable boiteux*: in *The Old Curiosity Shop*, needing to bridge the distance between country and city, he lifts his reader into the air to be propelled back to London 'at a greater rate than ever Don Cleophas Leandro Perez Zambullo and his familiar travelled through that pleasant region'. LeSage's devil usually hobbles on two sticks but is unimpeded when he flies; Dickens is equally aerodynamic and, as he boasts, can overtake Asmodeus.

In Defoe's *Political History* the devil is introduced as a 'prince of the air', reigning over a 'vastly extended empire'; he has 'the attribute of omnipresence', able 'to be everywhere and see everything'. Dickens claimed the same prerogative, which might have been handed down from what Defoe calls Satan's 'sublimated government'. In *Barnaby Rudge* he asserts that he and his fellow chroniclers are 'privileged . . . to ride upon the wind' and can surmount 'all obstacles of distance, time, and place'. *Bleak House* has an omniscient narrator, an observer whose breezy surveillance of human confusion alternates with sections of personal testimony from bashful Esther Summerson. Asmodeus satisfies Cleophas's curiosity about his near neighbours; Dickens's narrator flies higher and sees further, as when he reports that the legal profession has 'scattered over the face of the earth' during the summer vacation, with London barristers on holiday in Venice, at German spas, in Constantinople or on the Nile. At the start of the novel this anchorless guide conducts us from the fusty Court

of Chancery to the sophisticated West End 'as the crow flies'. Much
later an actual crow, scavenging at dusk, skims across a 'slice of sky'
visible above the street in which Snagsby the stationer has his shop
and continues its flight over Chancery Lane into Lincoln's Inn Fields,
where Tulkinghorn lives. That black bird might be in the service of
Defoe's devil, who as 'prince of the power of that element . . . we call
air . . . sends out his spies, his agents, and emissaries, to get intelligence'. When Inspector Bucket investigates Tulkinghorn's murder,
he too 'mounts a high tower in his mind' and reviews the 'night-land-
scape', wishing for 'an enchanted power' that would transport him to
the scene of a crime. The detective like the devil is exempted from the
physical laws that limit the rest of us, as the narrator acknowledges
when he remarks that 'Time and place cannot bind Mr Bucket.' More
thorough in his scrutiny than Asmodeus, he leaves the roofs of houses
intact but rifles through Lady Dedlock's drawers and closets.

Surveying the terrain from above, the narrator of *Bleak House*
points out that the novel's subplots connect 'many people in the innumerable histories of this world who from opposite sides of great gulfs
have, nevertheless, been very curiously brought together!' The gulfs
to which this refers separate social classes and geographical areas,
but for Dickens the word implied something more. When Snagsby
ventures into the stinking tenements around Tom-All-Alone's, where
'few people are known . . . by any Christian sign' and instead adopt
illicit sobriquets like Gallows or Toughy, he 'sickens in body and mind
and feels as if he were going every moment deeper down into the
infernal gulf'. The tautology in 'deeper down' creates a false step that
lurches beneath his feet and ours – another reminiscence of Milton's
Satan finding a lower depth beneath the lowest. Even when Snagsby
and Bucket struggle back out of the diseased pit, the crowd in the
surrounding streets is 'a concourse of imprisoned demons'.

'Gaslight Fairies', written for *Household Words* in 1855, investigates another 'dark, deep gulf of a place, hazy with fog'. 'Visible
people' do not belong in this cavity, which is blearily lit and enveloped by 'dusty palls', and Dickens seems to be 'at the bottom of a sort
of immense well without any water in it'. Democritus located truth at

the bottom of such a well, and Master Humphrey – who calls himself an alchemist and places 'the commonest and least-regarded matter' in his crucible to be transformed – follows the Greek sage when he says that he and his storytelling friends hope to retrieve 'coy Truth . . . from the bottom of her well'. The gulf in 'Gaslight Fairies' turns out to be the cavernous interior of a theatre, and what Dickens extracts from it is not truth but spangly, gauzy fiction. Hence the title: during rehearsals for a pantomime, the stage manager makes a request for thirty-five fairies, confident that the gossamer beings will be delivered the next morning, ready to take to the stage.

As the gas flares, Dickens hears 'hammers going, in invisible workshops' and salutes the 'unseen mechanist' who keeps up with 'the striding ingenuity of the age'. Wagner – a musical hypnotist and scenic wizard who shared the mind-bending gifts of Dickens – made that clamour audible two decades later in the theatre he built at Bayreuth. In *Das Rheingold* the offstage din came from percussionists whose hammering evoked the industrial hell of Nibelheim, where elves enslaved by Alberich toiled at their metalwork; the noise seemed to originate underground, since the musicians played in a sunken orchestra pit that Wagner called his 'mystischer Abgrund' or mystic abyss. In the opera, Wotan swoops down from the godly heights to expropriate riches that are secreted in the earth's bowels. Dickens undertook his own descent as a creative endeavour: the gulf was his subliminal recess of imagination.

In 1853 a troupe of Zulus, visiting London 'with the sanction of the Colonial Authorities', performed a tribal pageant at a gallery in Piccadilly. They pretended to labour in the fields, danced at mealtime, sang a 'charm song', traded women for cows, settled a dispute with a bundle of switches, and mimed a battle. When Dickens sampled the show he winced at its 'howling, whistling, clucking, stamping, jumping' hubbub and in his exasperation called the rites both 'demoniacal' and 'diabolical'. At one point a witch doctor was summoned to smell out an evil interloper, which he did while chanting 'O yow yow yow!' Dickens assumed that such frenzies had a medicinal use in Africa, where natives who fell ill would be diagnosed as victims of sorcery and cured by a 'learned physician' whose professional uniform consisted of a leopard's head with a collar of tigers' tails. The scenario is described with jocular bigotry in *Household Words*, but how different was it from the biblical episode in which Christ draws the impure spirit out of the afflicted man's body and transfers it to the herd of swine?

Dickens revealed his true interest in such transactions in a disagreement with Carlyle about African religion. In his historical epic *The French Revolution* Carlyle derided the 'new Deity of Robespierre', a substitute for God to be worshipped in deconsecrated cathedrals. He considered this so-called Supreme Being to be no more worthy of veneration than the 'Mumbo-Jumbo of the African woods', and although he expected gullible Africans to be taken in, he blamed the more educated French for bowing down before 'a *conscious* Mumbo-Jumbo' that was mere 'machinery'. As Dickens saw it, Carlyle had mistaken the Mumbo-Jumbo for 'the common Fetish', by which he meant a magus who cast spells using amulets or charms, called 'feitiços' by Portuguese colonists in Africa. Dickens pointed out that the Mumbo-Jumbo was a showman who knowingly spouted gibberish to terrify the shrewish wives of his fellow tribesmen. Carlyle failed to see that the act was an imposture, and he had no right to feel superior because such masquerades persisted in 'the improving world' of the mid-nineteenth century. The Uncommercial Traveller identifies a procession of contemporary medicine men who dress up for solemn observances that keep English society functioning: judges and lawyers don wigs to signify sagacity, while heraldically costumed courtiers strut at St James's Palace and undertakers choreograph 'preposterous enchantments' – perhaps with mutes like Oliver Twist and black horses adorned with nodding plumes – for which the bereaved pay at a premium.

Dickens practised his own form of witch-doctoring, known as mesmerism or animal magnetism, a technique introduced in the 1770s by the physician and astronomer Franz Anton Mesmer, who supposedly channelled the healing agency of an all-pervasive magnetic fluid. Dickens thought he could summon those invisible currents of influence, and in 1842 in Pittsburgh he used them to mesmerise his wife. Catherine first had a hysterical fit, then fell docilely asleep; her sister Georgina reacted in the same way on a later occasion. Convinced of his ability to 'magnetize a Frying-Pan', Dickens believed he could calm mental distress or cure physical pain, and he even joked to Forster that he ought to advertise his services with 'a large brass plate' at his door, charging twenty-five guineas per nap. Whereas mesmerists sometimes brandished magnets made of iron oxide, all Dickens needed was what Forster called his 'iron will', which turned the mumbo-jumbo into a demonstration of his hypnotic imaginative power. He could fabricate a character from the mesmeric metal – the porter Jerry Cruncher in *A Tale of Two Cities* has a second skin of iron rust, with hair that stands jaggedly upright like 'an animated bit of the spiked wall of Newgate' – and he drew on its polarising properties when working out his plots: coincidences for him were evidence of Mesmer's magical physics, bringing people together as if they were impelled by an electromagnetic charge. He commented on just such a providential concurrence in a letter sent from Rome to Emile de la Rue, a Swiss banker he befriended while living in Genoa in 1884–5. The hotel in which he was staying had been 'full to the throat' when he arrived, except for a single apartment that happened to be the very one recently occupied by de la Rue. '*I* say there is something Magnetic in it,' said Dickens.

During his months in Genoa, Dickens had administered therapy to de la Rue's overwrought wife Augusta, who suffered from tics, facial spasms, convulsions and insomnia; she would once have been stigmatised as a witch, just as Tattycoram's neurotic tantrums in *Little Dorrit* recall the distemper 'sent by the Demons of old'. Coaxed by Dickens, Madame de la Rue blamed her anxieties on a 'Phantom' who haunted her. Dickens also called this bogey a 'bad spirit' or 'bad figure'. Sometimes, losing focus, it became 'the shadow', the role Dickens had intended to assume in his proposed periodical. In his novels he let such malign agents run amuck, but now he spoke of 'beating down' the tormenter, promising that his 'Magnetic power' would shatter it like glass. It fought back, and at one point seemed to have the exorcist himself in its sights. Madame de la Rue reported, Dickens told her husband, 'that this creature was talking of me, and at my request, she tried hard to overhear what it said', but without success. Another familiar was perhaps preparing to tear the enchanter apart.

While travelling throughout Italy, he continued his sessions with Augusta de la Rue remotely. For this he set aside 'an hour's abstraction', which he described as 'shutting myself up within myself', so that he could beam his targeted thoughts back to Genoa. Once the energy that he transmitted somehow overflowed and again sent his own wife, who happened to be nearby, into a shuddering trance; he described his misdirected thoughts as 'the strongest instance of the strange mysteries that are hidden within this power'. Another misfire caused him to write to Emile de la Rue from Naples to apologise for having expressed himself undiplomatically in a previous letter, when he seemed to doubt de la Rue's earnest concern for his wife's health. Dickens explained that 'the vast extent of the danger by which I saw she was beset, made me clench the pen as if it were an iron rod – Made me use it too, as clumsily as if it were a poker'. The implement of his art had become a deadly weapon, aimed at de la Rue's head.

At first Dickens worried that Augusta de la Rue's fear of her persecutor was 'greater than her subservience to me'; after relieving her 'nightly horrors', he finally assured her husband that she now had 'no secret in connexion with the devilish figure'. Presumably he had taken ownership of that secret, although he may also have drawn out her devil by inviting it to lodge inside him. An incident in *Little Dorrit* briefly and wittily recalls these fraught psychic negotiations. When Cavalletto is asked to describe Blandois, with whom he once shared a prison cell, he identifies the killer by physiognomically becoming him. He pushes his eyes closer together, outlines an angular hooked nose with his hand, makes his upper lip jut out so that it seems to bristle with a thick moustache, and affects a sinister grin. Trifling with a malign spirit, he has invited Blandois to invade his body. No exorcism is necessary; Cavalletto ejects the 'noxious creature' by letting his facial muscles relax.

In Robert Louis Stevenson's story, sober Dr Jekyll activates feral Mr Hyde during a chemical experiment that he calls an exercise in 'transcendental medicine'. Dickens's experiments in transcendence released a mental propulsion that was as likely to harm as to heal. At work on *Bleak House*, he felt a warning tremor, 'as if my head would split like a fired shell!' He knew that the detonation could be dangerous, as the novel's narrator warns when Bucket and Snagsby close in on a secret that may at any moment 'take air and fire, explode, and blow up', like Krook spontaneously combusting. Dickens believed he had saved Augusta de la Rue from madness, but he found no respite from the inflammatory alarms of his own mind: the medicine man was never sure that he could cure himself.

7

In Arabia

For Dickens, *The Arabian Nights' Tales* qualified as a sacred book, whose charter of imaginative liberties he preferred to the Bible's killjoy commandments; it served, he said, as a 'mighty talisman', enabling him to work wonders of his own. The *Tales*, also known as *One Thousand and One Nights*, are a compendium of supernatural legends collated from Indian, Persian, Syrian and Egyptian sources, translated into English early in the eighteenth century. Dickens called himself 'one of the most constant and delighted readers of those Arabian Entertainments', though many others shared his infatuation. The book's un-Christian fantasia so enthralled Coleridge that his father confiscated his copy and burned it; a poem by Tennyson recalls his own youthful expeditions to the pavilions of the Caliphate in the days of Haroun al-Raschid, when he felt himself to be a 'true Mussulman'. Not wanting the journey on the magic carpet to end, both Edgar Allan Poe and Théophile Gautier added sequels by imagining a story with which the tale-teller Scheherazade might tantalise her Sultan on the thousand and second night.

When David Copperfield recalls the reading that, as he says, 'kept alive my fancy' during a miserable childhood, he adds *The Arabian Nights* to a list of favourite titles by Cervantes, LeSage, Fielding, Goldsmith and Smollett from his father's library. The novels supply David with a 'glorious host' of imaginary playmates, but for Dickens the Arabian tales did more than that. They served as a touchstone, a testament to the spiritual worth of his characters. Scrooge in *A Christmas Carol* begins to soften when he recalls his boyish fondness for Ali Baba and the Genii, and Sissy Jupe in *Hard Times* reads stories of 'the Genies' to her father, suggesting that adults can also profit from them. The sweetly ingenuous Tom Pinch in *Martin Chuzzlewit*, visiting a bookshop, browses among 'the Persian tales' and 'the rare Arabian Nights', which he admires as 'matchless wonders'. For Dickens, anyone who did not feel the same was hardly human. The Uncommercial Traveller complains about a hard-headed teacher who made Aladdin's lamp the pretext for a lecture on sperm oil and whale fishing, and in *Bleak House* the wizened Bart Smallweed knows nothing of Sinbad the Sailor, which means that he had no childhood.

The Arabian Nights also offered Dickens a preview of his own destiny. The young wastrel Aladdin resents being trained as a tailor and abandons that humble trade when he happens upon a sorcerer's lamp and releases the wish-fulfilling genie trapped inside. Dickens too escaped from a life of menial labour, but did so because he possessed talent or was possessed by genius. Having helped him into the future, the lamp later enabled him to erase the painful or embarrassing evidence of his past. He therefore recalled it when in 1860, wanting to detach himself from his earlier self, he incinerated decades of personal papers and sheafs of correspondence received from friends: the smoke from the pyre in the garden of his country house reminded him of 'the genie when he got out of the casket on the seashore' in the story of Aladdin, although because it soon began to rain he suspected that his act of arson had angered some other deity. Another Arabian tale provided him with an excuse for considering a second lucrative American tour. The idea first came to him in 1847, when he told Forster that he felt drawn towards a loadstone rock; he was alluding to a magnetic mountain that, in a story told by a dervish, tugs nails from the hull of approaching ships and causes them to fall apart and sink. In *A Tale of Two Cities* this legend explains the compulsion that near-fatally lures Charles Darnay back to Paris and lands him in the Bastille. Dickens eventually returned to America in 1867 for a tour that earned him a fortune but left him ill and exhausted: the fable was his horoscope, which he chose to ignore.

The Arabian tales concern the merchant class and those who aspire to membership of it, like the impoverished cobbler Marouf who brags about expecting a caravan laden with riches, which of course never arrives. Fantasies of conspicuous consumption are indulged, with palaces built overnight, chests of precious stones and wardrobes of embroidered silk, and sumptuous meals served on silver dishes. In *Our Mutual Friend* the snobbish freeloader Lady Tippins sneers that the Veneerings 'have a house out of the *Tales of the Genii*, and give dinners out of the *Arabian Nights*'. For Dickens, however, the fable of Aladdin's lamp was not about self-enrichment; instead it contained a prescription for kindling imagination. Shelley described 'the mind in creation' as 'a fading coal', roused to 'transitory brightness' by a poet's efforts, although its visions when transcribed are 'a feeble shadow'. Dickens knew how to control what Shelley calls 'this power [that] arises from within', and he joked about the self-stimulating effort that went into it in a comment on the beardless Fledgeby in *Our Mutual Friend*. Shamed by his lack of facial hair, Fledgeby surveys the whiskers of his more hirsute colleagues and decides which variety 'to produce out of himself by friction, if the Genie of the cheek would only answer to his bidding'.

Tom Pinch's perusal of 'the enchanted books' in the Salisbury shop prompts him to 'rub up and chafe that wonderful lamp within him', in an act that sounds almost as flagrantly sensual as the friction to which Fledgeby resorts; the warmth he arouses allows him to revisit in imagination the happiness of the years before he became Pecksniff's dogsbody. With the rows of books 'awakening instant recollections' of his carefree schooldays, Tom confirms the truth of Wordsworth's claim that poetry is 'emotion recollected in tranquillity'. The difference is that Dickens did not use memory as a tranquilliser: rubbing and chafing produce a vital heat, and Tom's wistful recollection gives way to hope for a happier future. Later – now living in London, which he sees as 'some enchanted city' – Tom watches as his friend John Westlock metaphorically 'rubbed an enchanted lamp or a magic ring' to summon up 'twenty thousand supernatural slaves'. In fact John is merely polishing wine glasses in preparation for dinner; the place of the multitudinous slaves is filled by a waiter from a nearby restaurant, who flourishes a napkin and unpacks a banquet from an oblong box that an assistant transports on his head as if it originated there, like an idea or a dream. At the age of seventeen, alight with the same expectancy, David Copperfield says that life is 'a great fairy story, which I was about to begin to read'. Living and reading are equated, although David like Dickens rereads reality to make it match his vision. The upside-down boat on the beach in which he stays while visiting Yarmouth is as fabulous to him as 'Aladdin's palace, roc's egg and all', and later a birthday picnic for his first wife Dora takes place in suburban Guildford on a 'green spot . . . carpeted with soft turf' laid out on purpose by 'some Arabian-night magician', who shuts it up again when the party ends. Meanwhile a djinn or bottled imp is intent on fulfilling wishes of his own, and David sees Uriah Heep ogling Agnes like 'an ugly and rebellious genie watching a good spirit'. At its most solemn and hieratic, the Arabian sorcery is a supreme fiction, capable of keeping death at bay. In *The Old Curiosity Shop* Dick Swiveller falls ill and for weeks is selflessly cared for by the put-upon servant he nicknames the Marchioness. Recovering, he says 'It's an Arabian Night; that's what it is. I'm in Damascus or Grand Cairo' rather than his unpalatially dingy lodgings. When the Marchioness claps her hands for joy, he remembers that in the tales this is a summons that ought to call up 'two thousand black slaves, with jars of jewels on their heads!' She laughs at his nonsense, but her intervention is magical as much as medical.

On Dickens's first trip to Washington in 1842, the long and as yet empty avenues laid out by the city's over-optimistic planners reminded him of a Barmecide Feast, the dinner of invisible dishes offered by a witty Persian prince to the famished Shacabac, who must pretend to be enjoying an un-nutritious meal. The joke demolishes the conceit of the American capital, and also hints that imagination may be self-deception by other means. More happily, in his essay 'Gone Astray' Dickens recalls a childhood incident when he got lost near the Guildhall in London. With no adult to contradict him, he could transform the merchant bankers who did their dreary business in the area into adventurers like Sinbad. He imagined the Baring brothers travelling across the desert in caravans to stock up on eggs laid by the mythological roc, while Nathan Mayer von Rothschild wooed 'a veiled lady from the Sultan's harem' in the bazaar at Baghdad. The experience left him 'inspired by a mighty faith in the marvellousness of everything'. This was the gospel of *The Arabian Nights*, and in following its precepts Dickens became the wizard of modern life, an urban fabulist whose aim was the re-enchantment of a drab workaday world.

Christmas appealed to him because then 'all lamps are wonderful, all rings are talismans': the implements employed by Aladdin were democratised and made available to all for as long as the festive season lasts. Dickens bestowed his own capacity for wonder on a retired Islington grocer in his essay 'Some Account of an Extraordinary Traveller', which tracks the intrepid Mr Booley as he explores the American wilderness, makes side trips to New Zealand and Australia, and ventures both south to Brazil and north to the Arctic – a hectic itinerary that never allows him to pause at home for more than a day or two before he resumes his voyaging. Eventually we discover that Booley in fact never journeys further than the West End of London, where he visits galleries that exhibit panoramas of those inaccessible places. Dickens does not belittle Booley: instead he says that 'His days were all Arabian Nights', which is a recommendation of how we all ought to live.

Booley's vicarious travels anticipate an episode in J.-K. Huysmans' novel *À Rebours*, published in 1884. Here the fatigued aesthete Des Esseintes plans a trip from Paris to London, but after envisaging the dank, smoky Dickensian city and picturing David Copperfield and other characters from the novels morosely poring over glasses of blood-coloured port in a pub, he decides to stay at home. Why trouble the body to plod through space when the mind can teleport you to any destination? Des Esseintes opts for imagination not experience; Dickens, on a journey of his own from London to Paris by express train, does not feel the need to choose between the two but instead enlists imagination to augment and intensify experience. He records the trip in an exclamatory rush, emitting non-verbal noises

– 'Whew!', 'Bang!', 'Whizz!', 'Bur-r-r!' – as the train plunges into tunnels or impressionistically scrambles the passing landscape. Feeling 'enchanted or bewitched' as he alights in Paris, he blesses the railway company 'for realising the Arabian Nights in these prose days'. Without the assistance of a fast train, Dickens knew how to jolt the diurnal into the uncanny or absurd: all it took in one case was some altered spelling. In 1855 in his satirical squib 'The Thousand and One Humbugs' he ridicules the government at Westminster by calling Parliament the Howsa Kummauns, which makes the parleying place sound like a rowdy proletarian greeting. Scheherazade is assigned a new scribal persona as Hansardadade, although rather than spinning tales to the Sultan she tediously transcribes every word spoken by the would-be rulers at Westminster.

Dickens unexpectedly consulted 'the imaginative people of the East, in the palmy days of its romance' in an article for *Household Words* in 1854 about Sir John Franklin's Arctic expedition, lost in the frozen north seven years earlier. At the behest of Franklin's widow, he denounced reports – which turned out to be true – that the icebound crew had resorted to eating their dead comrades. Relying on patriotic prejudice, Dickens declared that cannibalism was an abomination inconceivable for Englishmen. The practice, he claimed, was confined to 'ghoules, gigantic blacks with one eye, monsters like towers' and other members of 'this or that tattooe'd tribe' who worship 'goggle-eyed gods', and he pointed out that even Sinbad in *The Arabian Nights* refuses the 'dismal expedient' of eating human flesh when he is buried alive. But the taboo did not inhibit Dickens's own ravening imagination. To terrorise Pip into helping him escape his jailers, Magwitch in *Great Expectations* dreams up an accomplice who is, he says in a slavering reverie, waiting to tear open the boy's chest and remove his heart and liver, which he intends to roast and eat; the assault is described with unsettling vividness as this demon prepares to invade Pip's bed and ravage his body with a 'secret way pecooliar to himself'. Cannibalism may be unthinkable for Franklin's 'gallant band', but Magwitch makes it only too imaginable. For once the Arabian precedent proves too tame.

Other novelists sternly reconciled both characters and readers to a reality which in Charlotte Brontë's view was as 'unromantic as Monday morning'. Dickens resisted such disenchantment, and in *Sketches at Boz* he winces when daylight in the pleasure gardens at Vauxhall reduces the Moorish tower to a wooden shed patchily daubed with crimson and yellow paint. The domestic graces of Dickens's women are valued as a way of rehabilitating romance. As a charmingly inept young bride in *Our Mutual Friend*, Bella Wilfer studies *The Complete British Family Housewife* like an 'enchantress poring over the Black Art'. Less perplexed, Madeline in *Nicholas Nickleby* beautifies a room in the debtors' prison by filling it with flowers, a pet bird and her own handicrafts. Her decorative touches revive 'the halo with which old painters surround the bright angels of a sinless world', and Nicholas feels that 'the smile of Heaven' is 'visibly before him'. These are Christian graces; Nicholas supplements them by commissioning Madeline to paint some velvet, 'of the most elegant design', for an ottoman. The request is no accident: the ottoman was originally an Arabian footstool or hassock, and here it evokes a life of cushioned leisure that she is encouraged to dream about.

This wishful thinking is what Dickens, in a rare foray into art criticism, found lacking in John Everett Millais's painting *Christ in the House of His Parents*. He rebuked Millais for making the New Testament characters in the carpenter's shop look like a gathering of derelicts and guttersnipes from a grubby slum. Only an age 'very short of faith', he complained, could cheapen the 'pure spiritual condition' of redeemed humanity as Millais had done, and he mocked this apostasy with the help of *The Arabian Nights*. His essay on the painting is entitled 'Old Lamps for New Ones', alluding to the folly of the housekeeper who exchanges Aladdin's old lamp for a shiny replacement that is worthless because it contains no genie. Dickens suggests that Millais and his fellow Pre-Raphaelite painters entered into the same bad bargain, discarding the 'sublime and lovely' exaltation of Raphael in favour of homespun realism. The Italian Renaissance had kindled 'a certain feeble lamp of art'; his own aim, as a latter-day Aladdin, was to keep it alight.

The lamp began by comfortably glowing. Dickens, taking it over, infused that domestic amenity with his own fervour and made it blaze with industrial force. Introducing the first issue of *Household Words*, where he published the squib about Millais later in 1850, he described factory chimneys as 'swart giants, Slaves of the Lamp of Knowledge', which 'have their thousand and one tales, no less than the Genii of the East'. Dickens himself was not unlike those chimneys, 'spurting out fire and smoke' that attested to his creative labour, though he was enslaved not to the lamp of knowledge but to an imagination that flared up in the 'wild, grotesque and fanciful' stories he told.

'Arabesque' was at first a term of disparagement, even a psychological slur. In 1827 in an essay on the supernatural in fiction, Walter Scott permitted 'the young and the indolent' to enjoy 'eastern tales', but warned against the spooky stories of E. T. A. Hoffmann: Scott likened 'the grotesque in [Hoffmann's] compositions' to 'the arabesque in painting', and diagnosed his bizarre inventions – including a seductive female automaton, a snake with blue eyes and a seven-headed mouse king – as evidence that he was 'on the verge of actual insanity'. In 1840 Poe wittily adopted the term and emphasised geometry not grotesquerie as he laid down the law about interior design in an essay on 'The Philosophy of Furniture'. Floral patterns on carpets and wallpaper were unendurable, Poe said, 'within the limits of Christendom'. Rather than 'representations of known objects', he insisted on shapes *'of no meaning'*, and made it a rule that 'all upholstery of this nature should be rigidly Arabesque'. No longer a symptom of mental imbalance, arabesques were here liberated from any need to illustrate reality.

A few years later, Dickens alluded to that decorative creed while remembering Scott's wary recognition that our daydreaming can breed monsters. In *Dombey and Son* the bedridden Paul sees 'miniature tigers and lions' on the wallpaper and faces squinting from 'the squares and diamonds of the floor-cloth'. All this is the 'arabesque work of his musing fancy', and because Paul 'saw things that no one else saw' it almost qualifies him as an artist. Paul's literal-minded schoolfriend Toots does not share this gift of second sight. Dickens comments that 'Ideas, like ghosts . . . must be spoken to a little before they will explain themselves; the mist . . . issuing from that leaden casket, [Toots's] cranium' does not condense into the shape of a genie and instead 'it only so far followed the example of the smoke in the Arabian story, as to roll out in a thick cloud'. Whenever Dickens takes over, the ignition that Toots is unable to manage produces a flash or an impromptu explosion of delight as two ideas brought unexpectedly together strike sparks. A wedding dinner in Greenwich in *Our Mutual Friend* serves up 'samples of the fishes of divers colours that made a speech in the Arabian Nights . . . and then jumped out of the frying-pan', although Dickens apologises that their polychrome skin has lost its lustre while sizzling with battered whitebait. A similarly chimerical marvel occurs when Mr Dorrit, released from the debtors' prison, installs his family in a Venetian palazzo. The pompous Mrs General, hired as a companion for Dorrit's daughters, appears there enthroned on a small rug 'as if she had come into possession of the enchanted piece of carpet, bought for forty purses by one of the three princes in the *Arabian Nights*, and had that moment been transported on it, at a wish, into a palatial saloon with which it had no connection'. The words 'as if' were Dickens's equivalent to 'Open sesame', the command Ali Baba hears the thieves using when they unseal the cave in which they have hidden their loot. In *Tom Tiddler's Ground* a traveller apostrophises the gate behind which a hermit has his lair, and says 'Open sesame' in the hope that it will let strangers into the misanthrope's rancorous solitude. That doesn't entirely rid the password of its illicit or even sacrilegious associations: 'sesame' is a garbled cabbalistic word from the Talmud.

Whether Arabian or not, metaphor is a transporter like a flying carpet; it performs metamorphoses by prompting fish to speak as they leap from the pan or briskly conveying a ponderous matron through the air. As a conjurer, Dickens made such verbal transfigurations visible. Adopting the pseudo-Arabian persona of Rhia Rhama Rhoos, he transformed a box of bran into a guinea pig, or pocket watches into tea caddies. At Christmas his speciality was The Pudding Wonder, when he messily mixed flour and eggs in a top hat from which he then extracted a hot plum pudding. Miss Pross, Lucie Manette's maid in *A Tale of Two Cities*, shares this talent: she qualifies as 'quite a Sorceress' in the kitchen, where her 'wonderful arts' can change a fowl, a rabbit or a vegetable 'into anything she pleased'. Dickens's metaphors – specimens of what Carlyle's German savant in *Sartor Resartus* calls 'the grand Thaumaturgic art of Thought!' – achieve the same result by using words as their raw material. A thaumaturge has the power to perform miracles, and Teufelsdröckh points to industrial evidence of 'the Poet's and Prophet's inspired Message' which 'makes and unmakes worlds'. The steam engine, said to be 'stronger than any Enchanter's Familiar', here outstrips the train that speeds Dickens to Paris: taking to the water, it travels 'on fire-wings round the Cape, and across two Oceans'. Thaumaturgy is a devious business, and many of Dickens's metaphors are vanishing acts, showing off a sleight of hand that passes for everyday practice in the overlapping areas of politics, finance and crime. When Veneering in *Our Mutual Friend* purchases a seat in Parliament, the bribe is pocketed by no one in particular but 'disappear[s] by magical conjuration and enchantment'. Pecksniff, equally slick, appropriates Martin Chuzzlewit's architectural drafts, adds a few extra twiddles, and sells them as his own, which counts as an alchemical masterstroke: 'such is the magic of genius, which changes all it handles into gold!' On his tour of thieves' hide-outs in St Giles's with Inspector Field, Dickens notices trapdoors that spring open 'like the lids of the conjurer's boxes' so that felons can slip away; at the Liverpool docks, the Uncommercial Traveller joins forces with a police superintendent to summon supernatural assistance in tracing a suspect. 'Ring the wonderful stick, rub the wonderful lantern,' they command. In this case the genii who execute the order are officers of the law, though in *The Arabian Nights* they would probably be helping some scapegrace to make a getaway.

Dickens calls Mr Dombey the Sultan of his firm, with his treacherous deputy Carker installed in a nearby office as Grand Vizier. Thackeray saw the same balance of power between Dickens and

W. H. Wills, whom he employed as assistant editor on his period-icals. Thackeray identified Dickens as the Sultan, with Wills as his Grand Vizier. But despite Wills's long and loyal service, Dickens in 1861 declared him unfit for Arabia by remarking that 'Wills has no genius'; as an enchanter, he served as his own wizard. Killing charac-ters at will, Dickens helped himself to the prerogatives of the Sultan Shahryar, who executes successive brides after consummation to ensure that they will not have the chance to be unfaithful. Yet the postponements imposed by serial publication also schooled him in the delaying tactics perfected by Scheherazade, the last and most artful of the Sultan's wives, who ends each instalment of her tales on a suspenseful cliff-edge, calculating that her husband will spare her life in order to hear the sequel. David Copperfield inherits her role when he and Steerforth make 'some regular Arabian Nights' in the school dormitory. David tells Steerforth stories until he nods off, but 'like the Sultana Scheherazade' he is woken early next morning and told to continue.

In Dickens's childhood, his nurse Mary Weller officiated as a live-in Scheherazade; he renames her Mercy in *The Uncommercial Traveller*, adding that she was unmerciful to him. In a long-running serial, she told the young Charles bedtime stories about the exploits of the bucca-neering Captain Murderer, who marries a succession of naive brides and, like the Sultan Shahryar before Scheherazade's arrival, kills them on their wedding night. Scheherazade survives by canny subterfuge and teasing prevarication; Mary, however, took control of the situa-tion and derived a 'fiendish enjoyment' from making her audience of one suffer 'nightmares and perspirations'. The Captain also turned out to be a more savagely and greedily Dickensian character than the insecure Sultan with his fear of cuckoldry. He entombs each freshly beheaded bride under a pie crust that she herself has prepared with a golden rolling pin, seasons her to taste, eats her when baked and picks her bones clean, after which he laughs at his voracious practical jokes and, as the nurse reports, prospers exceedingly.

When Aladdin changes into a glamorously bedecked prince-ling in *The Arabian Nights*, Allah is thanked for permitting his metamorphosis: 'Glory be to Him who changes others and remains Himself unchanged!' Seasonal excitement prompted Dickens to make his own more skittish, wayward version of this prayer. 'Everything,' he says about the high-speed harlequinade of Christmas pantomimes, 'is capable, with the greatest ease, of being changed into Anything; and "Nothing is, but thinking makes it so."' He delights in the ease of those mutations, although he vaults in an instant from anything to nothing and backs up his claim with a nipped and tucked quotation from Shakespeare. Hamlet, imprisoned in his brooding mind, ruefully admits that 'There is nothing either good or bad but thinking makes it so.' Good or bad matter less to Dickens, who elides those words: waving away Hamlet's solipsistic moral scruples, his declaration concerns the untrammelled rights of imagination.

Fondly recalling the literary works that nourished his youthful fantasy, David Copperfield pays tribute to *The Tales of the Genii*, an Arabian pastiche published in 1764. This prompted Dickens's earliest literary endeavour: at the age of nine he adapted one of its episodes, 'The Enchanters', in a tragedy which he sonorously entitled *Misnar, The Sultan of India*. From then on, the book was one of his standbys, and what he did with it far outstripped the half-hearted exoticism of the source.

The Tales of the Genii came equipped with assurances that readers true to 'our Holy Christian Faith' would not be compromised by their sojourn in this heathen realm. An anonymous editor introduced the supposed translator Sir Charles Morell, 'formerly ambassador from the British Settlements in India to the Great Mogul'. Morell did not exist; this was the pseudonym of the Reverend James Ridley, an army chaplain who chose to remain incognito because his Arabian diversion might be 'inconsistent with the clerical character'. Ridley exposed his qualms by setting up a debate between Morell and the Persian imam Horam, who has been educated in the West and reveres Isaac Newton, one of the 'Genii of Mankind', for having mapped 'an immeasurable system of planets'. But when Horam criticises Christians for doing 'deeds unworthy of Pagans', Morell starchily reminds him that Christ is a saviour not merely a prophet and insists that any angel or genius is 'but a debtor to his Creator'. Horam eventually surrenders to Morell's Anglican orthodoxy by describing the *Tales* as 'Delightful Lessons' that disguise 'the true doctrine of morality under the delightful allegories of romantic enchantment'. In a second volume Ridley dispensed with his tale-telling surrogate and took responsibility for his own work: admitting that Horam was 'but the phantom of my mind', he went on to call the imam 'fiction himself, and fiction all he seemed to write'.

Ridley's apologetic misgivings did not placate the Irish Archbishop Richard Whately, who in 1849 revised – or, as he said, 'purified' – *The Tales of the Genii* to salvage 'a religious moral'. Dickens had his own subtler second thoughts about Ridley's work: rather than superimposing piety by force like Whately, he discovered an unexpected moral truth in Horam's whimsies. In *Great Expectations*, when Magwitch returns from Australia and upsets the London life of his protégé, Pip finds grounds for his dread in an unspecified 'Eastern story'. He is referring to 'The Enchanters', the tale dramatised by the juvenile Dickens, in which bestial magicians menace the regime of Misnar, a pious ruler who is forever praising Allah and his prophet Mahomet. The sorcerers change at will into a dragon, a scorpion, a vulture, a tiger, a spider, a toad, a serpent and an alligator; a wily vizier saves Misnar from their attacks with 'the help of several engines'. Having found the last two enchanters asleep in a pavilion, he suspends a crushing rock above them, holding it in place with a rope that is passed through 'a secret channel' drilled into the side of a mountain and fastened by an iron ring. As Pip reveals in his summary, Misnar uses an axe to cut the rope so that the ceiling above 'the bed of state' falls in, crushing the demons. This outcome is cruelly relevant to Pip's predicament, because when Magwitch reappears 'the roof of my stronghold dropped upon me'. Pip's body is not smashed to atoms like those of Ahaback and Desra, but his gilded existence capsizes. He realises that he is soiled by a convict's dirty money, and additionally sullied by his inability to feel grateful to his benefactor. The vizier in

'The Enchanters' congratulates himself on 'a device, which I hoped would put the enchanters in my power'; the return of Magwitch may be a plot device, but Pip stresses fatality not trickery, recognising in the contrivance a secret channel that leads back into his suppressed past. As the slab falls, it carries with it the weight of his guilt.

David Copperfield testifies that the Arabian stories 'did me no harm', but only because his juvenile ignorance protected him: 'whatever harm was in some of them, was not there for me; *I* knew nothing of it'. In fact, as he implies, *The Tales of the Genii* naughtily skirts corruption. During one of the quests, the Genius who guides Sanballad warns him against female votaries whose 'wild religion' incites orgies; other characters are tutored in villainy by 'licentious maxims'. In a footnote, Morell says that he has censored the details of these 'schools of vice' – though he adds, with a wink, that 'by the omission, the original beauty of the tale will be much lessened'. Dickens saw through this clerical hypocrisy. In *Oliver Twist* the benevolent Mr Brownlow unexpectedly compares religions when the prostitute Nancy complains about Christian bigotry. 'Between the Mussulman and the Pharisee,' he says, 'commend me to the first!' The decrepit flirt Mrs Skewton in *Dombey and Son* is gratified by the coincidence that brings her daughter and Carker together, and she mangles a quote from the Koran to make a chance meeting seem predestined. Like 'those wicked Turks', she reverently avows that 'there is no What's-his-name but Thingummy, and What-you-may-call-it is his prophet!' The god whose name she forgets is an obliging pandar, and Mrs Skewton herself is his meddlesome prophet. In 1857 at the Doncaster racetrack Dickens summoned a similar go-between to help him arrange a rendezvous with Ellen Ternan. He appealed to the 'Slave of the Lamp, or Ring', called him forth as if with 'Arab drums, powerful of old to summon Genii in the desert', and begged him to 'enchant this dusty barouche', the carriage in which the unnamed object of his infatuation, soon to be his mistress, sat watching the races.

Dickens's most titillating excursion into the ribald Arabian realm came in his contribution to *The Haunted House*, a set of tales about a group of ghost-hunters who stay overnight in 'an avoided house'.

The narrator is assigned to a garret that once housed the innocuous Master B., whose spirit he pursues in a nocturnal chase on a broomstick, a rocking horse and a headless donkey – dreamy voyages which he likens to those of Sinbad. 'I was myself, yet not myself,' he says of this liberating fantasy. In one of these whirlwind transformations he turns back into a misbehaving schoolboy and takes another lad behind a door to make him 'a proposition of the most astounding nature'. What he suggests, with startling sexual precocity, is that 'we should have a Seraglio'; he says that this scheme to set up a separate household for wives and concubines is blameless because Caliph Haroun al-Rashid, whose 'corrupted name . . . is so scented with sweet memories', provides a precedent. Their 'Oriental establishment' is kept a secret from Miss Griffin, the baleful gryphon in whose school at Hampstead the young narrator is apparently enrolled. Behind her back, others are awarded racy Arabian identities. Miss Pipson, a curly-haired tot aged eight or nine, becomes a Circassian slave girl, purchased by the narrator who vacillates between her and Miss Bule, his official Sultana. Tabby the household drudge is recast as Mesrour, 'chief of the Blacks of the Hareem'. Only Miss Griffin remains herself, secure in her 'Westerly' rectitude and unaware, as she parades her pupils through the London streets, that she is 'walking with a stately step at the head of Polygamy and Mahomedanism'. Despite their professed innocence, the children feel 'a mysterious and terrible joy' that derives from their 'knowledge of what Miss Griffin (who knew all things that could be learnt out of book) didn't know'. Their 'dreadful power' is that of Dickens, congratulating himself on his capacity to effect such transformations with no assistance from a genie.

It all falls apart on Sunday, under attack by the official theology. The narrator, obliged to attend church in an 'unsecular' capacity, reports on a reading from the Bible which describes 'Solomon in his domestic glory'. He gives no details, but presumably the congregation was regaled with an account of Solomon's seven hundred wives and three hundred concubines. 'A crimson blush, attended by a fearful perspiration', makes the narrator's shame and guilt visible, and 'the whole Seraglio reddened' as if in the setting sun: this sudden rush of blood – catching him 'at the full height of enjoyment of my bliss' – could hardly be more explicit. Miss Griffin glares at her charges, suddenly aware that they are 'children of Islam', illicit converts to a religion that took a more tolerant view of sensual foibles than Victorian Christianity.

Later, brooding on his 'Moosulmaun responsibilities', the narrator spots a stranger eyeing him suspiciously. Fearing arrest by this 'minion of the law' he runs off, bound for Egypt, but is detained. What follows is a reprise of a primal scene from *David Copperfield*, which was already a disguised reprise of Dickens's own parricidal plotting. The narrator receives a message about the death of his father, just as David is abruptly informed that his mother has also died; the family's worthless property is then sold off – surely a reminder of the indebtedness of the Micawberesque John Dickens. The narrator's 'own little bed' goes 'for a song', jumbled into the same lot with a coal scuttle and a birdcage, and he wonders what dismal song these battered souvenirs of a damaged childhood will be silently singing on the auctioneer's block. He is then banished to a 'great, cold, bare school of big boys', where the daily provisions are 'thick and clumpy, without being enough', like the miserly portions doled out to Oliver Twist in the workhouse. Chastened, he keeps quiet about his earlier fantasy life: 'I never whispered . . . that I had been Haroun, or had had a Seraglio.'

After this, the dreaming narrator awakens to a chilly reckoning. Master B.'s room, he realises, was haunted by a phantom representing his own lost self. He examines himself in a mirror and recognises that he has been 'shaving in the glass a constant change of customers', rehearsing his transmutation into other creatures as Dickens did when writing. He has also been 'lying down and rising up with the skeleton allotted to me for my mortal companion': that sounds fatalistic and funereal, although like Dickens the narrator reserves the right to rise up from the grave in which he buried his characters. When all the stories about the house have been told, Dickens in his editorial summing-up concedes that he and his fellow contributors – among whom were Wilkie Collins and Elizabeth Gaskell – have not been 'haunted by anything more disagreeable than our own imaginations and remembrances'.

Dickens returned to the theology of the Arabian tales in the last chapter of *A Tale of Two Cities*, published in the same year as *The Haunted House*. The French Revolution placed Christianity under an embargo, converting cathedrals into Temples of Reason, but that did not rationalise an ideologically inflamed society. Instead, as Dickens suggests, the eastern genii migrated west to put a curse on France: the 'powerful enchanter, Time' changed farm wagons into 'death-carts' that delivered condemned prisoners to the guillotine and warped humanity into 'tortured forms', producing the likes of the maenadic Madame Defarge. Treating the revolution as an upsurgence of fantasy and not the logical outcome of social and economic causes, Dickens glances at his own power as an enchanter in a tortuous sentence which declares that 'All the devouring and insatiate Monsters imagined since imagination could record itself, are fused in the one realisation, Guillotine.' He looks to 'the wise Arabian stories' for an explanation of this black magic and summarises a decree supposedly proclaimed by 'the seers', whose verdict is doom-laden. 'The great magician who majestically works out the appointed order of the Creator, never reverses his transformations', which means that those who have been 'changed into this shape by the will of God' must stay that way. Historical events are irrevocable, so there can be no reprieve for Sydney Carton and the others who are sentenced to death. But Dickens adds a waiver: the seers agree to spare those who have been changed into another form by 'mere passing conjuration'. Bending the deterministic rule, this allows France to recover from the malign enchantment of the Terror, so that Carton as he dies is able to foresee 'a beautiful city and a brilliant people rising from this abyss'. The same exemption applies to the victims of Dickens's metaphors. During his time in Genoa, the fowls and cats he saw scavenging in the courtyards of broken-down palazzi looked to him like 'transformed retainers, waiting to be changed back again': he has bewitched them, but only temporarily, and when it pleases him he will exercise his prerogative all over again by releasing them from the spell.

Although Dickens deferred to the will of the biblical God, his world was actually ruled by the caprices of the deity he called 'the great magician'. Hence his lifelong interest in the quest of the merchant Abudah, who in *The Tales of the Genii* is sent to search for the talisman of Oromanes, 'the magician of Fire, the great alchymist'. Abudah takes his orders from a sibyl, whose authority is disputed by two of Dickens's characters. During an account of his childhood reading, the Uncommercial Traveller says he is glad that he never personally encountered this schoolmistressy hag, and Tom Pinch, browsing in the Salisbury bookshop in *Martin Chuzzlewit*, likewise flinches from 'the terrible little old woman' in the story. Abudah, however, readily consents to the task she sets him, and in doing so he announces that 'I have a nocturnal monitor, who will not permit me to rest' until the prize is gained. Guided by his own nocturnal monitor of imagination, Dickens replaced Abudah's physical mission with a mental escapade; he already possessed the magic-making talisman, which was his pen. Misnar in 'The Enchanters' acknowledges that Allah has the right 'to dissolve this frame of earth, and every vision of the eye'. Dickens boldly appropriated the power before which Misnar abases himself, and by reframing reality he altered our vision of it.

8

Species and Origins

Planet Dick teems with an undifferentiated, anarchic life, a melee in which human beings no longer enjoy priority. On his visit to Washington in 1842, Dickens noticed a whirligig of activity in the yard behind his hotel: maids with handkerchiefs as their headgear bustled about, waiters ferried dishes to and fro, dogs frolicked and a pig luxuriantly sunned itself. At the front of the hotel, the view was more disruptive. There, on a grubby patch of land that seemed to have 'taken to drinking, and . . . quite lost itself' after stumbling in from the country, stood a lop-sided, one-eyed shack topped by a steeple with a flagpole poking out of it; this wooden crate, which was possibly a church, resembled debris 'fallen down from the moon' after some astral catastrophe. The occasional dusty tornado added to the instability.

A triangle set up in the yard was repeatedly struck to summon laggard servants. In *American Notes* Dickens calls this an 'enlivening engine', like a galvanic battery or a mesmerist's magnet, and hears it 'tingling madly', 'in full performance' all day, although 'neither the men, nor the women, nor the dogs, nor the pig, nor any created creature, takes the smallest notice'. Humans and animals are equalised by the tautologous phrase 'created creature', with the pig as the most enviable and eloquent in the group: it grunts as its upturned stomach absorbs the warmth, and Dickens translates its utterance as 'That's comfortable!' But who created those creatures, and why do the people work while the dogs play and the pig relaxes? Humanity has been

137

demoted, and the triangle might be the irritated voice of a God whose commands no one heeds.

In such jumbled panoramas, Dickens made a free-thinking contribution to the scientific and theological arguments about our species that raged around him and reached his own conclusions about our place in nature. He began with a reminder that the status of humanity is relative, conditional on good behaviour or good luck. Unemployed in London, Martin Chuzzlewit lazes outside a pub. He has slithered down what philosophers used to call the chain of being, taking only a month 'to reach the lowest round of this tall ladder!' Dickens, however, defends Martin from any Pharisees who might reproach him: before invoking the higher destiny of human nature, he advises them to 'see that it be human first', not transformed 'into the nature of the Beasts!' That ancient moral distinction between human and animal is upset again at Smithfield meat market in *Bleak House*. Here the 'scarcely human' waif Jo listens to a band whose music also entertains a drover's dog, which has delivered its flock of sheep to their fate and is now off duty outside a butcher's shop. With no offence to Jo, Dickens notes that the 'educated, improved, developed dog' has at least been taught a trade: 'how far above the human listener is the brute!'

Exploring the streets around Waterloo, the Uncommercial Traveller is taken aback by the impudence of what once were categorised as 'the lower animals'. A costermonger's donkey enters a house through the front door and goes upstairs to sleep, a bulldog keeps a man as its pet, cats behave like the slatterns who feed them, and fowls seem hardly to be 'products of Nature': a creature 'born of an egg and invested with wings' has no business hopping down a ladder into a cellar to roost. A speckled cock is observed 'defying the Universe' in support of an elderly hen as it attempts to invade a chapel, intent on 'entrusting an egg to that particular denomination'. The broody hen reminds the Traveller of the deranged prophet Joanna Southcott, who in 1814 at the age of sixty-four announced that she was about to give birth to a new Messiah. Mrs Southcott was a farmer's daughter, and a dairy maid in her early years; she claimed to be the Woman of the Apocalypse described in the Book of Revelation, which may explain why the urban litter in which the fowls are pecking is described as 'meteoric discharge', comparable to the lunar detritus in Washington – the fall-out from worlds that have collapsed or collided.

Poll Sweedlepipe, the barber in *Martin Chuzzlewit*, makes his peace with this destabilised state. At home Poll has game-cocks in the kitchen, pheasants in the garret, bantams in the cellar and owls in the bedroom, while his staircase is 'sacred to rabbits'. Merging with his fellow tenants, he develops a range of 'ornithological properties' and is likened to a sparrow, a dove, a pigeon, a magpie and a raven. Dickens kept ravens as pets, the first of which was the model for Grip, Barnaby Rudge's companion. Enjoying their baleful verbal catchphrases, he assured his friends that they could read and write as well as talk, and did not object when they bit the ankles of his children. His third Grip, resituating itself in the pecking order, browbeat the family's hulking mastiff and stole its food. In 1850 Dickens wrote a set of articles in the persona of one such raven, which beadily eyes the members of the household where it is kept caged. 'You are so proud of your humanity,' it croaks. 'Ha, ha!' A horse concurs, criticising equestrian statues. Man, it says, is 'an unmeaning and conceited creature', not fit for mastery over 'the nobler animals'. True, we are adept at debasing other species, often in the same breath as smarmily expressing affection for our own kind. Dickens's pet names for his wife ranged invidiously from Mouse to Pig, just as Amy Dorrit's sister Fanny calls her 'the best of small creatures' and likens her to an owl, a bat, a mole, a tortoise and a dormouse – small creatures that are nocturnal or subterranean or else fugitive. Kindness like this can kill.

Already in *Sketches by Boz* Dickens challenges accepted biological nomenclature. Animals are supposed to be animate, whereas inanimate objects should remain inert: how then do we categorise the 'animated sandwich, composed of a boy between two boards' that appears in the street to advertise Signor Billsmethi's dance classes? A creature is a living thing, a subject rather than an object, though that distinction is not respected by the fussy bachelor Mr Minns, who abhors 'two classes of created objects', namely dogs and children. A creature also has to be animal rather than vegetable, although Boz identifies exceptions. The Crumpton sisters are 'marigolds run to seed', while the four inseparable and indistinguishable Miss Willises, who 'have no separate existence', are said to have 'vegetated'.

Chemistry offers another way of explaining the maidenly merger of the Willises. Boz, referring to the affinity between polar or magnetic bonds and electric charges demonstrated by Michael Faraday's experiments during the 1820s, suggests that the sisters lived 'in Polar harmony among themselves'. Again borrowing from Faraday, whose lectures Dickens published in *Household Words*, Boz speculates about the affinity between men and the door-knockers on their houses, which he sees as an example of magnetism. The face of an ancient beau resembles 'a chubby street-door knocker' which is itself the product of a mongrelised graft, 'half-lion half-monkey'. Boz lists 'the most prominent and strongly-defined species' of knockers, flouting the requirement that members of a species must be alive and capable of interbreeding. The very word 'species' is twisted awry by Mr Omer, the elderly undertaker in *David Copperfield*, who explains that for him 'the two ends of life meet' now that his legs are untrustworthy and he is 'wheeled about for the second time, in a speeches of go-cart'. 'Species' derives from the Latin 'specere', meaning to look; Omer's mispronunciation replaces bodies that appear to be similar with words that sound the same, but in doing so he identifies a talkative new species that travels on wheels not legs.

When Henry James reviewed *Our Mutual Friend* in 1865 he deplored its assemblage of hunchbacks, amputees, freaks and imbeciles, and concluded that 'there is no humanity here'. That may have been the point: for Dickens, the notion of humanity was open to question. Do we really deserve to congratulate ourselves on the superiority of our species? Boz, having anatomised knockers, says 'This is a new theory.' The remark is more than a joke, because Dickens had many zanily ingenious theories about people and their position in or adjacent to nature. A bank director in *Dombey and Son* is 'reputed to be able to buy up anything', including 'human Nature generally, if he should take it in his head to influence the money market in that direction'. But if we are appraised as stock, our price fluctuates. Chadband, the pompous preacher in *Bleak House*, unctuously informs the wretched Jo that 'You are a human boy.' He means that Jo should live up to this privilege, although other characters live down to a less demanding standard. 'I am merely human,' whines Bella Wilfer's sister Lavvy in *Our Mutual Friend* after she recovers from a bout of jealous hysteria. The brutalised narrator of Dickens's story 'George Silverman's Explanation' knows how slippery and relativistic the idea is. To be human is not a birthright; he has had to work on 'the humanising of myself'. In Dickens's charitable campaigns to improve the welfare of foundlings or fallen women, humanitarianism was his corrective to a self-satisfied humanism; possibly it was also his rebuke to himself, since he often dehumanised the people he described. He categorised a Shaker shopkeeper in upstate New York, for instance, as 'something alive in a russet case, which the elder said was a woman; and which I suppose *was* a woman, though I should not have suspected it'.

Explaining his inflated use of the second-person pronoun, Pecksniff in *Martin Chuzzlewit* says that his 'we' refers to 'mankind in general; the human race, considered as a body, and not as individuals'. As Pecksniff sees it, all individuals except one are expendable, which is why he considers the subservient Tom Pinch to be merely 'an item in the vast total of humanity' – a particle, the lowest of single digits. The exemplary body that concerns Pecksniff is his own, and he marvels at the oiled efficiency of his digestive system. After having swallowed some 'enlivening fluid' from the hotel bar and regaled himself with an ample meal, he greasily gives thanks to the 'most beautiful machinery' of his alimentary tract. 'When I have wound myself up, if I may employ such a term,' he says, 'and know that I am Going, I feel that in the lesson afforded by the works within me, I am a Benefactor to my Kind!' This serves as 'a kind of grace', after which he falls contentedly asleep. Later, following a tiff with his daughter Charity, Pecksniff resigns from a species that he now thinks unworthy of him. 'Ah, human nature, human nature! Poor human nature!' he exclaims; he is seen 'shaking his head at human nature, as if he didn't belong to it'.

Mrs Gamp is just as much of an outlier. 'Gamp is my name,' she declares as she presents her business card, 'and Gamp my nater.' The formulation is absurd yet entirely apt. Because she is one of a kind, her name is a whimsical neologism that does not attach her to a family – although the type of bulbous, unwieldy umbrella she carries everywhere came to be known as a gamp, effectively making it her offspring. As a nurse, her professional function is to assist natural processes, helping babies into the world and tending the sick as they prepare to leave it, but she regards her patients as insentient puppets who need to be manipulated: she hustles the trembling dotard Mr Chuffey into bed by telling him 'you're a-shakin' all over, as if your precious jints was hung upon wires. That's a good creetur!' Her true vocation is not care for others but the embellishment of her own mystique, and Dickens stands back to marvel at the 'ecstasies' of her rhapsodic monologues. Arriving in Jonas Chuzzlewit's house, she distributes blessings to all the characters she encounters there, wishes that 'this tearful walley would be changed into a flowerin' guardian', warns of 'wot is wrote upon the wall behind', and salutes the non-existent Mrs Harris for having a face that is 'quite a angel's!' Her self-invention and self-exhibition make her an artist: Mrs Gamp, Dickens says, 'added daily so many strings to her bow, that she made a perfect harp of it; and upon that instrument she now began to perform an extemporaneous concerto.' Gamp is her nature because she is a nonpareil; she might be called a 'lusus naturae', although this sport of nature is the novelist's creation, not a biological freak. As Fernando Pessoa put it in *The Book of Disquiet*, Dickens's great characters are 'extra-human', and if they do not exist there must be a flaw in reality.

'What is man?' asks the dandy Horatio Sparkins in *Sketches by Boz*. He ought to be directing the question at himself, because his real name is Samuel Smith and he is drably employed at a draper's shop. Sparkins's musings do not take him very far: after noting that we breathe and have desires and appetites, he says 'We know that we exist, but there we stop.' Price tags in the dirty window of his shop complicate the problem by exposing the invisible abundance of the microscopic living things with which we coexist: they display 'dropsical figures of a seven with a little three farthings in the corner, something like the aquatic animalculae disclosed by the gas microscope', an instrument that used limelight to expose micro-organisms. Elsewhere Dickens extends this aborted enquiry into the status of humanity. Buzfuz the barrister drones through his own vacuous legalistic definition in court when he describes 'a being, erect upon two legs, and bearing all the outward semblance of a man, and not of a monster' who turns out to be Pickwick. Bucket, the detective in *Bleak House*, is 'man in the abstract'; physically ubiquitous, he functions as a detached mind intent on the 'observation of human nature' or scrutiny of 'the follies of mankind' – employment that suits him because he is himself not quite human. Jobling, a sleazy embezzler in *Martin Chuzzlewit*, also refers to 'the imitative biped man', but does the fact that we walk upright necessarily rank us above the quadrupeds in the Washington yard?

For some characters, a stark dread resounds in Sparkins's rhetorical question. Disgusted by Fagin's panic before his execution, the turn-key in *Oliver Twist* asks 'Are you a man?' 'I shan't be one long,' moans Fagin. Nicholas Nickleby materialises in the dimly lit lair of the grizzled usurer Gride, who gibbers 'Is it a man or a - a -'. 'For what do you take me, if not for a man?' sneers Nicholas. Gride peers into the gloom and ascertains that 'it is a man, and not a spirit. It is a man.' The narrator of the ghost story 'The Signal-Man' decides otherwise when he encounters a glowering form among 'lower shadows' at the entrance to a railway tunnel. Guarding a conduit that leads out of 'the natural world', the dark, grave stranger is another Dickensian psychopomp, who emerges from the future to foretell a death. 'This,' the narrator rightly suspects, 'was a spirit, not a man.'

Corpses, of which Dickens was a connoisseur, exist in an intermediate state. On one of his visits to the morgue beside the Seine, he was startled to see an attendant rearranging the bodies, as if they 'were all getting up!' At the Great St Bernard hospice in the Alps, he inspected the frozen bodies of dead travellers retrieved from the snow: upright in icy rigor mortis, they looked 'horribly human', their reaction to dying still recorded in their facial expressions, and Dickens welcomed them as 'the only human company out of doors'. The most daring account of this existential transition comes in *Our Mutual Friend*, in which John Harmon, given up for dead, returns to life to remember the experience of drowning. What Harmon took to be his death sounds very like birth. He says he experienced 'a downward slide through something like a tube, and then a great noise and a sparkling and crackling as of fires', after which 'the consciousness came upon me'. Mind has somehow come alight in matter, but who is the creature experiencing this pain? 'I cannot possibly express it to myself without using the word I,' he says. 'But it was not I. There was no such thing as I, within my knowledge.' As a 'living-dead man', he contemplates his demise and wonders whether or not to accept it:

> John Harmon is dead. Should John Harmon come to life?
> If yes, why? If no, why?

Having decided to stay dead, he performs 'the sexton-task of piling earth above John Harmon all night long' and drowns himself 'many additional fathoms deep'; he then begins a second life as John Rokesmith.

'Society,' James argued in his essay on *Our Mutual Friend*, 'is maintained by natural sense and natural feeling.' Harmon's eerie self-resurrection goes against both. In any case, Dickens was interested less in maintaining society than in constructing an autonomous world, and rather than identifying nature with humane sentiment he thought of it as a violent, amoral chaos. Attempts to uphold a norm are mocked in *Nicholas Nickleby* when Snawley, who pretends to be the captive Smike's stepfather, says that his urge to punish the runaway vouches for his natural instincts as a parent. Squeers takes this to be proof that 'She's a rum 'un, is Natur.' Snawley reverently adds 'She is a holy thing', and Squeers sums up by declaring that 'Natur is more easier conceived than described.' That reminded Dickens of his task: before he could describe nature, he had to reconceive it.

George Bernard Shaw said that Dickens's novels, taken all together, constitute 'a Bible in fact'. They are bright books of life, which D. H.

Lawrence thought that novels should always be, but also dark books of death, and they have their own heterodox version of the biblical beginning and end.

The Pickwick Papers starts as the Bible does, with a 'first ray of light which illuminates the gloom' and retrieves Pickwick from obscurity; in the second chapter the sun rises again while Pickwick arises from his bed 'like another sun' and opens the window onto Goswell Street in Clerkenwell to take stock of 'the world beneath'. Like God, he sees it all at once – the thoroughfare, Dickens says, is 'not more populous than popular' and it gives Pickwick 'an equal opportunity of contemplating human nature in all its numerous phases' – and presumably, like God at the end of the day, he finds the panopticon to be good. But Genesis is dim not luminous at the start of *Bleak House*, and in *Hard Times* the disaffected worker Stephen Blackpool anticipates a thermodynamic retribution when 'th' Sun turns t' ice' and 'God's work is onmade.'

Martin Chuzzlewit opens by joking that the Chuzzlewits are the direct descendants of Adam and Eve, which explains why they have always been 'closely connected with the agricultural interest'. Having remembered Eden, the first chapter of the novel – published in 1844, fifteen years before Darwin's *On the Origin of Species by Means of Natural Selection* – concludes with a nod at early evolutionary hypotheses. The Chuzzlewits are human but behave inhumanely, which prompts Dickens to mention 'the Monboddo doctrine'. In the late eighteenth century the Scottish lawyer Lord Monboddo speculated about the similarity between homo sapiens and the orangutan, and although Dickens hesitates to agree, he admits that men play ape-like tricks on one another. He also cites the even more opprobious 'Blumenbach theory': Johann Blumenbach, a German anatomist, thought that 'the descendants of Adam' were close kin to swine. The biblical narrative resumes when Martin crosses the Atlantic on an 'unwholesome ark', hoping to improve his prospects in a country that claimed to be an earthly paradise, although when the migrants disembark in New York, they 'might have fallen from another planet'. Revising the chronology and geography of Genesis, Martin travels west to a frontier settlement that presumptuously calls itself Eden. Rather than a pristine garden, it is a fetid swamp from which 'the waters of the Deluge' seem to have drained away only a week before. 'What are the Great United States for, sir,' demands a patriotic general, 'but the regeneration of man?' When Martin sickens and almost dies in malarial Eden, he experiences instead the degeneration of man.

Before he leaves England, an amusing error questions America's redefinition of humanity. The driver who takes Martin to London says 'All men are alike in the U-nited States, an't they?' No, America's founding faith is that all men are created equal, but for Dickens egalitarianism meant uniformity. On the voyage out, English, Irish, Welsh and Scots passengers are crammed together, merged in seasick squalor; once on shore they are all forcibly equalised as Americans. At best the country's creed licenses a brash, unkempt informality: a dishevelled New York journalist who accosts Martin has a waistcoat through which a shirt-frill obtrudes, 'asserting an equality of civil rights with the other portions of his dress, and maintaining a declaration of Independence on its own account'.

As Martin sees it, the American experiment produces people 'strangely devoid of individual traits', who have the national character – in its Greek source, 'character' refers to a stamping tool – typecast into them on an overworked assembly line. The same industrial process is responsible for the speechifying Congressman who shakes Martin's hand 'like a clock-work figure that was just running down', then rewinds himself when he chews tobacco and noisily squirts out a gusher of saliva. Looked at in perspective, his countrymen are as standardised as their footwear: a hotel verandah, seemingly occupied by boots and shoes stationed in mid-air on a rail and enveloped in cigar smoke, offers 'no other evidences of human habitation'. In a New York lodging house Martin notices 'a stove, garnished on either side with a great brass spittoon, and shaped in itself like three little iron barrels set up on end in a fender, and joined together on the principle of the Siamese Twins'. This refers to Chang and Eng Bunker, the first conjoined twins to be called Siamese; born in what is now Thailand, they toured America in a freak show and in 1839 settled in North

Carolina, where they married two non-conjoined sisters and between them fathered twenty-one children. Remaking the twins in brass as a cuspidor, Dickens treats them as human facsimiles duplicated in metal and soldered together. The cruel joke somewhat undercuts the appeal he made to 'the commonest of common humanity' when he railed against slavery in the southern states.

Dickens believed that America, by collectivising the people who migrated there, had brought about a mutation in the human species. For different reasons the change was happening at home as well. In 1847 the crusading hero of Disraeli's *Tancred* – a young aristocrat who tires of secular frivolity and abandons London for the Holy Land – explains his discontent with his English contemporaries by declaring that 'Individuality is dead; there is a want of inward and personal energy in man.' Perhaps people had been reduced to labouring units by capitalism, or else nature had adopted the routines of the factory. Chester in *Barnaby Rudge* cozens Mrs Varden by pretending to mistake her daughter for her sister, and when corrected says 'humanity is indeed a happy lot, when we can repeat ourselves in others'. The word he chooses is chilling because it turns reproduction into self-replication, rather than the creation of another independent existence. In Wilkie Collins's *The Woman in White* the hypochondriac Mr Fairlie sniffs at biology and its rowdy excess. He demands a 'reform in the construction of children', who as currently designed are 'machines for the production of incessant noise', and he blames nature for 'generating such a vast variety of co-existent productions'. The chatty governess Mrs Vesey in his opinion is the result of 'a vegetable preoccupation in the mind of the Mother of us all': he regards her as a cabbage, not a human being. Collins probably took the notion from *Martin Chuzzlewit*, where Montague Tigg, disowning the sneaky swindler Chevy Slyme, calls himself 'a premium tulip, of a very different growth and cultivation from the cabbage Slyme'. Dickens, however, at least found cabbages to be endearingly comical. Mrs Gamp's nightcap resembles one, and the boarding house run by Mrs Todgers is infused with the smell of them, 'as if all the greens that had ever been boiled there, were evergreens, and flourished in immortal strength'. Dickensian vegetables are organisms too, and they may inherit the earth.

When in the course of his quest Disraeli's Tancred reaches Mount Sinai, a visionary figure identified as 'the angel of Arabia' waves a sceptre the size of a palm tree at him and prescribes a remedy for 'morbid civilisation'. The seraph sermonises about 'the relations between Jehovah and his creatures', and tells Tancred that 'The equality of man can only be accomplished by the sovereignty of God.' Dickens preferred to emphasise the disparity of actual men, women and children, who make themselves sovereign by their gloriously unruly use of language. They have no relations with Jehovah, and their personal relationships are tenuous as well, because alienation from one another is the consequence of the freedom they enjoy.

At the end of his article about the night he spent exploring the criminal slums in London with Inspector Field, Dickens sees the thieves slinking to rest in their hideouts and says that 'as undistinctive Death will come here, one day, so sleep comes now'. He means that death is undiscriminating, that it refuses to distinguish between people, so distinctness ought to be treasured while it lasts. In *Dombey and Son*, Miss Blimber wrongly castigates Paul for being 'singular in your character and conduct', and when Miss Tox tries to stop Rob the Grinder referring to himself as a chap or a cove, he agrees to say he is an individual but stubbornly customises the word as 'indiwiddle', varying Mrs Gamp's 'indiwidgle'. Early in *Martin Chuzzlewit* Montague Tigg calls Chevy Slyme – with whom he is then still in league – 'an individual, of whom it may be said . . . that nobody but himself can in any way come up to him'. The remark is the ultimate Dickensian accolade, although it is indeed fortunate that there is only one Slyme. Dickens even respected 'the individuality of locomotives'. Some railway engines, he pointed out, had a taste for coke and water, others a bronchial objection to Scotch mists; each one had as much right to be indulged as 'the finer piece of work called Man'.

Henry James in his review argues that humanity consists of what we share not what differentiates us, but Dickens refused to think of his characters as interchangeable members of a species, and their eccentricity explains his repudiation of realism. Mimesis can be left to mirrors, like those which the Veneerings in *Our Mutual Friend* use to reflect the shallow veneer of their existence. An innocuous Chuzzlewit relative was 'born for no particular purpose but to save looking-glasses the trouble of reflecting more than just the first idea and sketchy notion of a face, which had never been carried out': no mirror could possibly reflect the unfinished face and unformed mind suggested by this verbal portrait of an uncreated character. For similar reasons Ralph Nickleby dismisses Miss La Creevy's portrait minia-tures. 'I have no eye for likenesses,' he snaps.

The nickname Dickens chose for himself was The Inimitable, and he wished this inimitability on all his people. Although David Copperfield's schoolfriend Traddles apologises that 'there never was a young man with less originality than I have', Dickens makes up for that by endowing Traddles with 'a comic head of hair' that bristles like a porcupine. Pickwick explains that he allows his servant Sam Weller to take cheeky liberties because 'I flatter myself he is an original, and I am rather proud of him.' In retaliation, Mr Magnus snorts 'I am not fond of anything original', which shows him to be an interloper on Planet Dick. Joe the fat boy – a figure of almost mystical self-absorp-tion, somnolent when not feeding and given to snoring while he waits at table – receives a similar accolade from Pickwick, who remarks that he is 'very odd!' His employer replies 'I'm proud of that boy – wouldn't part with him on any account – he's a natural curiosity!' In one of his most inspired puns Sam Weller reassigns Joe's species. The fat boy's gluttony, Sam says, makes him a 'young boa-constructer': with his distended physique he has no need to constrict what he ingests. Other human curios become museum pieces, preserved in vitro. Sikes tells Fagin that he is 'fit for nothing but keeping as a curiosity of ugliness in a glass bottle', though he supposes that 'they don't blow them large enough', and Mrs Gamp reports that Mrs Harris has a stillborn niece 'kep in spirits in a bottle' and exhibited at fairs 'in company with a pink-eyed lady, Prooshan dwarf, and livin' skelinton'.

Once or twice Dickens allows his creatures to baffle taxonomy. In *Martin Chuzzlewit* the self-dramatising 'genius' of Benjamin Bailey is said to have 'eclipsed both time and space', prevailing 'in defiance of all natural laws'. He is a genie who refuses to stay bottled, and as well as frequently changing names he impersonates a howling dog, a high-stepping horse and a monkey; his inexplicability makes a myth of him as 'a breeched and booted Sphinx'. When he reappears after his reported death, Dickens can only call him 'a something in top-boots'. At least he is still madly animated, at the opposite extreme from Mrs Gamp's manhandled patient Mr Chuffey who sits 'looking at nothing, with eyes that saw nothing, and a face that meant nothing. Take him in that state, and he was an embodiment of nothing. Nothing else.'

Dickens overcomes an initial uncertainty about Jenny Wren in *Our Mutual Friend* by allowing her to present herself as an exception to the human norm. Jenny is a cripple, at once juvenile and ancient, and she regards the dolls she dresses as her friends, perhaps her creatures; she appalled Henry James, who could not accept her as 'a possible person'. Dickens is also hesitant at first, describing her as 'a child – a dwarf – a girl – a something'. Much later she embarrasses Sloppy by demanding 'what do you think of Me?' When he fumbles, she lives up to her capitalised pronoun and takes the initiative, defining herself as 'a queer little comicality'. Jenny fits Darwin's category of 'monstros-ities', creatures with a 'deviation of structure in one part' like albino blackbirds which, as he specified, exist in nature but are 'not generally propagated'. Nor can comic monsters like Quilp, Krook, Mr Dick and Miss Havisham be propagated or duplicated, because unrepeat-ability is what gives them their value.

Darwin bred pigeons and enjoyed their 'wonderful' diversity: he was especially fond of the pouter pigeon, an avian Pecksniff whose preening could excite 'astonishment and even laughter'. In *The Origin of Species* he points out that breeders have demonstrated that 'an animal's organisation [is] something quite plastic', and he quotes an expert's opinion that natural selection is a 'magician's wand', able to 'summon into life whatever form and mould' is required. The phrase suits the talismanic artistry of Dickens, though his feelings about human breeding were more complex: he worried about his over-supply of offspring, especially the surplus sons he shipped out to India and Australia, as if he were not half responsible for having produced them all. On a Mississippi steamboat he observed a little wife who a year before had travelled to New York to visit her mother 'in that condition in which ladies who truly love their lords desire to be'. Her lord's desire seems secondary, at least until he belatedly turns up to collect her and their new baby from the wharf in St Louis. For Dickens, procreation was a side effect; what mattered to him was literary creativity.

Darwin admitted that nature discharges its function as a 'manufactory of species' with painful slowness. Dickens by contrast could produce a result instantly, and although Darwin argued against the notion of 'each species as a separate act of creation', that was how Dickens worked. His characters do not derive from a common stock, and each of them is proudly unique or unapologetically monstrous. Despite its frustratingly slow pace, Darwin believed that selection was 'as immeasurably superior to man's feeble efforts, as the works of Nature are to those of Art'. Dickens, whose efforts were never feeble, made the contest more competitive.

The Pickwick Club consists of amateur anthropologists who travel to observe the habits of their fellow humans, yet at their first meeting Mr Pickwick reads a paper about tittlebats, whose habits he has researched in the reservoirs on Hampstead Heath. These three-spined cuttlefish are as odd as the people at Dingley Dell, Eatanswill and the other places the Pickwickians visit, and that makes them worthy of study. Every living thing receives Dickens's fascinated attention, as do innumerable things like door-knockers that are strictly speaking not alive.

During an election campaign in the provinces, Pickwick and his friends find the journalist Pott vilifying his political adversary Slurk as 'a reptile contemporary'. In *Oliver Twist* that name-calling is replaced by a metaphorical fusion of species as Fagin is compared to 'some loathsome reptile, engendered in the slime and darkness through which he moved'. The loathing registered here is overcome in *Martin Chuzzlewit*, where Mark Tapley notices a slippery amphibian squatting in a neighbour's room in Eden. 'I ain't superstitious about toads,' Mark says, and with an authentically Dickensian eye he notices their likeness around the throat to 'a very partickler style of old gentleman', but he prefers them to remain outdoors. Tony Weller welcomes pond-dwellers into the intelligentsia when he recommends the lawyer Solomon Pell, who has 'brains like the frogs, dispersed all over his body, and reachin' to the wery tips of his fingers'. As Magwitch in *Great Expectations* tries to shake off his pursuers, he finds an extra reason to admire and envy creatures that can hop or slither to freedom. 'I wish I was a frog,' he says. 'Or a eel!'

When *Bleak House* first surveys the Dedlocks' estate in Lincolnshire, the weather is wet and dreary. The narrator is dejected because 'the liveliest imagination can scarcely apprehend its ever being fine again', and with Lady Dedlock and Sir Leicester away there is no 'superabundant life of imagination' on the premises. Then, unhindered by the absence of human society and even of articulate speech, he turns aside to find 'motions of fancy among the lower animals'. Horses shut in the stables day-dream about open country and engage in 'livelier communication' than any overheard in the local pub. A mastiff remembers days of sun when he has to migrate around the yard in search of a cooler spot, and with his limited brain wonders why the shadows are so annoyingly mobile. Rabbits pine for fresh greenery, a turkey frets about Christmas, and a waddling goose gabbles discontentedly. This all-comprehending account of nature is extended when Tulkinghorn retrieves a bottle of aged port from the cellar. The 'southern grapes', released from the bottle after 'fifty years of silence and seclusion', impart the secrets of their noble rot to the lawyer, who sits in the twilight 'pondering . . . all the mysteries he knows' while the 'radiant nectar', suddenly self-conscious, 'blushes in the glass to find itself so famous'. In his 'Ode to a Nightingale' Keats calls for wine 'cool'd a long age in the deep-delved earth' and imagines a glass filled with 'the true, the blushful Hippocrene', water from a spring on Mount Helicon frequented by the muses. Keats wants to be flushed with poetic inspiration; Dickens, who looks outwards not at himself, makes the grapes do the blushing, flushed by their vivid revival after that long entombment.

Dickens's well-stocked domestic menagerie vouched for the pleasure he derived from the inventive variety of creation. His aviary at different times included an eagle as well as a canary, along with his succession of ravens. A pony kept for his children took its name, appropriately, from the avuncular Newman Noggs. His first dog was a fluffy Havana spaniel called Timber Doodle, presented to him in America; later he owned larger St Bernards, Newfoundlands and bloodhounds, dignifying them with lordly or exotic names like Don, Sultan and Turk, although one of them was ingloriously dubbed Bumble. When his cat Bob died, Dickens had one of its paws stuffed and attached to an ivory blade for use as a letter-opener. He presented miniature versions of Noah's ark to his children, and one such model cheers the orphan Johnny in *Our Mutual Friend* as he lies dying in hospital. Johnny's ark is said to convene 'All Creation', but Dickens in his summary of the embarkees fixes on 'the elephant leading, and the fly, with a diffident sense of his size, politely bringing up the rear' – a comment which gently infers that the modest fly is no pest and saves it from being crushed by the elephant's foot. A more grimly selective version of the fable appears in *Great Expectations*, where Pip sees the black, iron-ribbed hulk in which the convicts are penned as 'a wicked Noah's Ark'. A vessel built to ensure the survival of all species has been replaced by one that functions as a prison or mortuary for a single stigmatised class of men.

The zoo in Regent's Park brought to London the scattered descendants of the animals that supposedly left the ark after it came to rest on Ararat. But Darwin's world-encircling voyage on the *Beagle* from 1831 to 1836 cast doubt on the biblical claim that all creatures had their origin in Eden: marsupials in Australia, armadillos in South America and lemurs in Madagascar obviously had no shared ancestry, as became clear when specimens from the separate continents were rounded up. Dickens, who lived not far away, often visited the zoo, where he mocked the monkeys, taunted a tiger, teased the snakes and admired the idyllic lassitude of the hippopotamus Obaysch which, as he said in *Household Words*, neither toiled nor spun but in an overly busy world 'bathed and slept, serenely, for the public gratification'. The heterogeneity on display in the enclosures confirmed his scepticism about the exceptional status of his own species.

Like an enchanter reviewing his bestiary of familiars, Dickens habitually made matches between people and their spirit animals: Quilp in *The Old Curiosity Shop*, for instance, resembles a rolled-up hedgehog. Boffin in *Our Mutual Friend* consists of layered folds like a rhinoceros, while superannuated Lady Tippins is 'a diurnal species of lobster – throwing off a shell every forenoon and needing to keep in a retired spot until the new crust hardens': her cosmetic armature is renewed daily, re-outfitting her for social circulation. Carker in *Dombey and Son* starts as a tortoiseshell cat kept to kill mice, evolves into a wolf, and ends as 'a scaly monster of the deep'; Mrs Skewton has the predatory vigilance of a lynx, while Major Bagstock is given an elephant's ears, a lobster's eyes and a horse's cough (but not all at once). Conducting their legal business as if in the wild, Stryver and Carton in *A Tale of Two Cities* operate in tandem as lions and jackals do. Pecksniff in *Martin Chuzzlewit*, more dangerous than Joe the fat boy in *The Pickwick Papers*, goes wooing like 'an affectionate boa-constrictor'. Uriah Heep in *David Copperfield* is 'a malevolent baboon', and when he hoodwinks his employer Mr Wickfield he is an ape leading a man astray. Not exclusively simian, Uriah skitters between species: he also writhes like a conger eel, and he and his mother are 'two great bats'.

Baudelaire in his 1855 essay on comedy emphasised the devilish malice of laughter but pointed out that sometimes we laugh with happy incredulity at 'fabulous creations, beings for whose existence no explanation drawn from common sense is possible'. That could be applied to dozens, even hundreds of Dickens's characters, and it also suits the 'Crorkindills' that Peggotty in *David Copperfield* takes to be a kind of foreign vegetable and the kangaroo whose habits preoccupy Mrs Micawber as she prepares to emigrate to Australia; it can be extended to Obaysch and to the plumed cockatoo that

Fosco, the villain in *The Woman in White*, donates to the keepers at Regent's Park before he absconds from London. Dickens's tropically florid zoology stretched ahead into a future when life might be engineered rather than engendered. On a visit to the Chatham dockyard the Uncommercial Traveller calls the shipbuilders' huge shears 'the Giraffe of the machinery creation', and says that an iron battleship looks so much heavier than the tiny anchors tethering it that he might just as well attach 'the largest hippopotamus in the Zoological Gardens to my shirt-pin'.

After the genealogical jokes in *Martin Chuzzlewit*, Dickens did not directly allude to the debate on evolution inaugurated by Monboddo, but he was by no means disengaged, and his novels supplement Darwin with their own account of what can only be called unnatural selection. *Bleak House*, serialised in 1852–3, is Darwinian before the event when it describes the usurer Smallweed and his clan. These malign parasites derive from myth, folklore or a sacrilegious angelology – the grandfather is a goblin, his grandson an imp, and the assembled family is 'a company of ghastly cherubim' – but Dickens also defines them biologically or geologically. To ensure that they are not mistaken for human beings, their surname marks them as vegetation, and at best they qualify as invertebrates. Grandfather Smallweed was begotten by 'a horny-skinned, two-legged, money-getting species of spider' and he remains in a larval state, 'a grub at first, and . . . a grub at last', never having 'bred a single butterfly'. Inching up the chain of being, he is also called a leech, a snake, a clawed lobster and a crow, although his extortionate practices give him a mechanical extension: Phil Squod says that he is 'a screw and a wice in his actions'. His granddaughter Judy bears 'the family likeness to the monkey tribe' and is shunned by other children as an 'animal of another species'. Her brother Bart, a wizened adolescent, looks so like a fossil from the lower depths that his 'terrestrial existence' is hard to explain, and Judy attains 'a perfectly geological age' as she hurls herself at a victim like a velociraptor 'from the remotest periods', which suggests that she may be a contemporary of the megalosaurus that Dickens imagines 'waddling like an elephantine lizard up Holborn Hill' at the start of the novel. Darwinian nature debarred different species from inter-breeding, but Dickens has no qualms about grafting an elephant onto a lizard, and in *Little Dorrit* Merdle's doctor views his patient as an even more eclectic crossbreed: he has 'the constitution of a rhinoceros, the digestion of an ostrich, and the concentration of an oyster'.

Our Mutual Friend, serialised in 1864–5, five years after the publication of Darwin's book, comprehensively undercuts our vainglorious species. When Boffin pointedly praises bees for their work ethic, the indolent lawyer Eugene Wrayburn resents the aspersion and says that 'as a two-footed creature' he dislikes being compared to insects. The moneylender Fledgeby is introduced as 'the meanest cur existing, with a single pair of legs', which prompts Dickens to add that instinct travels on four legs and reason on two: the meanness of the lower animals is never as calculating as that of their supposed superiors. Rogue Riderhood subsides into the murk as he plods down a path beside the river, his footprints leaving 'mere shapeless holes' in the slush as if 'the very fashion of humanity had departed from his feet'. Because humanity is an exercise in self-fashioning or dressing up, its pretences are belied by Riderhood's sodden cap, which is 'formless and mangey . . . like a furry animal, dog or cat, puppy or kitten, drowned and decaying'. Metaphors like these erode our confident morphology and show people devolving, declining through the species or elementally vanishing. Jenny Wren's alcoholic father Mr Dolls stumbles into the Covent Garden vegetable market to collapse among the 'squashed pulp of humanity'; Lizzie Hexam, grieving over her drowned father, laments that what once used to be his 'own shape' has deliquesced, 'soaking into this filthy ground'. But that mulch or sump is a creative source where new life irrepressibly germinates. The nouveau-riche Veneering, a 'mushroom man', sprouts overnight from this fertile ordure. Merdle is another idol whose substance is 'other than the commonest clay', and after he kills himself rumour-mongers declare that 'He had sprung from nothing, by no natural growth or process that any one could account for.' In fact he sprang fully formed from Dickens's head: speculation about origins inevitably led him to glance back at the source of his own imagined world and of the life that thrives in it.

Late in 1859 *All the Year Round* published a long review of *The Origin of Species* by an anonymous contributor who seems, as he contemplates 'the immense variety of living creatures', to have the productivity of the magazine's owner and editor in mind. Troubled by Darwin's heresy, the critic defends the prerogative of 'the Great Artificer' or 'the Author of Nature' – epithets that align religion and art, or authority and authorship, while taking care to stay doctrinally vague. But this idea of the deity splits apart when the review describes God as 'Continuous and Unyielding Law' on the one hand and 'Incessant Energy, and All-pervading Life' on the other. The first definition suits the forbidding Jehovah of the Old Testament; the second doubles as a succinct homage to Dickens.

9

In the Carvery

Casting an eye over the passengers on a Mississippi steam-boat during his first American tour in 1842, Dickens notices a talkative teenage girl whose physiognomy enables him to read her character: she has a 'loquacious chin' that is accustomed to wagging, a feature he ascribes to 'nature's handwriting'. Then later in the voyage he meets Peter Pitchlynn, a Choctaw chief whom he salutes as a 'stately and complete gentleman of Nature's making', although what sets him apart as 'another kind of being' is his literary taste: he enjoys the epic battles and chivalrous romances in Walter Scott's poetry. Nature is blamed for the chatterbox and given credit for the tribal elder; it is Dickens, however, who sketches both vignettes, just as he says that the caricaturally twisted face of the workhouse slattern Sally in *Oliver Twist* 'resembled more the grotesque shaping of some wild pencil, than the work of Nature's hand'. That wild pencil was wielded by Dickens, and some of his characters recoil from it. When the Artful Dodger objects to a jailer's 'deformation' of his character, and Micawber describes himself to David Copperfield as still 'your fellow-man, though crushed out of his original form', they might be remarking on the morphological experiments of the novelist who designed them.

Dickens admits the daring and perhaps the danger of his under-taking in *Dombey and Son*, where he speculates that 'It might be worthwhile, sometimes, to inquire what Nature is, and how men work to change her.' Analysing the emotional malaise of the rigidly business-like Dombey, he takes his lead from laboratory technicians 'who study the physical sciences' and track 'the noxious particles that rise from vitiated air' in over-crowded cities. Pollution has poisoned nature, and in a society obsessed with the pursuit of profit Dombey's heart is hardened by the 'enforced distortions' that dry up more tender, altruistic feelings. Yet Dickens's proposal to examine how we change nature remains hesitant, uncommitted: the inquiry, he says, 'might be worthwhile, sometimes' – or might it inconveniently reflect on his own creative procedures? Although he complains that the good health and sanity of the world 'as GOD designed it' has been altered by economic changes, Dickens also redesigns nature, sidelining God.

Enforcing distortions in his own way, Dickens pieces his characters together and then pulls them apart. In 1837 *The Mudfog Papers*, a set of sketches that follow the activities of the Mudfog Association for the Advancement of Everything, inaugurated a tortuous anatomy lesson that extends throughout Dickens's work. At a session devoted to Umbugology and Ditchwaterisics, Professor Ketch – who shares his surname with the barbarically clumsy executioner employed by Charles II – produces for examination a skull that supposedly belonged to James Greenacre, a murderer recently hanged at Newgate. Greenacre, a grocer from the Edgware Road, killed his fiancée, then sawed off her head and dropped it in a canal near Stepney; he deposited her torso up at Kilburn and took her legs down to Camberwell, using her quartered body, as if in some civic rite, to mark out the eastern, northern and southern extremities of London. Unfortunately what Ketch unpacks from his bag is a coconut, chiselled with indentations to ornament a baked-potato stall. When a more authentic head is located, a dispute about its provenance ensues: is it 'Mr Greenacre's, or a hospital patient's, or a pauper's, or a man's, or a woman's, or a monkey's'?

The pedantic dunce Mr Blubb submits the cranium to phrenological analysis, and after examining its bumps he opines that its owner 'possessed the organ of destructiveness to a most unusual extent, with a most remarkable development of the organ of carveativeness'. Carving is at once a way of committing murder and of creating art; Blubb's muddled tribute to Greenacre punningly amalgamates the two activities and also catches the contradictory motives of Dickens, who saw living bodies as what might be called carveative artefacts. At a Shaker village in upstate New York, for instance, he thought the grimly abstinent men looked as stiff as their high-backed chairs. On the beach at Boulogne he remarked with a keener appreciation that the young fishwives had 'the finest legs ever carved by Nature in the brightest mahogany'. Sometimes, joking about his own interventions, he faulted nature for sculpting people roughly. The face of Wemmick in *Great Expectations* is 'imperfectly chipped out with a dull-edged chisel', and the lawyer Grewgious in *The Mystery of Edwin Drood* says he began as a chip not a bud: the notches on his forehead might have signalled refinement, but Nature discarded the chisel, deciding 'I really cannot be worried to finish off this man; let him go as he is.'

In *Martin Chuzzlewit*, carving is an aesthetic skill, regardless of the blood it sheds. When Ruth Pinch buys meat for a pudding, she takes Tom along 'to see the steak cut, with his own eyes', and they are both enraptured by the finesse of the butcher, who chops up a section of the carcase as if he were painting a still life. 'There was nothing savage in the act,' Dickens extravagantly insists, 'although the knife was large and keen; it was a piece of art, high art; there was delicacy of touch, clearness of tone, skilful handling of the subject, fine shading. It was the triumph of mind over matter; quite.' The butcher handles the juicy slab with such tender indulgence that it might still be alive: meat, he says, 'must be humoured, not drove'. At Dotheboys Hall in *Nicholas Nickleby*, butchery and surgery overlap as Mrs Squeers deals with an abscess on one of the malnourished pupils. Awestruck, her husband exclaims 'To see how she operated upon him with a pen-knife!' On one occasion, no sharpened blades are required. At a fair in Flanders the Uncommercial Traveller watches a performance by 'Monsieur the Face-Maker', who in preparation for his act 'gouges himself' without making incisions; he then 'turns his mouth inside out' and, helped only by a wig and a pocket mirror, shows off a succession of visages belonging to a senile patrician, a bewildered conscript, a military leader surveying 'illimitable armies', a paranoid miser and a village idiot. With his plastic or elastic face this 'great Changer of Countenances' sleekly outwits nature, as Dickens set himself to do.

Ovid in his *Metamorphoses* describes bodies hurriedly changing into new forms, often in the course of an erotic chase. The wood nymph Syrinx, for instance, escapes from Pan by turning into a clump of hollow reeds beside the river, then into panpipes on which the frustrated faun blows a lament for her. Dickens also saw a metamorphic compulsion at work in the world. His people exist in a provisional state; he describes them while he is still making them, and when made they are likely to be unmade, only to be remade from another substance. The work of metamorphosis is done by his unstoppable flux of poetic metaphors.

Joe Gargery in *Great Expectations*, kindly but weak, appears to be still raw, with 'undecided' blue eyes that have 'somehow got mixed with their own whites', like eggs in the process of being scrambled. The puffy-faced Bazzard in *Edwin Drood* also needs to be cooked, with 'a doughy complexion, that seemed to ask to be sent to the baker's'. Squeers pinches and pokes the rubberised bulk of his spoiled and over-fed son Wackford and says admiringly 'Here's flesh!', but obesity is no guarantee that a character has the usual constituents of skin, muscle and insulating oil. A stout gentleman in *The Pickwick Papers* resembles 'half a gigantic roll of flannel, elevated on a couple of inflated pillow-cases'. A second portly gentleman constitutes 'the other half of the roll of flannel'; overlapping, their bodies are beds, fluffy yet so tightly woven that they muffle any prodding or pricking from outside. Images add extraneous layers to Mr Wardle's servant Joe, the fat boy. His cheeks, which at first have 'a blanc-mange motion' when he nods, grow to be 'mountainous'. Briefly roused from his sluggishness, he emits 'a horse's laugh' and has 'a semi-cannibalic leer' when he thinks of roast pork.

As the metamorphoses continue, flesh and blood are left behind and creation shades into fabrication or manufacture. The expendable poor relation Volumnia Dedlock in *Bleak House* has the glassy fragility of a chandelier, with a meagre stem and limbs like bare stalks, and in company can only give off a 'feeble prismatic twinkling'. Tulkinghorn, Lady Dedlock's lawyer, looks as inexpressive as a millstone; that changes to a gravestone when his face becomes 'as unperturbable as death'. Wood, less brittle than glass and less onerous than stone, is a frequent component. Bagnet the battle-hardened artilleryman in *Bleak House* is nicknamed Lignum Vitae after the densest of hardwoods, used in the nineteenth century for heavy machinery, and Doyce the engineer in *Little Dorrit* has a face made from the same material, with 'deep lines of cogitation' carved into it. The face of Sarah Pocket in *Great Expectations* is corrugated, with the texture of walnut shells. Two unfeminine women bristle metallically. Mrs Joe, Pip's gruff sister in *Great Expectations*, wears a bib with pins and needles stuck into it, and Miss Murdstone in *David Copperfield* arrives with suitcases initialled in 'hard brass nails' and 'a hard steel purse' that snaps shut 'like a bite' – an accessory as alarming as the razor-toothed vagina of Freudian psychology. Before his collapse, the 'lead-coloured' face of Jasper in *Edwin Drood* sweats in 'drops or bubbles, as if of steel'.

These eclectic beings are at constant risk of decomposition. Gride in *Nicholas Nickleby* looks like fruit out of season or withered vegetation: his sunken cheeks resemble dry winter apples and his ragged eyebrows evince 'the badness of the soil from which they sprung' and to which the seedy, senile man will soon return. Mrs General in *Little Dorrit* looks 'floury' and is 'a chalky creation altogether', apparently ground to powder in 'some transcendentally genteel Mill'. Jeremiah Flintwinch threatens that his abject wife Affery will be 'shaken to yeast', reduced – in botanical terms – to a fungal micro-organism. Even more bizarrely, the air-headed Flora Finching first describes Flintwinch as 'a rusty screw in gaiters' and then goes on to confuse him with his employer Mrs Clennam so that Mr Dorrit, bewildered by her prattle about people he does not know, pictures a hermaphroditic machine, a 'compound of man and woman, no limbs, wheels, rusty screw, grimness, and gaiters'.

Mrs Jarley, who manages a waxwork gallery in *The Old Curiosity Shop*, makes a partisan claim for the sticky substance from which her historical figures are formed. Their 'constantly unchanging air of coldness and gentility' gives them a neoclassical calm, which she contrasts with the plebeian fisticuffs in the Punch and Judy show. 'I won't go so far as to say that, as it is, I've seen wax-work quite like life,' Mrs Jarley declares, 'but I've certainly seen some life that was exactly like wax-work.' Dickens agrees: he gives Miss Lillerton in *Sketches by Boz* the complexion of 'a well-made wax doll' and a personality to match. But whereas Mrs Jarley admires the frigidity of the end result, Dickens draws attention to the fiery chemical process that uses paraffin or petroleum to liquefy the wax and make it ready for what Coleridge called the 'shaping spirit of Imagination'. In *Barnaby Rudge* that creative process goes into reverse, as a human figure regresses into molten shapelessness. A drunken rioter sets fire to the house of a Catholic, then sprawls on the ground with a bottle plugged to his mouth, unaware that lead from the roof is streaming down 'in a shower of liquid fire, white hot; melting his head like wax'.

In *Master Humphrey's Clock* Sam Weller tells a story about a barber who dotes on the four wax dummies that advertise his services – two couples, the men with blue dots for their whiskers, the young ladies simpering with fingers on lips. Like a blighted Pygmalion, the barber vows never to marry until he meets a facsimile of his favourite female mannequin. This prompts frustrated female customers to call his infatuation 'sinful' because he is 'wurshippin' a idle'. Then someone who is 'the wery picter' of the dummy turns up. 'Behold your imige in my winder, but not correcter than my art!' he tells her. However, her attention strays to the virile effigy of a pomaded soldier; in a jealous frenzy the barber smashes his rival's nose with a curling iron and immolates him in the parlour hearth. Aesthetics, eroticism and religion collude in Sam's tale. The accusation of idolatry is justified: *A Child's History of England* contains an account of an equally calamitous plot against Henry VI by the Duchess of Gloucester and 'a ridiculous old woman named Margery (who was called a witch)'. They fabricate 'a little waxen doll in the King's likeness', then roast it over a slow fire.

Margery and the chaplain who assists her are executed and the duchess is imprisoned, although they 'might have made a thousand dolls . . . and . . . melted them all' without harming the puny monarch.

Jenny Wren, the dolls' dressmaker in *Our Mutual Friend*, is more adept at this kind of sinister magic. The clothes she sews enliven the inert poppets, and she elaborates stories in which they go to balls, ride horses, get married and participate in 'all the gay events of life'. Researching designs, her methods are as sly as those of Dickens, who regarded life as a rehearsal for literature and living people as first drafts of his characters. At shows or fêtes, Jenny keeps an eye out for any lady whose costume is worth copying, then hurries home to 'cut her out and baste her'. Her scissors belong in Dickens's carvery: basting stitches pieces of cloth together. Wielding a needle, Jenny is equipped to puncture her dolls as witches do, though she chooses to deploy this tiny weapon against the usurer Fledgeby, at whom she aims 'two dabs . . . with her needle, as if she put out both his eyes'. When she loops and knots the thread 'to bowstring him into the bargain', a sudden metaphorical leap sharpens needlework into the deadlier sport of archery.

Clothes have a more than sartorial function for Dickens: like religion and law, they strain to keep a collapsible world from falling apart. The deranged astrologer in 'The Lamplighter' dresses 'with no braces, strings, very few buttons – in short, with hardly any of those artificial contrivances that hold society together'. More than that, garments confer an identity on those who wear them. Swaddled in a blanket soon after birth, the naked and nameless Oliver Twist could be a nobleman's heir; thrust into discoloured calico robes a little later, he is now 'badged and ticketed' as a foundling brat. When the criminal gang recaptures him after his time with Mr Brownlow, he is instantly re-costumed: 'Put off the smart ones,' Charley Bates orders. Later, on the scaffold at Newgate, 'strong and vigorous men' abruptly change to 'dangling heaps of clothes' once the trapdoor opens. These second skins symbiotically merge with the bodies to which they are attached, so that the bulging waistcoat of jolly Mr Varden in *Barnaby Rudge* is said to be 'smiling in every wrinkle'. Taken off and laundered, clothes acquire a strange autonomy, as fluttery and ethereal as wraiths or uprisen souls: Barnaby himself sees garments drying in the wind as 'shadowy people there, like those that live in sleep'. In a second-hand shop on Monmouth Street, Boz grieves over 'a deceased coat' and 'a dead pair of trousers'. Carlyle, describing the same street in *Sartor Resartus*, regards the empty suits as 'stainless Ghosts', no longer ruffled by the passions of those who once wore them, but Boz fancies that the items on display are eager to be reincarnated. Coats jump off their pegs and button themselves up around the bodies of new owners, 'waistcoats . . . almost burst with anxiety' to be filled out again by an ample stomach, and shoes find feet of the right size and contentedly plod off. These are a sorcerer's practical jokes, weighed down by an aching sadness: the most melancholy task for the bereaved is sorting through a loved one's wardrobe.

Mr Dennis, the obscenely nasty executioner in *Barnaby Rudge*, is immune to such regrets. His musty garments are scavenged from felons he has hanged; even his underwear, he explains, came from a corpse. Disgusted, Sim Tappertit wonders why he can't 'wear live clothes'. Like Jenny Wren, Dennis lets slip some of Dickens's macabre professional calculations. He shows off a knotted stick with his own face carved on the knob, and proudly polishes the wood of his 'fictitious nose'. A friend, he says, made the portrait with a penknife, after which Dennis repaid the favour by hanging him. Asked whether he served an apprenticeship, Dennis says he owes his occupation to 'natural genius . . . It come by natur'.' As proud of his technique with the rope as Jenny Wren is of her needle, Dennis boasts 'I may call myself a artist – a fancy workman – art improves natur' – that's my motto.' Once again, creating and killing overlap, with nature as an alibi for art at its most deviant. And if art improves nature, does Dennis mean that death improves life?

Medieval warriors fortified their soft, squashy bodies with armour, which for Dickens was no defence against implosion. In *The Mudfog Papers* Ned Twigger, woozily staggering through a mayoral parade in armour that makes him look 'like an intoxicated effigy from Westminster Abbey', is terrified that the metal cladding will reduce his innards to mashed potatoes. He has good reason to be concerned. At the armoury in Venice, Dickens paused before two iron helmets that were once clamped onto 'living sufferers', whose heads were crushed as the gadgetry was ratcheted tighter by some 'directing devil'. He found in them a 'grim resemblance . . . to the human shape – they were such moulds of sweating faces, pained and cramped – that it was difficult to think them empty'. Tempted by his own imagination, he filled the vacant space with a living body, then through the 'walled-up ear' eavesdropped on the inarticulate moans of the man who was squeezed, torn and twisted 'with the torment of a thousand deaths'. Describing people, Dickens always started from the outside and worked his way inwards from body to mind. Here the external carapace tightens around the vulnerable interior, and his creative method doubles as a means of torture.

Blake praised 'the human form divine': our merciful hearts and pitying faces, he believed, show us to be replicas of our anthropomorphised maker. Dickens saw things differently. Visiting Parma, he looked up at heaven in the cupola of the cathedral, where Correggio's fresco of the Assumption had become such a mouldy mess that he could make out only 'a labyrinth of arms and legs'. The flying stumps entangled willy-nilly, further handicapped by foreshortening, and angelic amputees ushered the Virgin into heaven. The carvery came instantly to mind, as Dickens declared that 'no operative surgeon, gone mad, could imagine [the scene] in his wildest delirium'. This was his challenge to himself: he draws on a similar smattering of ill-matched parts when making his characters.

Only the inflexible Dombey appears to be monolithically constructed 'as one piece', as if lacking the joints and limbs that would allow him to be humanly responsive. Otherwise, with no God to keep them in alignment, Dickens's people have a fearful asymmetry. Clemency in *The Battle of Life* is clumsily thrown together: 'To say that she had two left legs, and somebody else's arms, and that all four limbs seemed to be out of joint . . . is to offer the mildest outline of the reality.' In *Martin Chuzzlewit* the dishonest American land agent Zephaniah Scadder has a bifurcated visage: one sightless eye is fixed in its socket, so that 'with that side of his face he seemed to listen to what the other side was doing'. The crow's feet around his wary eyes are not metaphorical, and Dickens suspects that the cunning, predatory bird has recognised him as its kin. Scadder sits oviparously with one leg propped on the door of his office and 'the other doubled up under him, as if he were hatching his foot'. Internally he is made of moving parts like a machine, and when he speaks a twitching and jerking in his throat suggests 'the little hammers in a harpsichord when the notes are struck'. Like a happy-go-lucky vivisector, Dickens marks the man's fault lines, then starts carving.

Silas Wegg in *Our Mutual Friend* is so dry and knotty that he seems to have acquired his wooden leg naturally and is growing a second one as a pair for it. But he objects to having been 'dispersed' and buys back his pre-wooden leg from the taxidermist Mr Venus, who is 'glad to restore it to the source from whence it – flowed'. Alerted by the verb that causes Venus to hesitate, Wegg points out that human flesh and blood cannot be purchased, 'not alive' at least: how come there is a market in human bones? Despite being named after the goddess of love, Venus deals in death, or perhaps resurrection. Among his bottled babies and animals with glass eyes, he points with pride to a stuffed canary, poised to hop off its twig. 'There's animation!' he says. He has precursors in *Barnaby Rudge*, where the rioters stand the corpses of fallen comrades on their feet, fix weapons in their hands, and with 'horrible merriment' – a defining Dickensian mood – prop them up to march in a parade.

Although Dickens enjoyed the body's exhibitionism, its gymnastics often rehearse demolition. In New York he watched a black dancer spin and shuffle kinetically until, like a turning wheel, he dematerialised as he picked up speed: he seemed to cavort 'with two left legs, two right legs, two wooden legs, two wire legs, two spring legs – all sorts of legs and no legs – what is this to him?' The first Spirit to appear to Scrooge is a metaphysical athlete who whirls through every possible combination, 'now a thing with one arm, now with one leg, now with twenty legs, now a pair of legs without a head, now a head without a body'. Another feat of self-multiplication ends the tale when the reformed Scrooge bounds out of bed on Christmas morning and, simultaneously laughing and crying, makes 'a perfect Laocoön of himself with his stockings'. In Virgil's *Aeneid*, the gods send two sea serpents to strangle, crush and finally devour the Trojan priest Laocoön. Dickens's metaphor spares Scrooge, whose serpentine stockings flap harmlessly, without the muscular grip of the coils that fasten around Laocoön and his sons in the Hellenistic sculpture.

Mr Venus keeps a 'box of human miscellanies' in his shop, a warning that we are all motley compounds. To illustrate this divisibility, Dickens often introduces his people in segments, either sideways or upside down. Mr Trott in *Sketches by Boz* calls for the boot boy, who appears piecemeal: when the door opens, he 'thrust in a red head with one eye in it, and being again desired to "come in", brought in the body and legs to which the head belonged, and a fur cap which belonged to the head'. The miserable hero of 'George Silverman's Explanation' shudders as he remembers his mother's clogs descending into the cellar where they lived in his childhood. As he waited in trepidation, he would 'speculate on her feet having a good or an ill-tempered look – on her knees – on her waist – until finally her face came into view and settled the question'.

Herbert Pocket's ascent of a staircase in *Great Expectations* reverses that vertical order, though only after Pip, upstairs on a landing, opens a sash window that has rotted cords and nearly beheads himself when it slams down 'like the guillotine'. Then he hears steps, and says that 'Gradually there arose before me the hat, head, neckcloth, waistcoat, trousers, boots, of a member of society of about my own standing.' Standing refers to status as well as height, and by tallying his friend's wardrobe Pip appraises him as a social being; the notion of membership – used here in a civic or corporate sense – makes amends for the dissection of bodies elsewhere. When the vulpine Mr Hyde appears inside him, Robert Louis Stevenson's Dr Jekyll begins to understand 'the perpetual war between my members'. Jekyll is describing a psychological or moral discord; for Dickens's characters that war is brutally and yet hilariously physical, as limbs brawl with each other and organs transpose themselves or alter their function.

The shaky collage can come unstuck, as it threatens to do when Mrs Sparsit in *Hard Times* sneezes so violently that 'her stately frame . . . seemed in danger of dismemberment'. Characters need to keep a tight grip on themselves to prevent such explosions or to resist the novelist's incisions. Hence the clenched resistance of Louisa Gradgrind, who is 'shut . . . within herself'. Dickens, initially frustrated, comments that 'she baffled all penetration', and Louisa says she will guard her privacy until the time comes 'to direct the anatomist where to strike his knife into the secrets of my soul'. Anatomy dissects bodies, potentially breaking down the whole until it can be divided no further; at its most reductive, it finally singles out an atom, the smallest particle that can exist. Dombey lethally alludes to the procedure when he diminishes his son Paul by calling him a 'presumptuous atom'. Dickens can be equally gruesome, but his analytical carvery has other motives as well. As a maker or manufacturer of people, he was fascinated by the way bodies worked, with separate parts roughly cohering into a whole. We all aspire to match some blandly beautiful norm, but for Dickens what mattered was the deviations that are marks of our singularity. Antony in *Julius Caesar*, eulogising Brutus, says that the four elements were 'so mixed in him / That Nature might stand up and say "This was a man"'. The Dickensian recipe for a human being is less equable, indifferent to nature's upright formulae. His characters know themselves to be haphazard compounds, and they are forever riskily rehearsing their own disintegration.

The anatomy systematically descends from top to toe, beginning with heads. Lewis Carroll's Red Queen in *Alice in Wonderland* screeches for the axeman whenever she has a problem, but Dickens's characters obligingly behead themselves, dethroning rationality. Blushing as he admits his attraction to Estella, Pip tugs his hair as if he wants to lift his face off and throw it away, and Mr Grimwig in *Oliver Twist* backs up every blustering assertion by offering to eat his bewigged head, which with its seasoning of powder is too large to be easily consumed. In *Edwin Drood*, the clerk Bazzard has written an unperformed tragedy. Grewgious, his employer, is an uncreative fellow who declares that, if he were himself 'under sentence of decapitation, and . . . about to be instantly decapitated', then offered a pardon on condition he wrote a play, he would be 'under the necessity of resuming the block'. Dickensian heads can function without bodies, and vice versa. Pecksniff, bobbing up and down behind a pew as he eavesdrops on a conversation in church, looks like 'the small end of a guillotined man'. The deduction of the headpiece, worn as lightly as a hat, might even be an improvement. 'Now we look all compact and comfortable,' Sam Weller remarks, 'as the father said ven he cut his little boy's head off, to cure him o' squintin'.'

'Heads, heads – take care of your heads!' cries Jingle as the coach leaves St Martin's-le-Grand in central London to take the Pickwickians on their first excursion. Jingle warns the passengers to duck as they cross beneath a low archway, but the dashes that punctuate his speech serve as carving knives: 'Other day—five children—mother—tall lady, eating sandwiches—forgot the arch—crash—knock—children look round—mother's head off—sandwich in her hand—no mouth to put it in—head of a family off—shocking, shocking!' Here the loss of a head is a digestive inconvenience; then as the coach advances down Whitehall, Jingle recalls the public execution of Charles I in 1649. 'Somebody else's head off there, eh, sir?' he says to Pickwick as they travel past the Banqueting House where the regicide occurred. Dickens jocosely restaged that tableau in a charade at Gad's Hill when he draped a black handkerchief on his head and took a coal scuttle from the fireplace to decollate Wilkie Collins, and he transferred the same primal scene to his dotty half-namesake Mr Dick, who is rescued from an asylum by Betsey Trotwood in *David Copperfield*. Mr Dick plaintively asks why Charles I's attendants should have 'made the mistake of putting some of the trouble out of his head, after it was taken off, into mine?' The head's contents survive and consciousness can migrate elsewhere: Mr Dick has revived Pythagoras's belief in metempsychosis, which is the soul's transmigration into another body. When the unnamed

'Monseigneur', an aristocrat in *A Tale of Two Cities*, escapes abroad disguised as his own cook, he is said to have metempsychosed, although he has only changed clothes not exchanged bodies; Mr Dick is better proof of the Pythagorean theory. In a shrewd blend of psychoanalysis and literary criticism, Betsey says that he 'connects his illness with great disturbance' and the regicidal scenario is 'his allegorical way of expressing it', 'the figure, or the simile, or what-ever it's called, which he chooses to use'. Mr Dick's psychomachia expresses agitation and confusion rather than propounding doctrinal truths as allegories usually do, and its recurrent image – a severed head whose consciousness takes wing, monarchising the madman – suggests that we are surrounded by free-floating dreams, fantasies and manias that can randomly alight on any of us. Mr Dick tries to write his way back to sanity, and among his bundled manuscripts, superfluous pens and half-gallon jars of ink, David notices a 'large paper kite in a corner'. Flying that kite relieves his distress: it carries extracts from the personal history he is scribbling, and David watches it 'disseminating the statements pasted on it', just as the west wind in Shelley's ode distributes the poet's words like 'winged seeds' and scatters them among mankind. The kite aerates Mr Dick's troubled head, releasing his thoughts to flutter 'in the sky, among the larks'.

There is a less breezily therapeutic epilogue in *Our Mutual Friend*, where Eugene Wrayburn torments Bradley Headstone, the repressed schoolmaster who is his rival for the love of Lizzie Hexam, by leading him on a wayward nocturnal chase through labyrinthine London. Stalked by the funereally named Headstone, Eugene pictures him as 'a haggard head suspended in the air'. As the chase ends, this grimac-ing head, with no assistance from legs or anchorage to a trunk, sneaks through the gate to Eugene's lodging at the Temple. Nearby is Temple Bar, the demolished barrier that Dickens re-erected by so often remembering the heads of executed traitors that were once displayed there, after being boiled in salt or pitch to deter birds from pecking at them; as if removed from the spikes, Bradley's head floats up the stairs that lead to Eugene's chambers and eavesdrops at the door. The illusion is explained as a metaphor that has come to life.

The hatred coursing through his body is said to have been tugged upwards in a rush of blood, changing his physical rage to a madly concentrated mental fixation that seems to 'cancel his figure'.

Dickens also sections the heads that his characters are still wearing. Metaphors dismantle Gradgrind: his forehead is a square wall, his eye sockets are cellars, and his bald cranium sustains a plantation of pine trees around its edges as a windbreak. His knobbly skull is likened to 'the crust of a plum pie', though its contents are inedible because his head serves as the warehouse in which he stores arid facts. For better targeting, eyes often come singly rather than in pairs. In *Great Expectations* Magwitch's envoy watches Pip with one eye half shut 'as if he were taking aim . . . with an invisible gun', and on their nocturnal outing Dickens and Inspector Field meet an apparently monocular constable with 'a flaming eye in the middle of his waist, like a deformed Cyclops' – his lantern, colloquially known as a bull's eye. Mr Dennis, the hangman in *Barnaby Rudge*, has eyes so mean and small that only the intercession of a broken nose prevents 'their meeting and fusing into one of the usual size'. Alternatively, surplus eyes come in handy for Nadgett, the undercover agent who tracks Jonas Chuzzlewit: 'Every button on his coat might have been an eye', which vouches for his professional acuity. Eyebrows meanwhile lead a life of their own. Those belonging to Mrs Sparsit are so dense and bushy that she lives behind them; they do her thinking for her, and at one point are so 'creased with meditation' that they seem to need ironing out.

Noses are judged architectonically. The pathetically dependent Miss Tox in *Dombey and Son* has an aquiline nose with a knob as 'the key-stone of the bridge', announcing her determination never to turn it up at any offer. Mrs Nickleby needs guidance about the 'order of architecture' to which Frank Cheeryble's proboscis belongs. 'Do you call it a Roman or a Grecian?' she asks Nicholas, who replies that it is 'a kind of Composite, or mixed nose'. Miss Knag credits her mother with 'the most exquisite nose that was ever put upon a face', which redefines the organ as a decorative attachment. Trotty Veck in *The Chimes*, less of an aesthete, pities his nose when it turns numb in the winter. 'Poor creetur,' he says of it, grateful for the hard work of smelling that it does and sorry that he cannot treat it to a pinch of snuff. Proceeding to the mouth, Dickens defines Carker in *Dombey and Son* by fixing on his dental weaponry. In the street he 'bestowed his teeth upon a great many people' in lieu of a smile, and he transfixes Captain Cuttle 'with an eye in every tooth and gum'.

The neck is a precarious junction. Dickens witnessed the execution of a murderer in Rome, and after the head had been set up on a pole he was taken aback by the 'odd annihilation' of the neck: a detail that makes you want to clutch the connective stem that juts out of your own shoulders. Gride's begrimed bottles of liqueur in *Nicholas Nickleby* either have 'necks like so many storks' or 'short fat apoplectic throats', which tempts us to speculate about snapping the frail necks of the storks or strangling those greedy throats. The young mothers with 'enormous goîtres' noticed by the Uncommercial Traveller in a Swiss village are better protected. As they suckle the infants plugged to their chests, the Traveller remarks that 'it became a science to know where the nurse ended and the child began'. Enlarged thyroids and the attachment of those thirsty feeders turn the women into rotund totems of fertility, with no point of entry for the carver.

Looking within, the crone from the opium den in *Edwin Drood* complains that her wheezing lungs are 'wore away to cabbage-nets!', unable to deter rapacious butterflies. The filthy trader in used clothes who buys David Copperfield's jacket enumerates his organs as if they belonged in his tattered stock and had price tags attached. 'Oh, my lungs and liver,' he cries while haggling, 'no! Oh, my eyes, no! Oh, my limbs, no! Eighteenpence. Goroo!' The internal probe reaches a mystifying cul de sac when Mrs Tibbs in *Sketches by Boz* complains that her hypochondriac lodger 'has no stomach whatever', which her friend Mrs Bloss takes literally. The transparency of Marley's ghost reminds Scrooge that he 'had often heard it said that Marley had no bowels, but he had never believed it until now'. Can we be sure that our internal organs, which with luck we never see, are really there?

Appendages are problematic, dangling excrescently from the trunk. Joe Willet in *Barnaby Rudge* loses an arm in the American Revolution, and his father is puzzled when he returns without it. He inspects the sleeve of a military greatcoat where it might be hiding, and studies other people to confirm that 'the usual allowance' is two; he is bemused by Joe's compromise with 'bodily disfigurement' as he carves his meat with a single hand. Eventually he decides 'It's been took off!' Sim Tappertit bullies the locksmith Gabriel Varden into helping him force an entry into Newgate prison. Varden says he would rather have his hands 'drop off at the wrists', and from there he imagines them making a fantastical jump onto Sim's shoulders to serve as epaulettes. He is right to think of hands as tenuous not tenacious things. Those belonging to Mrs Merdle, for instance, are 'not a pair'. The left one, white and plump, is used for gesticulation; the other remains a teasing, possibly unsightly mystery. Her husband is also uneasy about a body part that is synonymous with human connection: he considers Mr Dorrit's proffered hand, then takes it 'in his for a moment as if his were a yellow salver or fish-slice', after which he condescendingly returns it. Legs for Merdle are equally detachable, to be parked like vehicles when not in use, and after a double-dealing negotiation he stands up 'as if he had been waiting in the interval for his legs and they had just come'. Other characters juggle those trailing members. Shiftily embarrassed by female guests, the men at Mrs Tibbs's boarding-house in *Sketches by Boz* slide about 'as if they wished their arms had been legs, so little did they know what to do with them'. When the Boffins visit Mrs Wilfer in *Our Mutual Friend*, 'three pairs of listening legs' that have been shut out of the confidential meeting eavesdrop from high up on the stairs.

Dickens had a special interest in wooden legs, especially if they started to feel or move of their own volition. Silas Wegg's 'timber fiction', as Dickens calls it, shares its owner's indignation at Boffin's sudden good fortune: 'A wooden leg can't bear it!' he protests. Mrs Gamp in *Martin Chuzzlewit* blames her dead husband's alcoholism on 'a wooden leg . . . which in its constancy of walkin' into wine vaults, and never comin' out again 'till fetched by force, was quite as weak as flesh, if not weaker', and she reports that he thought of selling it 'for any money it would fetch as matches in the rough' so he could buy liquor. Wooden legs possess an erotic allure for Pecksniff, who drunkenly says he 'should very much like to see Mrs Todgers's notion of a wooden leg, if perfectly agreeable to herself!' Carving, even if done with a lathe or a chisel, overlaps with caressing. At home, Dickens once watched a visiting dog called Bully cast off all inhibitions. As he reported in a letter, it 'fell into indecent transports with the claw of the round table' and was 'madly in love' with the boots of its owner, a high-minded Anglican priest who observed this frottage with unperturbed innocence.

The seamstress Miss Knag in *Nicholas Nickleby* recalls an uncle who possessed 'the most symmetrical feet', matching 'those which are usually joined to wooden legs'; her employer Madame Mantalini acidly comments that 'They must have had something of the appearance of club feet.' While scattily reminiscing about people whose vanity extends to their legs, Mrs Nickleby cites poor Miss Biffin, then reconsiders: 'I think she had only toes, but the principle is the same.' Can you have toes without legs? Perhaps so, if you think that the body is modular or custom-made, as Dickens did. Having begun at the top with those severed heads, his anatomy lesson ends at the bottom. The Hamlet at an amateur performance in *Great Expectations* dies 'by inches from the ankles upward', while a goblin in *The Chimes* vanishes in sections, dwindling 'to a leg and even to a foot, before he finally retired'.

The problem of the jerry-built structure we live inside is summed up in *Our Mutual Friend* when Eugene Wrayburn says that as he grew to self-consciousness he realised he was 'an embodied conundrum'. He then tried 'to find out what I meant', but became bored and gave up. Conundrum – mock-Latin slang, coined in the seventeenth century – has come to mean a puzzle, which suits the jigsaw of arms, legs and head slotted together by Dickens's people. Eugene applies the word to his own mixed motives: he is by turns indolent, rogueish and cynical, vindictive when persecuting Bradley Headstone yet loyal and liberal in his decision to marry Lizzie Hexam. But the true conundrum, as his phrase makes clear, is the tragicomic incongruity of our embodiment.

Romantic poets had their own view of 'what Nature is' and resisted human efforts to change it. Wordsworth's sonnet about the view from Westminster Bridge surveys 'ships, towers, domes, theatres, and temples', but specifies that these structures 'lie / Open unto the fields, and to the sky'. From a vantage point down the river nearer the docks in *Martin Chuzzlewit*, Dickens sees 'steeples, towers, belfries, shining vanes, and masts of ships; a very forest', then adds a lower stratum of life that takes in 'gables, housetops, garret-windows, wilderness upon wilderness' – except that this forest is made from felled trees and the wilderness consists of slums. Wordsworth's London is placidly dormant, its air 'smokeless', its 'mighty heart . . . lying still', reliable but inaudible; Dickens hears the city breathe more heavily, choked by 'smoke and noise enough for all the world at once'. On the Iron Bridge at Southwark, Amy Dorrit is pained by the sight of 'the river, and so much sky, and so many objects, and such change and motion' because she knows she will have to return to the cramped prison. Solitude, which Wordsworth enjoys in the early morning at Westminster, is for her a penance.

Walter Bagehot said that Dickens had 'nothing Wordsworthian in his bent'. Certainly an unpeopled landscape looked dead to him: 'Nothing of life or living interest' was his verdict on the Alps. But he transfers Wordsworth's pantheism to the city, where it changes to a kind of pandemonism as the built environment stirs into life. Coleridge spoke of 'one Life within us and abroad', and Wordsworth sensed

A motion and a spirit, that impels
All thinking things, all objects of all thought,
And rolls through all things.

For the romantic poets, this continuum airily enveloped us or oceanically buoyed us up; in Dickens's novels the shared life is invasive and uncomfortably compressed rather than rolling expansively outwards, and insentient things suffer from fleshly distempers and disabilities. Buildings stare sullenly at each other across a Soho square in *Nicholas Nickleby*, their chimneys dismal 'from having nothing better to look at'. Mayfair tenements in *Little Dorrit* suffer from cramp, and the balconies of Georgian mansions, propped up by thin columns, 'seem to be scrofulously resting on crutches'. A Liverpool tavern in *Martin Chuzzlewit* is recessively cranial, with 'more corners . . . than the brain of an obstinate man' and 'full of mad closets'. Like a wooden conundrum, it has 'mysterious shelvings and bulkheads', with 'indications of staircases in the ceiling'. 'A little below the pavement', it appears to be subsiding into the earth; instead of being set back, it abuts on the street so that passers-by scrape it, their buttons and baskets grating on the window panes.

A few characters are safe in secular shrines. Willet the jolly publican in *Barnaby Rudge* has kegs, bottles and pipes as his 'household gods', and Jarndyce wants to make Woodcourt, the charitable physician in *Bleak House*, 'rich enough to have his own happy home and his own household gods – and household goddess, too, perhaps?' Most of Dickens's people lack such psychological and spiritual shelter. Alone at school, Paul in *Dombey and Son* looks 'as if he had taken life unfurnished, and the upholsterer were never coming'. Paul may be better off that way, since Dickens's houses are haunted by their fixtures and fittings. In *The Pickwick Papers* the carved back of a chair becomes a shrivelled face, with its cushions as a waistcoat; it turns out to be 'a very ugly old man, of the previous century, with his arms akimbo', who starts griping about his rheumatism. Gaunt fire-irons in the Clennam establishment in *Little Dorrit* constitute 'the skeleton of a set deceased', and in another victory for the anatomist, 'four bare atomies' of bedposts terminate in spikes on which the sleepers are free to impale themselves.

A muffled chandelier in Dombey's mansion resembles 'a monstrous tear depending from the ceiling's eye', and swathed curtains hang in 'cumbrous palls', with mirrors as dim as ageing eyes and boards that creak arthritically. After Dombey's firm collapses and his house is emptied, the removal men 'delight in appropriating precious articles to strange uses'. Mattresses are parked in the dining room, china is sent to the conservatory, and 'the stair-wires, made into fasces, decorate the marble chimneypieces'. Dickens the resurrectionist allows such second-hand items an afterlife in the Bishopsgate shop of the appraiser Brogley, whose stock includes a banqueting set of plates and glasses laid out on a bedstead and some chairs hooked to wash-stands poised on top of sideboards that teeter on dining tables, 'gymnastic with their legs upward'. Despite the wooden-legged orgy, Brogley belongs to 'that class of Caius Marius who sits upon the ruins of other people's Carthages', mimicking the exiled Roman general who was a frequent subject in neoclassical paintings. In Dombey's gutted mansion the 'chaotic combinations of furniture' revert to the mayhem that was nature's original, unorganised state; in the Bishopsgate shop they are the debris of a fallen civilisation.

One imperishable article regularly lifts itself out of this scrambled disarray: an umbrella. For Dickens this frisky canopy was a versatile symbol of the human condition. Awakening after his long illness, Dick Swiveller in *The Old Curiosity Shop* is embarrassed to find that all his clothes have been sold to pay for medicine. 'In case of fire,' he moans, 'even an umbrella would be something': like the cane carried by Charlie Chaplin's tramp, it might attest to the status he has forfeited. On a Channel steamer in bad weather, the Uncommercial Traveller only recognises another passenger as his fellow-creature because he has an umbrella raised; otherwise his blurry figure would merge with the vessel's bulkhead or with the murky air. The Traveller calls the umbrella 'that instrument' and says that the stranger desperately grasps the shaft for 'moral support', not just to keep him dry. This leads him to wonder if there might be an 'analogy . . . between keeping an umbrella up, and keeping the spirits up', and indeed Dickens did once see an umbrella haul its owner closer to salvation. At the Scala Santa in Rome on Good Friday, he noticed a wily penitent who spared his knees during the climb by 'unlawfully' hoisting himself up the twenty-eight steep steps with the aid of an umbrella which he brought along 'on purpose, for it was a fine day'.

When the Uncommercial Traveller refers to the umbrella as an instrument, he awards it a status beyond mere utility: like a violin or a piano, it exists to be played upon or played with, and the slightest pressure can bring it to life. During Pickwick's trial for breach of promise, Mrs Sanders studies the judge intently and keeps her thumb on the spring of her large umbrella, 'prepared to put it up at a moment's notice' in an act of protest. That spring is a trigger, simultaneously activating two sexes as female skirts billow out with a male rod to stiffen them. On a coach trip, the 'battered brass nozzle' of Mrs Gamp's priapically cheeky umbrella in *Martin Chuzzlewit* pokes 'from improper crevices and chinks' as she fusses over stowing it. It proliferates biologically and seems 'not one umbrella but fifty'; extending its tentacles, it terrorises Tom Pinch as the handle clutches his throat, the ferrule stabs him in the back, and the hook trips his ankles. In *Nicholas Nickleby* the 'most persevering umbrella' of lovesick Mr Lillyvick salutes the actress Miss Petowker from a box, and whenever she smiles in his direction, 'the umbrella broke out afresh'. Squeers treats his umbrella connubially and takes it to bed with him: it is surely better company there than his brutish wife.

Surrealist poets and painters sometimes justified their apparently random imagery with a slogan from the Comte de Lautréamont's *Chants de Maldoror*, published in 1868, in which the beauty of an English boy is inanely compared to 'the chance meeting of a sewing machine and an umbrella on an operating table'. Dickens could have arranged that encounter, but he would have done more than simply drop an umbrella into an accustomed place and leave it to be dissected. His umbrellas arise from the surgical table and effloresce in flurries of metaphor-making. The one that belongs to tiny Miss Mowcher in *David Copperfield* retreats down a wet street 'without the least appearance of having anybody underneath it', hopping along 'like an immense bird'. Silas Wegg owns an umbrella that resembles an 'unwholesomely-forced lettuce', and in a letter Dickens beautifully describes yet another as 'a faded tropical leaf' that provides shelter or shade. Mrs Bagnet in *Bleak House* employs her umbrella in a spirit of 'affectionate lunacy'. She never actually opens it; instead its purpose is to semaphore feeling, and she softly prods her husband with it to convey her fondness for him. Dickens first sutures it onto Mrs Bagnet by calling it 'her faithful appendage', after which he awards it new functions by saying that she employs it 'at home as a cupboard and on journeys as a carpet bag'. The umbrella's flabby waist is corporeal, but its wooden handle has 'a prow, or beak' that is both nautical and avian, supplemented by an 'ornamental object' made of metal like 'a little model of a fanlight over a street door or one of the oval glasses out of a pair of spectacles'. We now look through it, as through a window or a lens, rather than at it: Dickens's writing hand once again moves faster than our eyes.

Whether dealing with bodies or with buildings and their contents, Dickens carves things up or anatomically breaks them down, then finds quirky new ways of reassembling them. His gesticulating umbrellas obey the same impulse. They serve every conceivable purpose except the mundane chore of keeping out the rain, and the ultimate demonstration of Mrs Bagnet's prowess comes at the market when she 'uses the instrument as a wand' and points it at 'joints of meat or bunches of greens' that she wants to buy. The image returns us to the Soho bazaar where the young Dickens says he begged to be given the harlequin's caduceus, and these displays of twirling virtuosity confirm that his wish has been granted.

10

In the Forge

Elucidating Augusta de la Rue's nervous malady, Dickens said that for her the world was 'a Great Electrifying Machine' which subjected her to 'all sorts of unaccountable shocks and knocks and starts'. He often felt the same way, though he was unsure whether to be alarmed or elated by the barrage. On his Atlantic crossing in January 1842 the ship's tossing and lurching terrified him, and in *American Notes* he commands the reader to 'Picture the sky both dark and wild' and 'Imagine the wind howling, the sea roaring, the rain beating' as the vessel fights to stay upright, yet his account of the storm goes on to turn panic into farce. Above his cabin he hears the 'gambols' of loose ale casks, along with 'truant dozens of bottled porter': he might be aboard the 'bateau ivre' in Rimbaud's poem, inebriated by imagery. He offers brandy to some women huddled in 'ecstasies of fear' on a sofa, only to see the furniture suddenly back away as he approaches. Blundering onto the deck, he behaves like an imbecile and is 'humanely conducted . . . below' by the captain, who assumes the role of psychopomp. In sight of the harbour in Nova Scotia, the ship gets stuck in a quagmire. 'We were in as lively a state of confusion as the greatest lover of disorder would desire to see,' says Dickens, which amounts to a personal testament: he equated disorder with life and found it both desirable and loveable.

The energy that so exhilarated him was elemental and also mechanical. The arrival of a train in *Hard Times* is announced by a cacophony of clashing nouns that give off a blitz of colour and noise: 'Fire and steam, and smoke, and red light; a hiss, a crash, a bell, and a shriek.' Lightning jaggedly zigzags on the iron rails and the uproar causes the station to undergo 'a fit of trembling', the symptom of a seizure. Then the departing train projects the jittery station backwards into the rumbling dark and reduces it to 'a desert speck in the thunderstorm'. This brief scene is a verbal equivalent to Turner's *Rain, Steam, and Speed*, in which a train charges out of the mist on a viaduct. Hazlitt called such paintings 'pictures of nothing', which brought back 'the first chaos of the world'; Dickens's words add movement and noise to Turner's maelstrom of light, making it all the more atavistic.

Meteorology and melodrama collude on the night when Steerforth drowns in *David Copperfield*. The sea is lashed by 'showers of steel', a metallic onslaught from some over-productive factory in the sky. In a 'dread disturbance of the laws of nature', the storm is militarised, causing the wind to blow great guns while surging waves roar like a cannonade. Elsewhere the elements play practical jokes rather than making war. A boisterous gale that flattens Pecksniff blows out a candle 'incontinently', slams a door, then frisks away towards the sea, 'where it met with other winds similarly disposed, and made a night of it'. Shelley's autumnal ode salutes the west wind for speeding seasonal change and announcing political upheavals that lie ahead; the wind in *Martin Chuzzlewit* hunts and harries fallen leaves as cruelly as Shelley's does, and it rehearses social revolt in its own way by capsizing Pecksniff. In *Bleak House* bad weather has an ideological agenda. As Sir Leicester Dedlock returns home across the Channel, the choppy sea that provokes a nauseous 'revolution' in his stomach is 'the Radical of Nature', with no respect for his rank. Nature is not only liberal but also irrepressibly licentious. Speculating about the inhabitants of the nunnery in *The Mystery of Edwin Drood*, Dickens suspects that not all of them obeyed their vows: surely they had 'some ineradicable leaven of busy mother Nature', the unchaste impulse that 'has kept the fermenting world alive'. The same chemical notion – referring to the effervescence that causes substances to bubble and fizz – is extended to machinery during the railway excavations in *Dombey and Son*, where 'throbbing currents' of people and engines in Camden Town produce 'a fermentation in the place', with geysers spouting through the churned-up ground.

Once Dickens suffered through a soaking typhoon that was entirely man-made. On a canal boat in Pennsylvania he shared a rough dormitory with five fellow passengers who spent the night spitting, apparently managing to do so in their sleep. Between them they discharged a gale of fluid whose progress Dickens marked with the help of a recent book by William Reid, a military engineer who studied Caribbean hurricanes and charted the rotation of winds around a still eye: the spittle 'moved vertically, strictly carrying out Reid's Theory of the Law of Storms', as if the men were able to 'expectorate in dreams, which would be a remarkable mingling of the real and the ideal'. Reality is once again instantly overwhelmed by this fantastical idea, and although the men in the cabin are blamed for their drooling and dribbling, it is Dickens who dreamily whips up an indoor tempest.

Charles Lyell's *Principles of Geology*, published between 1830 and 1833, upset believers by questioning the assumption that God created our world some six thousand years ago as a stable, permanent home for mankind. Producing evidence of changes in strata of rocks over several hundred million years, Lyell demonstrated that the earth was being sucked away by water or burned up by subterranean fire, under siege from 'great antagonist powers' that he called 'aqueous' or 'igneous'. Those forces can be found remorselessly at work all over Planet Dick.

In *Pictures from Italy*, water is 'an old serpent', slickly furthering the scheme of the devil in Eden as it coils around the foundations of Venice and makes plans to submerge it. Less patiently, the sea at Dover in *A Tale of Two Cities* 'did what it liked, and what it liked was destruction'. In 1853 in a *Household Words* essay Dickens spends a night on the Thames with the police and watches as the black water – 'such an image of death in the midst of the great city's life' – swills its refuse towards the sea. A toll-collector, another Charon, describes the people who plunge from Waterloo Bridge 'making holes in the water'; the indifferent river immediately fills in the cavity and erases them.

Looked at in another way, the world seems scarily flammable. Durdles in *Edwin Drood* lights his lantern by striking 'a spark of that mysterious fire which lurks in everything' from a cold hard wall; Grewgious in the same novel is grateful that fire-proofed stairs in a London hotel offer protection from 'the devouring element'. Even the festal pudding in *A Christmas Carol* brings an incendiary threat to the table: it gives off 'a great deal of steam', which clears to reveal 'a speckled cannon-ball, so hard and firm, blazing in half of half-a-quartern of ignited brandy'. *A Child's History of England* contains an excited account of the Great Fire of London in 1666, with showers of hot ash, houses crumbling to cinders, and flames that made night brighter than day. Dickens himself joked about being a one-man conflagration, and in 1841 he toyed with a scheme to tantalise his readers by taking a year off, after which he would deliver a three-volume novel and 'put the town in a blaze again'.

Although the geological 'eras of paroxysmal violence and chaotic derangement' evoked by Lyell were prehistoric, on his travels Dickens visited places where those planetary beginnings or endings could still be observed. At Niagara, he told Forster that he 'went down alone, into the very basin'; on the way he was drenched by spray and mist which had hung there 'since Darkness brooded on the deep'. The primal light, he thought, must have gushed forth in just such a deluge, 'rushing on Creation at the word of God'. Blocking out the downpour and uproar, he claimed, not very persuasively, that this ongoing Genesis left him in a state of Wordsworthian tranquillity. A more unholy excitement thrilled through him during his own creative sessions, when the mist was replaced by fumes: 'I feel quite smoky when I am at work,' he informed Forster as he torched London in *Barnaby Rudge*. Ascending Vesuvius, as he told Thomas Mitton, he 'gave the word to get up, somehow or other', so determined was he to reach the rim by nightfall. While a courier predicted doom, Dickens looked into 'the flaming bowels of the mountain', dodging solidified cinders that felt 'like blocks of stone from some tremendous water-fall'. The mountain was a hot Niagara.

On Vesuvius as at Niagara, Dickens was watching the earth's birth pangs – a kind of parturition that was comparable to his own industrious labours: touring Naples, he contrasted the laziness of the populace with 'the burning mountain, which is ever at its work'. Byron defined poetry as 'the lava of imagination whose eruption prevents an earthquake'. For Dickens the process did without that safety valve. In *David Copperfield* Micawber, preparing to denounce Uriah, declares that he is determined to move 'Mount Vesuvius – to eruption – on – a – the abandoned rascal – HEEP!' Flushed and steaming, he emits the words like lumps of phlegmatic lava that sputter in 'hot haste up his throat, whence they seemed to shoot into his forehead'. Lyell pointed to steam as a 'moving power' in Icelandic geysers, and Dickens relied on this scalding energy to motivate or even motorise his writing. Once he likened his volatile state to that of a hot-air balloon, and as he worked on *Nicholas Nickleby* he worried that he might '"bust" the boiler'.

Reviewing a book by the mineralogist Robert Hunt in 1848, Dickens complained that science had demystified nature. Researchers venturing into mines and coal-pits with the aid of safety-lamps had expelled 'the Gnomes and Genii of those dark regions'; sirens and mermaids, he added, no longer had a safe haven underwater. The protest was premature, since there are gnomes and genii aplenty in his novels, where amphibious nymphs also enjoy walk-ons. Pecksniff forgets the name of 'those fabulous animals (pagan, I regret to say) that used to sing in the water', dismisses swans and oysters when these are suggested, then remembers sirens and the 'delusions of art' associated with them; in *Little Dorrit* Flora Finching, who is half a flirty juvenile and half a wistfully middle-aged matron, has turned herself into a 'moral mermaid'.

Lyell's geology had its own mythical sponsors. Bypassing the Bible, he identified the agencies that inundate or incinerate creation with two classical gods, Neptune and Vulcan. Dickens claimed a personal acquaintance with both. His seasickness on the Atlantic left him light-headed with 'fiendish delight', and he would not have been surprised 'if Neptune himself had walked in, with a toasted shark on his trident'. The god of fire – the mythical smith whose mouthpiece is a volcano and who sets up shop in a forge – qualified as one of Dickens's professional helpers. In 1855 *Household Words* published his account of the magazine's manufacture, written in tandem with Henry Morley: here, after the type is set by compositors, the 'iron-bound tablets of lead' are lowered into 'the domains of Vulcan' to be cast, which involves trials by fire and water in 'a pan of Vulcan's broth', evidence of creativity's white heat.

Lyell described 'subterranean fire' as 'the most violent instrument of change' and studied 'the modern theatres of volcanic action' as symptoms of 'some great crisis in nature'. Dickens brought that fire to the surface and lodged it inside his characters. The thermo-dynamic demon Quilp might have emerged through one of the fissures described by Lyell, from which 'hot vapours, thermal springs, and . . . red hot liquid lavas' seethe and spew. Fuelled by boiling tea and seething grog, Quilp is akin to a salamander, a reptile reputed to be fireproof. Long before Dickens made the alcoholic Krook in *Bleak House* burn up, leaving behind only cinders, ash and a residue of foul-smelling grease, he itched to put the pseudo-scientific notion of spontaneous combustion to the test. When Pecksniff's daughters quit Mrs Todgers' boarding house, the male guests farewell them with a caterwauling serenade that could not have been more tunelessly doleful 'if the two Miss Pecksniffs and Mrs Todgers had perished by spontaneous combustion', and in *A Christmas Carol*, before the Second Spirit appears, Scrooge lies in bed 'at the very core and centre of a blaze of ruddy light', wondering – expectantly, not in gibbering terror – whether he might be 'an interesting case of sponta-neous combustion'. At first what tantalised Dickens was a vanishing act that caused people to go up in smoke as if in a conjuring trick, but in Krook's case he turned the dissolution into an allegorical death, 'inborn, inbred, engendered in the corrupted humours of the vicious body'. Creation goes into reverse, breeding and birth are negated, and an internal fire returns the old sot to gaseous non-existence.

Two theoretical conjectures discussed by Lyell, which he calls 'the schools of the nether and of the upper world', continue their dispute in Dickens's novels. The first proposes that the earth's foundation is stratified rocks that were warmed and softened by volcanic fire, which makes it likely that as their heat increases the globe will eventually incandesce. Lyell calls this 'the system of the Gnome', in tribute to the dusky malevolent sprite Umbriel from Pope's *The Rape of the Lock*; it could equally well be the system of the calorific Quilp. The opposing theory reverses the chronology, suggesting that our earth began as 'a fiery comet' that has slowly cooled and will one day end as 'a frozen icy mass'. This, Lyell says, is the 'doctrine of gradual refrigeration', and its proponent in Dickens is Sir Leicester Dedlock, whose self-satisfied nonchalance makes him 'a magnificent refrigerator', the personification of bleakness; he has a colleague in *Little Dorrit*, Lord Lancaster Stiltstalking, a 'noble Refrigerator' who has 'iced several European courts in his time' and is still able to turn the gravy cold at dinner. The damp aggravates Sir Leicester's gout and the hot-water pipes 'fail to supply the fires' deficiencies', but his ancestral prestige is legitimised by nature's stealthy decay – encroaching ivy and moss in his gardens, elms 'gnarled and warted' with age, oaks embedded in 'the fern and leaves of a hundred years'. His disagreement with the factory-owner Rouncewell, an 'iron gentleman' from the industrial north, dramatises the opposition between Lyell's nether and upper worlds. Sir Leicester sniffily views Rouncewell as 'that ferruginous person': the adjective is a favourite of Lyell's, used in *Principles of Geology* when he refers to strata of rocks in which 'shingle and sand have been agglutinated firmly together by a ferruginous or siliceous cement . . . to bind together materials previously incoherent'. Rouncewell is obdurate and durable, made from the chemical element that supplies the earth with its outer crust and inner core, whereas Sir Leicester moulders like those rotting leaves and elderly trees.

Matthew Arnold's elegy for Wordsworth, written in 1850, pities the poet for surviving into an 'iron time / Of doubts, disputes, distractions, fears', and remembers that Byron's 'fount of fiery life' had also long ago dried up or cooled off. In Rouncewell's 'iron country' the stalwart metal regains its fiery life in a noisy prose poem. Iron is seen 'glowing and bubbling' in furnaces or exploding into 'bright fireworks' under the blows of a steam-hammer; 'mountains of it' lie about, 'broken up, and rusty in its age'. Noticing 'red-hot iron, white-hot iron, cold-black iron', Dickens races through the millennial course of what Lyell called 'the secular refrigeration of the entire planet'. At last the metal acquires sensory powers: it emits 'an iron taste, an iron smell, and a Babel of iron sounds', as the tower toppled in Genesis is rebuilt by a percussive din that outshouts language.

Wherever they turn up, forges or foundries are replicas of Dickens's creative consciousness. The astrologer in 'The Lamplighter' has 'a stove or furnace . . . in full boil'; in this he prepares the alchemical tincture that he hopes will reward him with 'all the riches of the earth'. In *Martin Chuzzlewit* a blacksmith's den shines at night 'in all its bright importance' while the villagers gape at the forge in awe, 'spellbound by the place'. The bellows roar lustily and the sparks dance, performing a combination of opera and ballet, while 'the gleaming iron' sparkles 'in its emulation': its reflective sheen shares Dickens's gift for mimicry. In *The Old Curiosity Shop* a mill hand tells Nell about the hypnotic allure of a furnace he tends. Other workers are 'flushed and tormented by the burning fires', but this grimy mystic communes with the blaze. 'We talk and think together all night long,' he says as he stares into the iron hearth. For him, all the arts emerge from this crucible. It is 'like a book to me,' he explains, 'the only book I ever learned to read'; in addition it is music, for 'there are other voices in its roar', and it has 'pictures too', enabling him to trace 'different scenes ... in the red-hot coals'. Joe Gargery's establishment in *Great Expectations* is shadier. Pip 'believed in the forge as the glowing road to manhood and independence', identifying it with honest, virile toil rather than the leisured amateurism of his later life when he is cushioned by his bequest from Magwitch. Yet Joe's swarthy apprentice Orlick, who threatens to feed Pip's body to the kiln, alleges that the devil dwells in a dark corner of the smithy, and when Pip wants to know why Magwitch and the other convicts are chained in floating prisons, his sister replies with a pronouncement that includes a biting pun. 'People are put in the Hulks because they murder,' says Mrs Joe, 'and because they rob, and forge, and do all sorts of bad; and they always begin by asking questions.' The gratuitous mention of forgery is a jab Dickens aims at himself: is the artist who questions reality and trades in fictions a counterfeiter?

In 'Kubla Khan' Coleridge describes 'a miracle of rare device', a 'sunny pleasure-dome with caves of ice!' that, like his poem, is at once warmly sensual and coolly controlled. Dickens localised the contending extremes of Coleridge's exotic fantasy on the railway line between Birmingham and Wolverhampton. In 1847 his *Household Words* article 'Fire and Snow' follows a train that battles through a blizzard past blast-furnaces and 'a cold white altar of snow with fire blazing on it'. The same paradoxical clash is present on Vesuvius. On the way up the cone, light bounces back from 'the snow, deep, hard, and white'; in the intense cold, 'the air is piercing'. Then at the crater Dickens and his companions feel 'giddy and irrational, like drunken men' as they view 'the region of Fire' – nature's smithy, 'reddening the night' and singeing their clothes. On the way back down, they slither and stumble because 'the usual footing of ashes is covered by the snow and ice', which recalls Lyell's image of a thin crust on the earth's surface above 'a central ocean of incandescent lava'. In a human avalanche, an overweight gentleman hauled on a litter by bearers has 'his legs always in the air', while someone else falls and by grabbing a pair of nearby ankles starts a chain reaction. Another member of the party rolls all the way, 'skimming over the white ice, like a cannon-ball'.

Notwithstanding the dangers and the damage, Dickens notes that they reeled along 'quite merrily'. One of Lyell's ancient cataclysms was still happening inside the volcano, but for Dickens the world began and ended with a guffaw.

In *Sartor Resartus* Carlyle's Teufelsdröckh shifts the responsibility for creation from God to ourselves. Mankind, he proposes, is 'in continual growth, re-genesis and self-perfecting vitality'. But in what Teufelsdröckh calls the 'ever-working Universe' that headlong progress threatened to leave mankind behind. Having vitalised society, industrial machines set about re-engineering people rather than regenerating them. When a sententious alderman in *The Chimes* is informed of a banker's suicide, he laments the contemporary human lot, overstretched and exhausted by the demands of progress. 'Oh the nerves, the nerves; the mysteries of this machine called Man!' he exclaims. 'Oh the little that unhinges it: poor creatures that we are!' Nerves are wires, and hinges belong on doors. Are we creatures or contraptions?

Today we fear being outsmarted by electronic brains. What both troubled and tantalised the nineteenth century was the prospect of a mechanical body, more agile and longer-lasting than the human model. In Genoa, Dickens watched a troupe of marionettes dancing for an enchanter and marvelled at their 'impossible and inhuman' pirouettes and 'the revelation of their preposterous legs'. 'There never was such a locomotive actor, since the world began,' he said of a figure with extra joints: it might have been on wheels, like a train. Then during a little play about Napoleon's demise the puppeteers lost control. The emperor's boots dangled in mid-air; the doctor, due to 'some derangement of his wires', croaked medical bulletins while hovering over his patient's deathbed like a vulture – a truly Dickensian affray. The Punch and Judy show in *The Old Curiosity Shop*, encountered by Nell and her grandfather on their wanderings, operates across the border between life and death, so often traversed by Dickens. Punch slumps on a tombstone when not on stage, and when packed away he is 'utterly devoid of spine, all slack and drooping in a dark box' with 'not one of his social qualities remaining'; he will be revived for the next performance, with the puppeteer supplying a Promethean spark to ignite his 'constant fire of wit'. In *Our Mutual Friend* the fashionable Podsnaps engage a 'well-conducted automaton' to play quadrilles at their party. A robot or a human being who behaves like one? Dickens leaves the matter unclear; what matters to the Podsnaps is that the automaton conducts itself or is conducted properly. Caleb Plummer, the toymaker in *The Cricket on the Hearth*, is less scrupulous. He designs automata that are 'ready to commit all sorts of absurdities on the turning of a handle', and Dickens adds that 'very little handles' can prompt human beings to similarly foolish or vicious displays.

The Mudfog Papers looks ahead to a showdown between the animate and the automated. At a meeting of the town's Association for the Advancement of Everything, Mr Coppernose exhibits models of a recreational park stocked with 'automaton figures' representing policemen, cab drivers and harmless old ladies, stationed there to be manhandled by young noblemen on the razzle; the victims, the promoter explains, will vent their groans through artificial voice-boxes. After the fisticuffs, magistrates with wooden heads are to oversee a 'pantomimic investigation' and at the touch of a spring will pronounce emptily sententious verdicts on the aristocratic hooligans. 'This is a great invention,' enthuses Professor Muff, though Mr Mallett suggests that true bluebloods would insist on 'thrashing living subjects'. But the automata would also surely have fought back: machines could now easily flatten men, and Dickens twice tested this new balance of power by sacrificially offering himself to a factory as raw material.

In 1850, assisted by Mark Lemon, he wrote an account of a visit to a paper mill in which, rather than touring the place to study its operations, he literally puts himself through it. He impersonates a bundle of dusty waste as it is swallowed up by 'a mighty giant'; 'labouring hard' inside the ogres as it is digested, it emerges as clean, white, fresh-smelling sheets, sorted into quires and reams that are ready 'to be written on, and printed on'. The process is explained to Dickens by a worker whom he describes as 'my conductor', again using the word he confers on guides who preside over existential rites of passage. This mentor sets him a mental task, as in a game of charades: 'I am to suppose myself a bale of rags.' Eager for any exploratory venture beyond humanity, Dickens instantly reports 'I *am* rags.' What follows – being sliced into shreds, stewed in cauldrons, consumed like gruel – ought to be painful, but the experience is cathartic and results in a resurrection. The laundered rags feel 'purified' and then 'quite ethereal', and Dickens finally announces 'My metempsychosis ends with the manufacture. I am rags no more.' Metempsychosis should be a mind's migration to another body, although here that mind migrates into some bundles of discarded cloth in a rag-store, which are described at the outset as 'the grave of dress'. The result, however, is a regenesis. Leaving the mill, Dickens notices a paper kite flying above it. A similar plaything, he says, was his 'airy friend' in childhood, and a kite also serves as a therapeutic aid for Mr Dick in *David Copperfield*. This one as it flutters in the sky reminds him that 'paper has a mighty Duty' to promulgate 'love, forbearance, mercy, progress' in the wider world. Meanwhile, back on the ground, another cycle resumes: the 'virgin paper' will be fed into Dickens's mental mill, there to be sullied all over again by his words or slashed by the flourishes of his pen.

The Uncommercial Traveller's tour of the dockyard in Chatham is less purgative: the place is a carnivore, which gobbles him up. Devoured by the gates, as when the paper mill laps up its ragged gruel, he says 'I became ingested into the Yard.' At the mill, Dickens is grateful to 'the subtle mind of this Leviathan' for massaging him so gently; now the process is more violent as he typographically transcribes a din that concusses the brain: 'Ding, Clash, Dong, BANG, Boom, Rattle, Clash, BANG, Clink, BANG, Dong, BANG, Clatter, BANG BANG BANG!', which is the noise made by twelve hundred men hammering the hulk of an armour-plated warship to be given the heroic name *Achilles*. Then he thinks he spots two large mangles, domestic equipment that is out of place in this militarised precinct. Mangles were laundry utensils, with hand-operated rollers that wrung washing dry; they fascinated Dickens, who considered the mangle to be a 'curious British instrument' and put it to work as a multi-tasking metaphor – Jingle in *The Pickwick Papers* describes the crush at a party as a 'regular mangle' because the crowd squeezes every crease out of his coat, and Lorry in *A Tale of Two Cities* considers his bank to be 'an immense pecuniary Mangle'. In the dockyard, what the Traveller takes to be mangles have 'a swarm of butterflies hovering over them', which looks odd. Approaching, he sees that the mangles are in fact machines that saw planks to shape them into oars, while the butterflies are shavings that swirl from the blades. For as long as the engine runs, it propels those dancing insects into the air; as soon as it stops, they 'drop dead' and flop to the earth. The metaphor in its turn gives life, then abruptly takes it away, and although the Traveller praises 'the exquisite beauty and efficiency of this machinery' he seems to wonder whether his little act of poetic revivification is merely a brief, sad illusion. He ends feeling 'torn to pieces (in imagination) by the steam circular saws, perpendicular saws, horizontal saws, and saws of eccentric action'. The machine age is already on a war footing: thinking along the same lines, the Traveller worries about an electric battery that can transmit an order to send steamships off to war.

Mounting a verbal defence against such assaults, Dickens set two of his most invincibly eloquent characters to upbraid a pair of industrial heavyweights. In *Master Humphrey's Clock*, Tony Weller, a coach driver by trade, fulminates against a steam train that threatens his livelihood: he calls it 'a nasty, wheezin', creakin', gaspin', puffin', bustin' monster, alvays out o' breath, with a shiny green-and-black back, like a unpleasant beetle in that 'ere gas magnifier'. Mrs Gamp turns up beside the Thames in *Martin Chuzzlewit* and rages at the shrill, hooting Antwerp steamboat, wishing that it would end in 'Jonadge's belly'. She shakes her umbrella at 'them Confugion steamers', and vents some steam of her own as she rails about the income she has lost as a midwife because of the intemperate roaring and hissing of such behemoths. A railway guard known to Mrs Harris, she says, is godfather to twenty-six infants born prematurely, 'all on 'um named after the Ingeines as was the cause!'

These tirades are cockneyfied epilogues to the outbursts of romantic poets as they confront the sublimity of nature – Coleridge likening a gale to a 'Mad Lutanist', Byron encouraging the 'dark and deep blue ocean' to swamp the land. The poets succumb, elated by danger: in Kant's theory, the sublime first exalts and then stuns the rational mind. Mr Weller and Mrs Gamp are tougher and more valiant, and they shout down the mechanomorphs that have taken over from the forces of nature.

––––––––

When discussing his own creativity, Dickens preferred to use a word that saved him from explicitly encroaching on God's monopoly. Instead he allied his art with the latest scientific and technological innovations. 'Invention, thank God, seems the easiest thing in the world,' he told Forster in 1844, and in 1855, in a letter of apology for arriving late at the theatre because he had been writing, he referred to 'my inventive capacity', which he said that he held 'on the stern condition that it must master my whole life'.

A creator in theory produces something out of nothing, while an inventor makes something new by using ingredients that already exist. The point is underlined in *Oliver Twist* when Fagin asks a dealer in stolen goods if he knows the whereabouts of Bill Sikes. '*Non istwentus*, as the lawyers say,' the fence replies. The phrase requires only a slight adjustment: it should be 'non est inventus', which means not found, not in the inventory. Doyce in *Little Dorrit* is introduced as 'a smith and engineer' and also as 'the inventor', which places him 'out of the beaten track of other men'. Although he is 'an originator', he has no responsibility for the origin of the world. He devises technical marvels by tinkering with wheels, cogs and levers, then humbly shows off each new gadget that he fabricates 'as if the Divine artificer had made it, and he had happened to find it'. In case that sounds drearily utilitarian, there is an antidote in the inventive capacity of Mr Dick, who 'could do anything that could be done by hands'. David Copperfield says that 'his ingenuity in little things was transcendent': in feats of bricolage that match Dickens's own conjuring tricks or his extravagant metaphors, 'he could turn cramp-bones into chessmen; fashion Roman chariots from old court cards; make spoked wheels out of cotton reels, and bird-cages of old wire'. Mr Dick's inventions are works of art.

Dickens cunningly manoeuvred around the inventor's secondary status in a speech at the Birmingham and Midland Institute in September 1869. Although his subject was 'the material age', he argued that the novelties that had transformed modern life were supernatural: what could be more immaterial than electricity? He attributed the spark, the flame of gas and the beneficent properties of 'certain chemical substances' to 'the good providence of God', and said that they 'might have been disclosed by divine lips nigh upon two thousand years ago, but that the people of that time could not bear to hear them'. It is a strange supposition, which implies that our remote ancestors would have refused to accept the boons of technology. Did their religious faith make them shun such alleviations of their lot? And why did God keep mankind waiting for two millennia? Quickly moving on, Dickens professed himself 'a child of Adam the dust' and allowed 'that Shining Source' to guard 'the unapproachable mysteries of life and death'.

To protect his own not always shiny sources, Dickens made sure that the idea of invention remained mysterious. He divulges no details about Doyce's masterpiece, 'an invention (involving a very curious secret process) of great importance to his country'; after failing to patent it, Doyce sells it abroad. Captain Cuttle in *Dombey and Son* subscribes to the same devout obscurantism. He declares science to be 'the mother of invention, which knows no law', and beams with pride as he surveys a shop full of navigational instruments, even though he has no idea how to use them. A single instance of literary invention gives Dickens the chance for a sour joke. During his time with Crummles's theatrical troupe, Nicholas Nickleby is commissioned to write a new play at a few days' notice. 'My invention is not accustomed to these demands,' he haughtily replies. Crummles scoffs that invention has nothing to do it, and tells him to translate a French script and put his own name on it – exactly the kind of piracy that infuriated Dickens, whose novels were adapted for the theatre without his permission, sometimes while the monthly instalments were still appearing. In these circumstances he was the creator whose exclusive rights had been violated.

As an inventor, Dickens engineers a symbiosis between bodies and machines, which trademarks certain characters as new-fangled products of the material age and its hectic metabolism. Between them, the Wititterlys in *Nicholas Nickleby* measure a change in human emotions and reaction. Mrs Wititterly is a throwback: she has the palpitating sensibility of an early romantic heroine, like Marianne in Jane Austen's *Sense and Sensibility*. Although her husband says that her soul 'swells, expands, dilates – the blood fires, the pulse quickens', she remains insipid, affecting ardour rather than genuinely feeling it, unequal to the storm and stress of daily life. Wititterly himself, more up-to-date, expresses himself industrially, and after rhapsodising about his wife he blows his nose 'as fiercely as if it had been done by some violent machinery'. The rent collector Pancks in *Little Dorrit* appears to be less a man than a dynamo. He is coal-coloured, with hair as resiliently upright as springs, black eyes that sparkle 'electrically', and a heart that jangles faster than the bell at a shop door. Words shoot out of him like cinders, by 'mechanical revolvency'. Never without a lighted cigar as he snorts and puffs on his monetary rounds, he resembles a pushful steam-tug with a refractory ship in tow. Sam Weller, perceptive as always, takes a dim view of his fellow servant Job Trotter's weepy pretence of remorse. 'Tears never yet wound up a clock,' Sam scoffs, 'or worked a steam ingin'.' He has a point, because the output of energy requires hot water, not this cold drizzle. The next time Job cries, Sam calls him 'you portable ingine': he now has in mind a fire engine quenching flames from its tank. Trotter's waterworks are automated emotion, and because the word refers to an internal movement – a spasm that causes us to feel more intensely – it can be applied to machines. As a steamboat on the Thames creaks and pitches in bad weather in *Sketches by Boz*, the upset is attributed to 'a slight emotion on the part of the vessel'.

People in Dickens's novels do not exist because they think, as Descartes proposed; they are alive thanks to a power that activates their bodies and tingles round the circuits in their heads. Boffin in *Our Mutual Friend* describes his wife as 'a thinking steam-ingein', and Toodle the stoker in *Dombey and Son* has his own cerebral version of the intersecting railway lines on which he spends his life: 'What a Junction a man's thoughts is,' he says in amazement. Rob the Grinder exhibits some gratuitous scientific know-how during his interrogation by the sinister Mrs Brown. 'You expect a cove to be a flash of lightning,' he says. 'I wish I was the electric fluency.' He is referring to the effluvium that Benjamin Franklin believed to be the source of electricity, which he hoped to entice from the air into the kites he flew. Wishing that he possessed what Walt Whitman called 'the body electric', Rob mutters that he'd like to give Mrs Brown a shock. The same jolt is emitted metaphorically by old Martin Chuzzlewit when he dismisses Pecksniff: the rebuff causes the oily fraud to start backwards 'as if he had received the charge of an electric battery'.

Carlyle's Teufelsdröckh expected such batteries – a technical novelty at the time – to give off 'vitreous and resinous Electricities' that would shake up the 'Chaos of Life' and stimulate social mingling. For Dickens they supplied the body with its bristling nervous weaponry. Yet this technology merely harnessed psychic capacities that some people already possessed. In a *Household Words* article about séances, Dickens mentions a purported medium who behaves 'like a telegraph before the invention of the electric one'. On an early visit to inspect the telegraph office in Tonbridge, he marvelled at 'electric communication'; in person, the way he communicated could be a kind of electrocution, intensely exciting for the enthralled audiences at his readings but perilous to Dickens himself. Thomas Cooper de Leon, who attended one of his performances in New York, commented that 'the electric genius of the man fuses all into a magnetic amalgam that once touched cannot be let go until the battery stops working'. In his poem about London, Blake hears the clatter of 'mind-forg'd manacles' in the streets: the fetters are bans, prohibitions that stifle life. Dickens considered the mind itself to be a forge, whose flaring violence threatens to demolish all restraints. After quarrelling with Edwin Drood, Neville Landless staggers away with a 'steam-hammer beating head and heart'. Pip in *Great Expectations* has a nightmare during which he is 'a steel beam of a vast engine, clashing and whirling over a gulf'; he pleads for the engine to be halted and for his section of it to be bludgeoned into insensibility. When David Copperfield arrives for his wedding to Dora, he notes how calm the church is but adds that 'it might be a steam-power loom in full action, for any sedative effect it has on me'.

To convey the frantic tempo of the world outside, Dickens turned to the myth of Ixion, who was punished by Zeus for sexual infractions by being bound to a fiery wheel that circled unstoppably across the sky. In Byron's *Don Juan*, Ixion prefigures the 'perpetual motion' and 'grindstone's ceaseless toil' of modernity. *Sketches by Boz* repeats the point while adding some whimsical technicalities: Ixion is credited with having 'discovered the secret of the perpetual motion', and his torment is linked to the discomfort of travelling for months on end in the kind of post-chaise in which Dickens sped to and fro across the country during his time as a parliamentary reporter. Steerforth takes the idea further by yawning about Ixion's fate, which he pretends was entirely voluntary. When David Copperfield accuses him of making only fitful use of his abundant powers, he disparages the rotating wheel as a symbol of middle-class careerism. 'As to fitfulness,' he says, 'I have never learnt the art of binding myself to any of the wheels on which the Ixions of these days are turning round and round.' Steerforth's contempt for the grindstone is authentically Byronic, but he may have a point about the momentum dictated by machines. Did progress mean a rush towards death? In *The Pickwick Papers*, when Tony Weller in a dolefully humorous letter tells Sam about the demise of his stepmother, he describes her body as a coach on its last, over-hasty journey. After she caught a chill, 'her veels wos immedetly greased and everythink done to set her agoin as could be inwented', with a 'drag . . . put on directly by the medikel man'. Nevertheless she 'vent down hill vith a welocity you never see' and 'paid the last pike' the previous evening, 'havin done the journey wery much under the reglar time'. Such speed, commendable in vehicles, is less welcome when it comes to human lives.

The industrial economy, which relied on consuming fuel to produce movement, accelerated the exhausting pace of life. As Dickens strove to keep up with monthly deadlines for his novels as well as editing and contributing to periodicals, delivering public speeches and conscientiously answering a daily influx of letters, he often urged himself on with a glance at competing modes of transport. *Barnaby Rudge*, he groaned, was inching ahead, but 'not at race-horse speed'. With *Nicholas Nickleby* he began as a rider, then advanced to an engine driver: 'I must buckle-to again,' he told Forster, 'and endeavour to get the steam up.' He felt at first that he was 'lumbering on like a stage-waggon' with *David Copperfield*, but after this regression to coaching days he charged ahead 'like a Steam Engine'. Figurative language of this kind is actually called a 'vehicle' by analysts of rhetoric: metaphors, for instance, change an object into something else – a man into a tugboat, a dying woman into a runaway coach – or move it elsewhere, as when the railway in *Dombey and Son* causes such disruption that 'the very houses seemed disposed to pack up and take trips'. In 1868 Dickens urged Sarah Palfrey, the daughter of a Unitarian minister he befriended in Massachusetts, to make use of just such a carrier. 'Convey yourself back to London by the agency of that powerful Locomotive, your imagination,' he told her. That analogy also occurred to Ralph Waldo Emerson, who after a reading in Boston called Dickens's genius 'a fearful locomotive to which he is bound': he was Ixion on rails rather than strapped to a solar wheel. While the engine in his head ran away with Dickens, others wracked his body. In 1865 he was travelling to London on a train that overturned on a viaduct in Kent. Unharmed himself, he helped care for the injured passengers, ten of whom died in the wreckage. He remained jittery long after the incident, worried about 'railway shaking', and on his final reading tour 'the constant jarring of express trains' that rushed him between engagements became a bone-rattling torment. According to Forster he calculated that a trip from London to Edinburgh had administered 'something more than thirty thousand shocks to the nerves'.

The doctor who delivered David Copperfield asks when they meet again many years later about the strain of his career as a novelist. 'There must be great excitement here,' he says, tapping his forehead with his forefinger. 'And this action of the brain now, sir? Don't you find it fatigue you?' David politely brushes off these enquiries, although when Dickens's hard-driven regime began to catch up with him he admitted that his work 'could not have been achieved without some penalty'. After a cardiac scare in 1866 he obtained a prescription for some medicine to 'set [his heart] going, and send the blood more quickly through the system'. By 1869 the machine was not so easy to regulate. Now he diagnosed a 'low action of the heart' and complained about its inefficiency as a pump. Shortly before his death the following year he applied electrodes to his agonisingly painful leg; the current was discharged by a so-called 'magic band' that consisted of galvanic batteries attached to a hydro-electric belt. Linking magic and medicine, Dickens here for the last time called on the vivacious yet potentially deadly impetus that sears through nature and matches the dizzy leaps and bounds of his writing.

11

Arranging the Universe

In 1853 Dickens moved his family to Boulogne for the summer. He likened the modestly sized villa they occupied to a doll's house, but the proud owner, a linen draper by trade, had a more expansive notion of its scale. He provided his tenants with a floor plan, fearing, as Dickens put it, that 'without such a clue you must infallibly lose your way, and perhaps perish of starvation between bedroom and bedroom'. Outdoors, the grounds were equally hyperbolic. A map inflated the garden to the size of Ireland and identified fifty-one 'amazing phenomena' that included a bower, a hermitage, a labyrinth, a cottage designed for Tom Thumb, and bridges that commemorated Napoleonic battles at Austerlitz and Jena. Dickens told Forster that he could not be sure which of these features was which, but he assured the portly draper that he was 'enchanted' by the place. The cramped estate was a home-made world, and he might have invented it himself.

Such all-encompassing cartography came naturally to him. In *Bleak House* the clogged lamps in the windows of Lincoln's Inn are said to be 'the eyes of Equity', recalling 'bleared Argus with a fathomless pocket for every eye and an eye upon it'. According to the myth, Argus Panoptes had a hundred eyes and could see in all directions, although at the barristers' headquarters the vigilance of the omniscient monster falters because he can only 'dimly blink at the stars'. A genuinely panoptic vision was Dickens's prerogative: all points on his planet were visible to him, from both above and below. In *Barnaby Rudge* he defends his 'soarings up and down' as he takes to the air in pursuit of his characters, and he hovers aloft at night in *A Tale of Two*

Cities with all of France 'concentrated into a faint hair-breadth line' beneath him. He plunges underwater in *A Christmas Carol* to inspect 'a dismal reef of sunken rocks' and the caverns in which the sea gnaws at the earth's foundations. The Uncommercial Traveller imagines himself at an even lower depth when he explores an empty theatre: looking up from inside the proscenium arch at 'a shipwreck of canvas and cordage' suspended from the flies, he says he feels 'much as a diver might, at the bottom of the sea'.

Pretending to possess the same spatial range, Miss Twinkleton, the schoolmistress in *The Mystery of Edwin Drood*, places 'a terrestrial and a celestial globe' on show in her parlour. These 'expressive machines' are meant to suggest that she spends her leisure hours 'scouring the earth and soaring through the skies in search of knowledge', although her sublunary mind has no such reach. Dickens is more indulgent to Paul Dombey, who during his illness roams the schoolhouse at night and enters the headmaster's study to 'turn the globes softly, and go round the world, or take a flight among the far-off stars'. The softness of Paul's touch is a tenderly sympathetic detail: his travels remain hypothetical, because he dies soon afterwards. The crooked attorney Sampson Brass treats himself to a more puffed-up astral foray in *The Old Curiosity Shop* when he informs an employee that the law is 'the first profession in this country, sir, or in any other country, or in any of the planets that . . . are supposed to be inhabited'. The boast is bogus, but if there were such planets Dickens could surely have described the people in them.

One of the ghost-hunters in *The Haunted House* is the narrator's cousin John Herschel, named in homage to an astronomer who tracked comets, nebulae and double stars: 'a better man at a telescope does not breathe', says the narrator in a tribute to the original Herschel. As this suggests, Dickens was fascinated by observatories like the one that opened at Greenwich in 1676. The first Astronomer Royal to study the motions of the heavens there was John Flamsteed; in homage to him and to others who mapped the universe, the astrologer in 'The Lamplighter' over-ambitiously christens his son Galileo Isaac Newton Flamstead. The mad stargazer in this story conducts alchemical experiments in an 'observatory' stocked with telescopes, a crucible and an inexplicable assortment of crocodiles and alligators, while his equally eccentric assistant Mr Mooney climbs a ladder onto the roof to look for omens in the night sky. In *Hard Times*, Gradgrind's windowless study serves as 'an astronomical observatory' in which he presides like a magus, exercising his right to 'arrange the starry universe solely by pen, ink, and paper'. That was also Dickens's project, but with a difference. Gradgrind cannot see 'the teeming myriads of human beings all around him', even though he presumes to 'settle all their destinies on a slate'; Dickens makes room for the teeming myriads, whose destinies are not so easily settled.

Individuals are measured against this vast vacancy. In *Our Mutual Friend* the self-important acquaintances of the Veneerings, 'like astronomical distances, are only to be spoken of in the very largest figures', whereas Miss Tox, an officious hanger-on in Dombey's household, is described as 'a by no means bright or particular star', who 'moves in her little orbit in the corner of another system'. Fashionable London in *Bleak House* fancies itself as a galactic hub: a 'tremendous orb, nearly five miles round', it demands a distanced respect from the entire 'solar system'. The narrator takes a wider view, reducing the city to 'a very little speck' that 'does not stretch *all* the way from pole to pole', and those who traverse it are warned that they will soon 'come to the brink of the void beyond'. After Silas Wegg in *Our Mutual Friend* gains control of Boffin's property, he announces a purge with a learnedly illiterate pun. Expelling Sloppy from the house, he declares that 'The atomspear is now freer for the purposes of respiration.' His coinage warps both parts of the Greek word 'atmosphere', which pictures the envelope of gas surrounding us as a ball of breathable vapour. Atmos, the oxygen on which life depends, is twisted into atom, bringing with it a hint of the anatomical division that Dickens found irresistible; the rotund sphere becomes a weaponised spear, as if a blitz of spiky umbrellas was raining down. Wegg's own word belies the purification he is seeking.

Upheavals impend in other novels. Space and time are jolted awry when Tom Pinch finally wakes up to Pecksniff's villainy in *Martin*

Chuzzlewit: he feels that 'the star of his whole life' has exploded into 'putrid vapour'; as if after a maritime disaster, 'his compass was broken, his chart destroyed, his chronometer had stopped'. Pecksniff himself does little enough to maintain the grand universal scheme, and he idly contemplates 'mathematical diagrams' that resemble 'designs for fireworks'. Although he is an architect, nothing could be further from the secure, grounded practice of building than those pyrotechnics, but perhaps they match the instability of our existence. The occupants of grace-and-favour apartments at Hampton Court in *Little Dorrit* rail against public visits to the palace on Sundays, and expect the ground to open and swallow the profane intruders. When this fails to happen, they blame 'some reprehensible laxity in the arrangements of the Universe'.

There is a remedy for these metaphorical hazards in *Dombey and Son*, where the ships' chandler Solomon Gills sells navigational aids that help the disoriented regain their bearings. Though his shop is situated within earshot of Bow bells, these instruments enable it to set sail and travel 'securely to any desert island in the world', and in the novel it functions as a kind of omphalos, like the oracle's shrine at Delphi which two eagles sent out by Zeus identified as the exact centre of the earth. Solomon, named after the wise biblical king, is fondly known as old Sol: he stands in for the sun as the rubicund centre of the planetary system, and his red eyes are 'like small suns looking at you through a fog'. As a one-man meridian, he has a chronometer that tells the time with absolute exactitude, and to defend its accuracy he would cast doubt on 'all the clocks and watches in the City, and even ... the very Sun itself'. But with that last enthusiastic exaggeration Dickens undercuts the attempt to fix a still point of anchorage: the model worlds assembled by art cannot alter the inexorable routine established by the sun.

Although Sol's technical knowhow extends across oceans, the man himself is disconnected from his immediate urban surroundings. He has 'a newly-awakened manner', as if he has been staring for days 'through every optical instrument in his shop, and suddenly come back to the world again, to find it green'. Like Adam in Eden, or

Noah after the flood waters recede? Or perhaps like Dickens, whose defamiliarising vision can make an ordinary setting look strange? A list of the ships' chandler's wares begins by attesting to a scientifically verifiable reality: Sol has 'chronometers, barometers, telescopes, compasses, charts, maps, sextants, quadrants' and much else. Then the temptation of metaphor prompts Dickens to liken a utilitarian box containing one apparatus to 'something between a cocked hat and a star-fish', after which he adds that this miscegenated shape is quite 'mild and modest' by comparison with others in Sol's stock. So much for any attempt to get our bearings. As the grizzled mariner Captain Cuttle sits in the shop, he feels he is 'weighed, measured, magnified, electrified, polarized, played the very devil with'. Like magic and mesmerism, these stress tests channel the combative, possibly devilish forces in Dickens's world.

Another of Sampson Brass's rhetorical outbursts in *The Old Curiosity Shop* inadvertently admits the truth. As he bewails the treachery of Kit Nubbles, whom he has falsely accused of theft, he looks first 'at the walls, at the ceiling, at the floor' and then dismantles the mental dwelling inside which we feel safe. 'And this,' he exclaims with mock incredulity as he scans outer space, 'is the world that turns upon its own axis, and has Lunar influences, and revolutions round Heavenly Bodies, and various games of that sort! This is human natur, is it! Oh natur, natur!' The earth's rotation suddenly seems improbable; lunar influences must include lunacy, and the planetary motions observed by Galileo dwindle to games, airy amusements. As for human nature and nature itself, they too are conventions, easily flouted.

In a *Household Words* article about a manufacturer of bone china in Stoke-on-Trent, written in 1852 with help from his colleague W. H. Wills, Dickens again unexpectedly glances at the workings of the universe and relates them to his own concerns. The potters' wheels cause him to reflect that the manufacture of crockery depends on 'the rotatory motion that keeps this ball of ours in its place in the great scheme, with all its busy mites upon it' – a typical reminder of his concern for the welfare of his multitudinous characters, even if they have dwindled to insects. Yet that motion halts as the clay models are taken from the lathe and placed in the kiln, and then the manufacture of plates starts to sound like the creation of the world, or at least of the world as Dickens conceived it. The shapes hardened by fire are said to be 'Pre-Adamite' – an allusion to Adam's formation from red clay, and also to a fluorescent zinc named after the French mineralogist Gilbert-Joseph Adam. Flinty clay is the 'nursery and seminary' of the potters, which they mash and mill into 'dough', the raw material of life-giving bread and of the floury Mrs General in *Little Dorrit*. But the kilns are also 'dread chambers', fiercely ablaze like Dickens's imagination as, in stages marked by his rhythmic punctuation, he shapes his planet, peoples it and opens it to view: the furnace, he says, subjects 'human clay' to a gradually intensifying heat, by turns 'white hot – and cooling – and filling – and emptying – and being bricked up – and broken open – humanly speaking, for ever and ever'.

Humanly speaking, the cycle repeats itself for ever and ever because there are whole worlds of stories still to be told, both here below and up above, on a scale that is alternately domestic and celestial. Jarndyce in *Bleak House* calls Esther 'little Cobweb' because her mission, while presiding over the daily routine under his roof, is 'to sweep the cobwebs out of the sky': Dickensian housekeeping involves setting the universe to rights.

Esther's task would be harder in Tulkinghorn's office, where an indoor sky proves indecipherable. The room in which the lawyer does business has a painted ceiling which, like Correggio's mouldy heaven in the cathedral at Parma, offers a glimpse of our supernatural overseers. But the central figure in the design, sprawling 'among balustrades and pillars, flowers, clouds, and big-legged boys', puzzles the novel's narrator. This classical personage sports a battle helmet, yet he is attired in 'celestial linen': is he a warrior or a deity? With 'cheeks like peaches, and knees like bunches of blossoms, and rosy swellings for calves', his physique is too lush to belong to a soldier, and if he is a god he has followed the trajectory of Milton's fallen angels, 'for ever toppling out of the clouds'. Tulkinghorn's visitors invest the scene with 'mystery and awe', but only because they find it so obscure. The narrator, equally flummoxed, identifies the presiding figure simply as Allegory. Other tableaux in *Bleak House* readily interpret themselves. Grandfather Smallweed's dark parlour is 'no bad allegorical representation' of his mean mind, and Phil Squod, busy with a whitewashing job, wordlessly recommends a way to cancel a debt with 'many allegorical scoopings of his brush and smoothings of the white surface'. The scene on the ceiling, however, is so puzzling that it 'makes the head ache – as would seem to be Allegory's object always'. Tulkinghorn's encounter with his killer happens when it is 'too dark to see much of the Allegory over-head'; after the murder this enskied looker-on remains 'a paralysed dumb witness', because the real allegory is on the floor not the ceiling. An empty chair, candles snuffed out, a blood stain, a bottle of vintage wine that remains nearly full – all are emblems of mortality, props in a still life that symbolises death. Now the bemused interpreters are the painted figure and his attendants, who try to make sense of the clues laid out underneath them, and despite their head-scratching, the conclusion reached by the 'excited imagination' is that 'the very body and soul of Allegory, and all the brains it has' have been driven 'stark mad'. We might be back inside the allegorically addled head of Mr Dick.

Forster, borrowing a phrase from Carlyle, said that Dickens's comedy possessed 'a sort of inverse sublimity' because rather than reaching towards 'what is above us' he habitually exalted 'what is below us'. But while he certainly lavished affection on the lowly, Dickens also looked up, as he does during his perusal of the painted ceiling. Then, having taken in the panorama, he was often inclined to pull the sky down.

A sublime inversion happens in *Great Expectations* when Magwitch grabs Pip in the churchyard and holds him in the air by his feet to turn his pockets inside out: suddenly the order of creation does a somersault so that from Pip's viewpoint 'the church jumped over its own weathercock', with its steeple under his feet. In a universe that is liable to suddenly stand on its head, the unlikeliest characters turn out to be light-headed metaphysicians. Speculating about the discontent of Miggs, the maid in *Barnaby Rudge*, Dickens suggests that she may be wondering 'what star was destined for her habitation when she had run her little course below'; lifted aloft by her reverie, Miggs marvels that 'those glimmering spheres' can bear the sight of the terrain occupied by 'that perfidious creature, man'. In *The Old Curiosity Shop*, on one of her rural walks at nightfall Little Nell watches as the darkness is pierced by successive pinpricks of light. The universe opens out, as potentially endless as one of Dickens's lists: 'new stars burst upon her view, and more beyond, and more beyond again'. Nell wonders at the 'changeless and incorruptible existence' of the galaxy, a reproach to the urbanised, industrialised earth with its 'noise of tongues and glare of garish lights'. Then as she bends over a river she sees the reflected stars 'shining in the same majestic order as when the dove beheld them gleaming through the swollen waters, upon the mountain tops far below, and dead mankind, a million fathoms deep'. Here Dickens again reimagines the biblical deluge, but without the ark and the surviving species: the river swells into an ocean that engulfs mountains and drowns humanity. The Uncommercial Traveller has a similarly macabre vision on a bridge in London as street lamps instead of stars shining back at him from the black Thames. 'The reflected lights seemed to originate deep in the water,' he says, 'as if the spectres of suicides were holding them to show where they went down.' Sublimity inverted equals horror.

Dickens came to delight in such metaphorical vendettas against what we think of as reality. The Uncommercial Traveller remarks that 'imagination gloats' at the thought of Gray's Inn mouldering, occupied by rats and feral cats. In this dismal future, a newspaper seller outside the gate resembles Caius Marius exiled in the ruins of Carthage, previously invoked when *Dombey and Son* introduces Brogley and his used furniture. Acknowledging the weary antiquity of the allusion, the Traveller admits that Caius Marius has already 'sat heavy on a thousand million of similes'. Dickens relies on more abstruse and unprecedented similes to connect things as dissimilar as cobwebs and galaxies, or a mythical giant and the windows of a law office; that is how he makes his disparate creation crazily cohere. The arrangement requires strenuous efforts, and will eventually come apart: as Paul Dombey dies, a grandly apocalyptic image looks ahead to a time when 'the wide firmament is rolled up like a scroll'. The specifications for Planet Dick are inscribed on that scroll, and the writing will be erased when the page is retracted.

In art, Dickens loved mayhem and uproar, pandemonium and topsy-turvydom; in life, he was a stickler for discipline. He was always precisely on time for appointments, and in *The Pickwick Papers* he compliments the sun on its reliability, calling it the 'punctual servant of all work'. Respectful of the earth's electrical currents, he took care to align himself with those force-fields. He always positioned his bed on a north–south axis, and when travelling he used a compass to check the coordinates in unfamiliar rooms. At home he policed the correct placement of chairs and drilled his children to use their assigned coat hooks. The same strictures prevailed inside his head. He told an American editor that his ideas were stored 'on different shelves of my brain, ready ticketed and labelled': he may have despised bureaucrats, but he had an office in some annex of his dreamily riotous head. His 'love of order', as he said in a letter, amounted to 'almost a *disorder*', of the kind we now call obsessive–compulsive.

Meticulous about the arrangement of utensils and ornaments on his writing desk, Dickens smiled at this ritual in *Nicholas Nickleby*, where the clerk employed by the Cheerybles sets out his parapher-nalia – 'paper, pens, ink, ruler, sealing-wax, wafers, pounce-box, string-box, fire-box' – as curatorially as if he were displaying the 'choicest curiosities' in a glass case at a museum. Naval discipline regulates the chambers occupied by Tartar the sailor in *Edwin Drood*. His cutlery is so neatly stored that a slack spoon 'would have instantly betrayed itself'; among his toiletries, no toothpick dares to exhibit 'slovenly deportment'. This is a matter of propriety but also of piety, and Dickens approvingly notes that 'No speck, nor spot, nor spatter soiled the purity of any of Mr Tartar's household gods, large, small, or middle-sized.'

Dombey and Son hints at the anxiety that underlies this shipshape regimentation. For extra security the charts and tools in Sol Gills's shop are 'jammed into the tightest cases, fitted into the narrowest corners . . . and screwed into the acutest angles'; the tight fit maintains the 'philosophical composure' of the shop and fancifully resists 'the rolling of the sea'. Captain Cuttle's rooms in Mrs MacStinger's lodging house are micro-managed with the same paranoia: his possessions are 'stowed away', battened down to guard against the prospect of there being 'an earthquake regularly every half-hour'. That disaster is only too probable, and when Walter Gay reports on Sol's depressed state, Cuttle's reaction suggests that 'a gulf had opened up in the City'. Under a collapsing sky, on a turbulent sea or an eruptive earth, Dickens's characters struggle to remain physically and mentally steady.

The anarchy they fear cannot be kept outdoors. When Dickens staged Wilkie Collins's melodrama *The Lighthouse* at his house in Bloomsbury in 1855, stormy weather was whipped up under his roof by a sheet of iron that gave off thunderclaps, a silk grindstone that mimicked the wind, and a dozen cannonballs rolled along the floor to simulate the noise of breakers assaulting the Eddystone beacon. Backstage at the theatre where her sister Fanny dances, Amy in *Little Dorrit* finds herself outside the world mapped by Galileo and Newton. In 'a maze of dust' with 'a mixing of gaslight and daylight', she is puzzled by beams and bulkheads that have not been assembled into a building; all this seems to be 'on the wrong side of the pattern of the universe'. Amy may be disconcerted, but for Dickens this zone of misrule and interstellar havoc had a seductive appeal.

Hence his decision to send Bill Sikes and Oliver Twist on a gratuitous detour through Smithfield meat market at the start of their expedition to Surrey. Sikes ignores the 'discordant sounds' and 'numerous sights' of the place, but for Dickens it was an irresistible descriptive opportunity. Herds of animals are led to slaughter through filth and mud, and the steam from their bodies mingles with the fog, once more reverting to Mudfog where, in the novel's serially published version, Oliver is born. After noting the quantity of sheep and oxen, Dickens next scans the mass of human livestock, which includes 'countrymen, butchers, drovers, hawkers, boys, thieves, idlers, and vagabonds of every low grade', although gradations are blurred in this seething mob. Negative attributes recall irrelevant standards as 'unwashed, unshaven' figures run about, and verbs do duty as nouns to convey an impersonal energy: the whistling, barking, bellowing, bleating, grunting and squeaking of the beasts and their human or canine handlers is followed by a 'crowding, pushing, driving, beating, whooping, and yelling' that are attributed to no one in particular because particularity has been lost in the mass. In another case of inverted sublimity, the 'stunning and bewildering scene . . . quite confounded the senses'.

As the new railway into Euston churns up Camden Town in *Dombey and Son*, Dickens disarranges the universe more dangerously. A street known as Staggs's Gardens – considered by its scruffy inhabitants to be 'a sacred grove', the sylvan abode of deities – is deconsecrated. With geysers, 'fiery eruptions' and 'enormous heaps of earth and clay thrown up' as if by some manic demiurge, the excavations expose the world's arbitrary muddle, producing 'a steep unnatural hill' and an accidental pond among 'a chaos of carts'. Architectural efforts to impose form are sabotaged by bridges leading nowhere and 'unfinished walls and arches'. 'Mounds of ashes' and 'tumuli of oyster shells' forewarn of our ultimate destination. After exulting in this bedlam, Dickens then admits that it has all been imagined, concocted – like everything he wrote about – inside his agitated head: the 'hundred thousand shapes and substances of incompleteness, wildly mingled out of their places, upside down, burrowing in the earth, aspiring in the air, mouldering in the water', are as 'unintelligible as any dream'.

To make such dreams intelligible, Dickens rejigged the dimensions of our existence. Carlyle's Teufelsdröckh considers both time and space to be mere 'Thought-forms', and Charles Darnay, rescued from his trial for treason in *A Tale of Two Cities*, feels the same. He says 'I am frightfully confused regarding time and place', and Carton wonders if he has re-attached himself to 'this terrestrial scheme'. Taking note of such disorientation, Planet Dick has its own laws of fictional physics.

Time is dismissed by Teufelsdröckh as a 'grand anti-magician', a 'wonder-hider' that leaves the world stalely predictable, tarnished by repetition. As a dealer in magic and wonderment, Dickens was bound to agree. In *The Chimes*, the Goblin of the Bell expresses the official view when he declares that 'Time is for [man's] advancement and improvement' and chastises Trotty Veck for his regrets, because in wishing that things had turned out differently he interferes with the 'mighty engine' that was set in motion in Genesis, 'when Time and He began'. It is this sacrosanct engineering that Dickens questioned. Captain Cuttle imagines that Sol Gills 'could make a clock if he tried', and he mimics the chronic mannerisms of this 'ideal timepiece' by tracing 'a species of serpent in the air' with the hook that has replaced his amputated hand. 'Lord,' says Cuttle, 'how that clock would go!' But the line he traces wriggles and twists, rather than leading straight ahead with every minute precisely measured.

We all have to live according to time's dictates; Dickens, however, exempts himself from this wearisome duration. In *Barnaby Rudge* he covers a gap in the novel's chronology by remarking that 'the world went on turning round, as usual, for five years, concerning which this Narrative is silent'. As well as varying the tempo of events as they occur, he claims a prophet's rights to dictate in advance events whose time has not yet come. At the end of *Hard Times* the banker Bounderby is said to be 'projecting himself . . . into futurity', which provokes Dickens to ask 'Into how much of futurity?' Able to see further than Bounderby, he previews providential outcomes that lie ahead and decrees that 'These things were to be.' Scrooge is allowed to appeal against this mandate. Told about his unregretted death and shown his unvisited grave, he asks the Spirit whether these are shadows of things that must be or only of what might be. He secures himself a remission by reforming, and rescinds the future when he announces 'I will not be the man I must have been' if the Spirit had not frightened him into reforming.

Control of time also gave Dickens authority in mortal matters. Oliver Twist is expected to die soon after birth, in which case the novelist realises that his book would be 'the most concise and faithful specimen of biography', exactly one page long. What saves Oliver is the fact that his name is already 'prefixed to the head of this chapter', so Dickens assumes responsibility for keeping him alive. Once his survival is settled, the imperative is to prolong the tale at all costs. Mr Brownlow lends a hand: having travelled abroad to gather information that will unravel the plot, he justifies Dickens's artful postponements when he stipulates 'that I shall be asked no questions until such time as I may deem it expedient to forestall them by telling my own story'. To be kept waiting is an annoyance in daily life but an edgily painful pleasure when we are reading. The laggard progress of lawsuits in Chancery in *Bleak House* reminds the narrator of fairy tales in which time stands still, as it does for Rip Van Winkle or Sleeping Beauty. Although the court's slow grind may be frustrating, suspended time is a means of enchantment.

In *Hard Times* the hard time of industrial society, set to a relentless pace that boosts productivity, disrupts the softer, seasonal time of nature. Even so, the novel's three sections are named after the rural cycle of sowing, reaping and garnering, and the old circular routine resumes outside Coketown, where the mineworks have been abandoned and the grass has grown up again, allowing 'the great wheel of earth . . . to revolve without the shocks and noises of another time'. As a narrator, Dickens prefers acceleration. He hurries through the adolescence of the Gradgrind children in *Hard Times*, breezily reporting that 'Time, with his innumerable horse-power . . . presently turned out young Thomas a foot taller', which transfers the credit for the boy's growth from the stealthy gradualism of biology to the jerky, abrupt propulsiveness of machinery. In the world outside the novel, time-keeping was changed by official decree. The horsepower Dickens invokes when explaining Thomas Gradgrind's growth spurt faded into a figure of speech: in *Sketches by Boz* 'omnibus horses smoked like steam-engines', anticipating the industrial acceleration of society. Then during the 1840s all parts of Britain were hustled into synchronicity, so that trains throughout the country could arrive and depart on an agreed schedule. In *Dombey and Son* the adoption of the standardised regime known as railway time suggests that 'the sun itself had given in' now that duration was no longer measured by its passage across the sky, and an article in *Household Words* sympathises with the distress of a passenger who finds 'the annihilation of time, the stupendous reversal of the natural sequence and order of things' to be 'too much . . . for the endurance of humanity'.

The vagaries of Dickensian time are at their boldest in his two historical novels. In *A Tale of Two Cities* the years from 1775 to 1793 are both the best and worst of times, simultaneously progressive and regressive. Rather than relating past to present, the novel is framed by prophecies that look beyond the historical record. At the beginning the millenarian ravings of a private in the Life Guards announce 'arrangements . . . for the swallowing up of London and Westminster' in a terminal catastrophe, and at the end Carton anticipates a period, 'generations hence', when the cycle of revolution, reaction and restoration will show history 'gradually making expiation for itself and wearing out'. Reviewing the riots of 1780, *Barnaby Rudge* likewise disposes of history as lost time, best forgotten. Catatonic after his pub is wrecked by rioters, John Willet sits among the ruins, to all appearances 'perfectly contented'. 'So far as he was personally concerned,' Dickens comments, 'old Time lay snoring, and the world stood still.' Barnaby is swept up into the mob, arrested, accused of crimes he did not commit and sentenced to death, only to be rescued from the scaffold at the last minute. All this causes him to suffer a mental collapse, but when he recovers he chooses to regard his experience as 'a terrific dream'. History is a nightmare from which he has luckily woken up.

Having recalibrated time, Dickens played similar tricks on space. The narrator of *Bleak House*, viewing human affairs from a vertical distance, mocks Jobling's facile faith in 'things coming round', which is a variant of Micawber's belief in *David Copperfield* that something will turn up. Left to themselves, flat things will never become round: the narrator points out that they must be 'beaten round, or worked round', and only a fool would 'trust in the world's "coming" triangular!' That may be a physical impossibility, but Dickens took it as a challenge. His plotting, like an exercise in three-dimensional geometry, relies on short cuts that make space flexible, compressing geography to bring about just such a triangulation. Some characters, dispensed from taking the long way round the curved earth, penetrate it diagonally. Mrs Varden in *Barnaby Rudge* reconsiders her life while staring at the ground 'as though she saw straight through the globe, out at the other end, and into the immensity of space', while Wemmick in *Great Expectations* says that his guileful employer Jaggers is 'deep as Australia' and points at the floor to indicate the continent that lies 'symmetrically on the opposite spot of the globe'.

Dickens often assured Forster the world was 'much smaller than we thought it', and in his novels this is an article of faith. Bumping into Martin Chuzzlewit in a pawnshop, the swindler Montague Tigg declares that 'this is one of the most tremendous meetings in Ancient or Modern History!' Although Martin responds that London is a 'large town' and hopes that they can 'easily find different ways in it', Dickens ensures that they remain intertwined. He felt no need to apologise for such improbable encounters, because in his view coincidences were not contrivances: they functioned like the gravity that maintains equilibrium throughout the universe. A clerk in the office of the Cheerybles in *Nicholas Nickleby* praises London as the best place in the world for coincidences; when a happy chance brings Nicholas and his adored but unattainable Madeline together, the chapter title attributes their conjunction to an unseen 'Gentleman Usher' who is none other than Dickens the conductor or manipulative plotter, here cast as a beneficent go-between. A guard in *A Tale of Two Cities* inadvertently underlines a truth when he refers to a 'coincidence', placing the stress on the wrong syllable: his error is a small revelation, because it emphasises the way that people have been made to coincide or collide in space. During Darnay's trial at the Old Bailey, his treacherous servant Roger Cly subjects the word and the process to further scrutiny by remarking on 'a particularly curious coincidence' that is actually the result of a wily conspiracy. For Cly, 'most coincidences were curious', employing another word that Dickens always loads with meaning: etymologically, a curio is something worth inspecting or enquiring into, as are the supposed accidents that entrap Darnay.

On his wanderings, the Uncommercial Traveller is guided by instinct to destinations that are somehow predestined. Bound for Wapping, he worries at first about getting lost in the mazy streets but adopts a fatalistic 'Turkish frame of mind', by which he means that he surrenders to some higher power; having done so, he soon finds himself at the workhouse he is looking for. Telegraphy excited Dickens because it wired the air, using electrical currents to connect continents. This was his equivalent to the Aeolian lyres of the romantic poets, which were played upon by breezes that made nature's music audible. In 'The Signal-Man' Dickens's narrator hears the telegraph along the railway line humming in the wind like a 'wild harp'. But instead of tinkling lyrically, the taut metal sounds an 'imaginary cry' to relay an alarm and foretell a death: could the telegraph transmit a message from the future? Dickens thought of technology as a paranormal or supernatural power, which he sought to harness for his own purposes. He planned a story in which two groups of people in different parts of the world would be linked 'by means of an electric message', and in his notes he instructed himself to 'Describe the message – *be* the message – flashing along through space, over the earth, and under the sea.' Captain Cuttle imagines such a venture in his rhapsody about the nautical instruments that fly and dive on Sol Gills's behalf: 'Earth, air, or water. It's all one. . . . Up in a balloon? . . . Down in a bell? . . . D'ye want to put the North Star in a pair of scales and weigh it? He'll do it for you.' Sol, however, is sedately old-fashioned and believes that 'the world has gone past me'; it is Dickens who can lift us to aeronautical heights and plunge us to subaquatic depths.

———

London, sprawling amorphously in space and growing both backwards and downwards in time, was Dickens's universe in little. In *Our Mutual Friend* the city seems to expand across continents, sifting at its outer edges into a 'suburban Sahara', a thirsty waste 'where tiles and bricks were burnt, bones were boiled, carpets were beat, rubbish was shot, dogs were fought, and dust was heaped by contractors'; meanwhile the knotty wood in a waterside pub looks as if it has regressed into a 'state of second childhood', since the walnut planks are relics of ancient forests. A metaphor can return the commercial metropolis to the age of the dinosaurs, as when a bridge over a canal near the India Docks swivels open in *Dombey and Son* to let 'a stranded leviathan' or some other 'monster of a ship' come foraging up the street.

Sketches by Boz affably attempts to establish London as God's favoured domain. But Greenwich Fair, overrun by dancing revellers, is at best an 'artificial Eden'. No longer installed in a garden, the first human beings lend their names to a dim, unparadisial alley off Oxford Street, from which 'the celebrated Mr Sluffen, of Adam-and-Eve court' emerges to propose a toast to chimney sweeps on Mayday. Eden's presumably balmy weather is not appreciated here. After five consecutive days of sunshine, 'hackney-coachmen became revolutionary, and crossing-sweepers began to doubt the existence of a First Cause', since both groups are out of work if there is no rain or mud. Londoners remain superstitious, not confident that they enjoy divine patronage. After Scotland Yard is rebuilt on the embankment, Boz commemorates the area's 'original settlers' as 'a race of strong and bulky men' employed on the wharfs, and he eavesdrops on coalheavers in a pub who relate 'old legends of what the Thames was in ancient times, when the Patent Shot Manufactory wasn't built'. Those ancient times are very recent – the first lead shot towers on the south bank were erected in the 1780s, and the last, beside Waterloo Bridge, was only demolished in 1962. Nevertheless the drinkers worry about 'the advance of civilisation' and are alarmed to learn that London Bridge is to be replaced. They believe that if the old piers are uprooted, 'all the water in the Thames [will] run clean off, and leave a dry gully in its place'; fortunately it remains wet.

Dickens had his own version of their foreboding. For him the river represented the life that flowed into and out of London, reducing Londoners to flotsam. When Florence in *Dombey and Son* hurries across the city from west to east, the 'stream of life' in the streets advances in parallel with the course of the Thames. The river too begins with naively infantile 'dreams of rushes, willows, and green moss' in the countryside, then awakens to roll, 'turbid and troubled', through 'the works and cares of men' in the city it bisects, before it flows on to spill into 'the deep sea', where it ceases to exist. After the riots in *Barnaby Rudge*, a metaphorical torrent recedes, like a river that is now dry or fiery: 'when the human tide had rolled away, a melancholy heap of smoking ruins marked the spot where it had lately chafed and roared'. That doleful verdict is echoed at the end of *Little Dorrit*, when Clennam and Amy are submerged by passers-by in the street who 'fretted and chafed, and made their usual uproar'. All that remains, as Dickens listens to London, is a retreating wave of sound, the echo of the noise the vainly assertive populace once made.

This urban flux ought to be stabilised by monuments, which recruit gods, military victors and political potentates to act as the city's warders, but they too are insecurely founded. *A Child's History of England* notes that St Paul's Cathedral arose on the site of a little church dating from Saxon times, which in its turn had supplanted a temple to Diana; Westminster Abbey likewise took over an inauspiciously 'muddy marshy place . . . where there had been a temple to Apollo'. Dickens acknowledged St Paul's as a landmark, but had doubts about its spiritual efficacy. Oliver Twist, locked in Fagin's den nearby, is unable to see anything of the city through the dirt-encrusted windows, and might as well have been living inside 'the ball of St Paul's Cathedral'. That small ball supports the cross on top of the dome, though here it is a sightless prison and its elevation gives it no power as a moral superintendent. The guilty Jonas Chuzzlewit is unaware that he is being tracked by a private detective, and 'would as soon have thought of the cross upon the top of St Paul's Cathedral taking note of what he did', while Jo in *Bleak House* regards that 'sacred emblem' as 'the crowning confusion of the great, confused city', because it stands 'so high up, so far out of his reach'. The admonition that tolls from the cathedral is hollow rather than commanding: a dandy described by Boz is 'as empty-headed as the great bell of St Paul's'. In *Our Mutual Friend* the dome still seems to be bogged down in an atavistic murk, appearing 'to die hard' as it struggles to lift its head out of a 'foggy sea'. Pip, arriving in London in *Great Expectations*, undergoes a foul initiation as he passes through Smithfield, 'all asmear with filth and fat and blood and foam', after which he glimpses St Paul's, 'bulging ... from behind a grim stone building' that turns out to be Newgate prison. Peggotty in *David Copperfield* has a version of the black dome prettified in pink on the lid of the box where she keeps her sewing kit, and when taken to see the original she considers it 'a rival of the picture' and prefers her homely painted miniature. David himself doubts the eternality of the building. On his return to London, he finds the nearby streets so drastically altered that he says he 'half expected to find St Paul's Cathedral looking older'.

Master Humphrey has an irreligious theory of his own about the cathedral's purpose. He owns a longcase clock in which he stores the manuscripts of the tales he reads to his friends, and when visiting the cathedral he chooses to inspect its clock, which he calls 'the very pulse' of the building. Its time-keeping, like that of Dickens when his story-telling is most doomily emphatic, proceeds with a 'sledge-hammer beat' that hustles the fleeting seconds towards the Day of Judgement. Watching the clock's 'great, sturdy, rattling engines' at work, Master Humphrey worries about the mechanism catching 'a finger put in here or there, and grinding the bone to powder': one way or another, time turns us to dust. He calls the clock 'London's Heart' and says that 'when it should cease to beat, the City would be no more'. Despite the thunderous tone of the chimes, London shares our cardiac frailty.

Mistrusting the cathedral, Dickens preferred to rely on the figures Gog and Magog, the giants whose grotesquely bug-eyed statues glare down from a balcony in the Guildhall. In folk tales they were the spawn of demons who impregnated the sinful daughters of the emperor Diocletian; Brute of Troy – a descendant of Aeneas, credited by legends with founding and naming Britain – is said to have tamed them and made them do penance as London's watchmen. *Dombey and Son* brings them up to date, pointing out that a ten-minute walk takes you from the Guildhall, where Gog and Magog 'held their state', to the Royal Exchange with its haggling traders, the Bank of England which hoards the nation's wealth, and the repository of colonial plunder at East India House. Imperial London needs the two ogres as its brawny enforcers. On his youthful wanderings, Dickens hoped that Gog and Magog would sponsor an 'opening of a Whittington nature' for him. Although they did not endorse him as a future Lord Mayor, they helped him to become a novelist: as a boy he knew them to be 'images made of something that was not flesh and blood', but in a trial run at creating characters he 'invested them with attributes of life', and when St Paul's strikes midnight in *Master Humphrey's Clock* they step down from their pedestals and carouse over a cask of wine until they resume their statuesque silence at dawn. Magog, goggle-eyed and physically stumpy, here has an expression 'that would have been very comical if he had been a dwarf or an ordinary-sized man'. He and Gog are the city's 'guardian genii', and this vocation vouches for their geniality. Disarming them, Dickens awards Miss La Creevy in *Nicholas Nickleby* 'a heart big enough for Gog', with a surplus of kindliness 'to spare for Magog'.

Another of London's sentinels is the Monument, a column erected to commemorate the city's recovery from the Great Fire; this too Dickens bent to his will. In *Martin Chuzzlewit* Tom Pinch, newly arrived from Wiltshire, asks the ticket-seller at the base for directions and discovers that 'the Man in the Monument was quite as mysterious a being . . . as the Man in the Moon'. 'Aloof from all mankind', this cynical hermit is as supercilious as the pillar itself; he charges visitors for the privilege of toiling up more than three hundred steps to see the view, but chuckles that they should pay double to stay on the ground. Tom therefore resolves 'to put no confidence in anything he said'. And can the Monument itself be trusted? Alexander Pope protested against an inscription at its base – expunged in 1831 – that wrongly blamed 'the treachery and malice of the Papists' for setting the fires in 1666, and in the third of his *Moral Essays* he likened 'London's column, pointing at the skies', to 'a tall bully' because it 'lifts the head, and lies'. This leaves Tom in a quandary: 'if Truth didn't live in the base of the Monument, notwithstanding Pope's couplet about

the outside of it, where in London . . . was she likely to be found!'
Probably nowhere, in which case fiction is our best guide to understanding the city.

At the top of the Monument a gilded urn sprouts metal tongues of
fire. Dickens saw this as a featureless face surmounted by an inflammatory hairdo: treated to masculine pronouns, the Monument has
'every hair erect upon his golden head, as if the doings of the city
frightened him'. In *Our Mutual Friend* Twemlow shampoos his sparse
hair with egg yolks which he leaves to dry for two hours, and as the
locks stiffen he looks 'equally like the Monument on Fish Street Hill,
and King Priam on a certain incendiary occasion'. That refers to the
fall of Troy as described by Homer; poets from William Dunbar in
the fourteenth century to Edmund Spenser in the sixteenth honoured
Brute of Troy as the founder of Britain by referring to London as
Troy Novant, but the image of Twemlow with his hair standing on
end as if 'for the receipt of startling intelligence' subverts that heri-
tage and rekindles the flames lit by the conquering Greeks. Cities
aspire to stability and permanence; Dickens's metaphor, at once
absurd and disturbing, warns that all resplendent capitals are likely
to end in ashes.

At his most sombre, Dickens thought of London as a necropolis.
During a holiday on the Kent coast in the summer of 1855, he wrote an
essay imagining his return journey to a West End that has lapsed into
bucolic calm, containing 'no animated existence'; then in Belgravia
he encounters an ostler 'eating straw, and mildewing away', whom
he identifies as 'the last man' left alive on earth. In Mary Shelley's
The Last Man, published in 1826, a pandemic that extinguishes
humanity spares only the narrator, who sets out with his dog to hike
across the evacuated continents. Dickens was happy to assume this
role, although he regarded his solitary state as a boon: on a weekend
stroll through the City, free from its usual crowds of merchants and
lawyers, he relishes his 'Sunday sensation . . . of being the Last Man'.
Entering a theatre after hours, he likens the orchestra pit to one of the
mass graves dug for victims of a plague, remarks that the chandelier
has 'gone dead like everything else', and sees the dust covers on the

tiers of unoccupied seats as winding-sheets or shrouds; a watchman on patrol appears to be a ghost carrying a 'corpse candle' as he haunts the upper gallery.

Restive in Lausanne, Dickens complained to Forster about the lack of 'suggestive streets' for his nocturnal walks. 'I don't seem able to get rid of my spectres,' he said, 'unless I can lose them in crowds.' Having released these phantasmal beings into London's thoroughfares, he was sometimes unsure whether the people he saw there actually existed or had been invented by him. On walks with friends, he occasionally pretended to spot one of his more obnoxious characters in the distance and would suggest an urgent detour. Not altogether in jest, he worried about the over-population that his necromancy might encourage: if the 'enormous hosts of the dead' who 'belong to one old great city . . . were raised while the living slept, there would not be the space of a pin's point in all the streets and ways for the living to come out into'. Near the Tower, the Uncommercial Traveller comes upon two such revenants, an old man and woman who rake a patch of dry grass inside the rusted railings of a churchyard. 'Gravely among the graves, they made hay, all alone by themselves,' he reports. The Gothic vignette prompts him to speculate that 'Perhaps they were Spectres, and I wanted a Medium.' As this sly wink intimates, Dickens was the medium and these were spirits he had revived.

One year in August, the Traveller finds himself in a 'city of the absent', which has temporarily died while its fashionable inhabitants are away in the country. Disconcerted by the 'pleasant open landscape' of Regent Street, he asks whether this is 'the Golden Age revived, or Iron London', and he is relieved that the usual traffic will soon be back to 'grind Arcadia away, and give it to the elements in granite powder'. In a lament for the materialistic 'iron time' of the mid-nineteenth century, Matthew Arnold regretted that 'the age had bound / Our souls in its benumbing round'. Dickens's Traveller, more resilient, is glad that 'the iron age will return' to enliven London, not benumb it.

Our last view of this grandiose Dickensian universe comes after Edwin Drood and Rosa amicably end their romance. Edwin files away his fond memories 'among the mighty store of wonderful chains that are for ever forging, day and night, in the vast iron-works of time and circumstance'; this bond is in turn 'riveted to the foundations of heaven and earth, and gifted with invincible force to hold and drag'. The industrial imagery sounds like a doleful reminiscence of Magwitch's leg irons and the furnace in which Orlick wants to incinerate Pip, yet here the chains are wonderful, while the rivets that connect present to past are a gift. Having varied the dragging pace of time and abridged space, Dickens could even metaphorically liquefy heavy metal. At the circus in *Hard Times*, customers are promised that they will see Signor Jupe 'throwing seventy-five hundred-weight in rapid succession backhanded over his head, thus forming a fountain of solid iron in mid-air' – preposterous of course, but no more so than the rotation that keeps our ponderous globe upright in space. Here the gravity of iron is lightened by comic grace: the feats of cosmic juggling performed by Dickens rival those of Jupe the clown.

Heroes of His Own Life

The hearty conviviality with which Dickens invited friends to his birthday dinner in 1844 was not the whole truth about him. At other times he regretted what he called his 'conspicuous position' in public view, and in a letter from Niagara Falls he complained that his American fans disrupted the introspection on which he depended. He worked in solitude, occupying a 'chamber of cogitation' like that in which the magnate Dombey broods; from there he was able to exercise a remote control over the emotions of the strangers who read his books.

Closer to hand, he could be ruthless in deploying his power. In 1838 he tested his verbal voltage on his wife by reading to her the murder from *Oliver Twist*, which left her, he contentedly remarked, in 'an unspeakable "*state*"'. Twenty years later, after he accused Catherine of a 'mental disorder' and attempted to commit her to an asylum, Elizabeth Barrett Browning said he had used 'his genius as a cudgel', almost as if he had turned into Sikes battering Nancy. As Dickens saw it, the break-up was a clean, cold erasure like a textual revision: he refused a friend's offer to broker a reconciliation and insisted that 'A page in my life which once had writing on it has become absolutely blank.' In his published statement on the marital separation he dismissed the 'fabulous stories' told about him and asserted his probity for the benefit of the 'great multitude who know me through my writings, and . . . do not know me otherwise'. Not to be known otherwise was his preference.

In his introduction to *Master Humphrey's Clock*, Dickens adopts an impersonal alias as 'the Author'. His earliest version of this persona was the jaunty Boz, who hopes that his trial balloon will 'catch some favourable current, and . . . *go off well*'. Later, less flightly, he planned to call himself The Shadow, working under cover of dark. He ended as the dourly professional Uncommercial Traveller, who is employed by 'the great house of Human Interest Brothers' to journey down back-roads 'seeing many little things, and some great things'. The Traveller defines himself negatively, and after a series of disclaimers he says that he should not be mistaken for the kind of itinerant salesman who waits on rural railway platforms like 'a Druid in the midst of a light Stonehenge of samples'. Yet that denial hints at a positive identification: the Druids, as Dickens pointed out in his *Child's History*, were priestly mystagogues, and that megalithic baggage is surely suspect.

Misgivings about the authorial role are voiced by characters who serve as Dickens's second selves. Esther Summerson in *Bleak House* apologises for her first-person narrative: 'I don't know how it is I seem to be always writing about myself', she declares, even though her purpose in the novel is to do exactly that. She affects embarrassment if someone pays her a compliment, says 'I must write it even if I rub it out again', then chooses to leave the flattery on the record 'because it gives me so much pleasure'. The more artless Esther claims to be, the craftier she seems. Oliver Twist, asked by Mr Brownlow if he might like to write books when he grows up, replies that he would rather read them, then decides that he would sooner be a book-seller than a book-writer. Yet Oliver is arrested after a theft at a bookstall and is recaptured by Fagin's gang when he goes on an errand to the same stall, which must count as an ill omen. Brownlow chuckles 'We won't make an author of you, while there's an honest trade to be learnt, or brick-making to turn to.' Perhaps authorship is as dishonest as the trades Fagin teaches to his gang of larcenous boys; brick-making may be psychologically safer than writing, because it does not involve self-revelation.

***

David Copperfield, the 'written memory' of a novelist whose initials are those of Dickens in reverse, has a fuller title which vouches for its authenticity at elaborate lengths but then nonchalantly admits its bad faith. In the first serial edition it was called *The Personal History, Adventures, Experience, & Observation of David Copperfield The Younger Of Blunderstone Rookery* – a self-advertisement belied by a parenthetical afterthought, printed in almost unreadably tiny type: *(Which He never meant to be Published on any Account)*.

Although David calls himself the younger, he never knew David senior; he supplements this plaintive attempt to establish a lineage by asserting that he belongs at the Rookery, from where he was soon expelled by his stepfather. His bolstering of his identity is understandable, because even in infancy he seems to realise how provisional our lives truly are. With the benefit of almost pre-natal hindsight, he recreates the domestic scene immediately after his birth. His aunt arrives expecting to greet a niece not a nephew and departs in a huff. This leaves David – still in his basket, while his mother recovers in bed – to brood about the unconceived sibling whose place he has seemingly usurped: that imaginary female child remains 'in the land of dreams and shadows, the tremendous region whence I had so lately travelled'. Then in the darkness outside the house he pictures his father's grave, 'the mound above the ashes and the dust that once was he, without whom I had never been'. His awkward phrasing makes it sound as if he too still hovers on the border of non-being, waiting to be salvaged by a progenitor or by a novelist. Asked to explain the origin of his characters, Dickens once said that they somehow materialised out of 'fine filmy webs of thought' and became 'instinct with life'. The process was not so involuntary, and those webs are too diaphanous to be truly Dickensian. One of David's asides is more candid. He reveals that he was born with a caul, and when he learns that this protective membrane was sold in a raffle, he shudders to think of 'a part of myself being disposed of in that way'. Novelists dispose of parts of themselves in another way, objectifying those fractions or fragments as the people they cast in the stories they tell.

David begins by wondering 'whether I shall turn out to be the hero of my own life, or whether that station will be held by anybody else'. He surely knows that it will be the latter: we read his book to make the acquaintance of the comic characters he incidentally encounters, not to follow his sentimental education or the progress of his literary career. Either hoping to transform himself into someone else or relying on others to do him this service, David undergoes a series of mutations. His aunt renames him Trotwood, which she briskly abbreviates to Trot; Steerforth gives him the girlish nickname Daisy; with his child bride Dora he answers to the pet name Doady. His London land-lady associates him with her day for doing the laundry and addresses him as Mr Copperfull 'because', as David points out with quizzical illogic, 'it was not my name', though it might well have been equally quaint: when planning the novel, Dickens considered calling him Copperboy, Copperstone and Topflower. Names are arbitrary labels, but novelists assign them as definitions, guides to character. Betsey Trotwood insists on believing that Peggotty chose her pagan-sounding surname, and says it would have been easier for her 'to be born a Jackson, or something of that sort'. Perhaps so, but the word evokes or even creates her. Mr Dick takes clever advantage of that onomastic liberty. Born Richard Babley, he changes a name that Betsey says he 'can't bear' and in the process becomes a homonym of Dickens and his dotty, distracted self-image.

David's second chapter is entitled 'I Observe', which defines his vocation. At first he observes only scraps: 'as to making a net of a number of these pieces, and catching anybody in it, that was, as yet, beyond me' – a telling admission that the future novelist's purpose is entrapment. His earliest recollections are of his mother and Peggotty as pictorial volumes in space. One of them is a 'youthful shape', the other has 'no shape at all'; together they obtrude as 'a distinct presence' in 'the blank of my infancy'. Much later, in a London coffee room, he refers to 'the person who had come in', using the word impersonally since all he notices here too is a shape or a physique, 'the figure of a handsome well-formed young man'. Then the stranger becomes a 'real presence' – a theological term, used to assert Christ's bodily participation in the Eucharist – and David realises that this new arrival is Steerforth, though his schoolfriend shares David's initial indifference and does not recognise him. G. K. Chesterton said that Dickens's characters were more real than their creator: here we see David gradually conferring that reality on one of those characters as he gives the shape a face, a name and a past.

The word Dickens uses more often than 'person' is 'creature', which fondly acknowledges an act of creation that can be religious, biological or aesthetic. Peggotty calls Barkis 'a good plain creature' and Mrs Gummidge says she is 'a lone lorn creetur'. When Mr Peggotty describes Emily as 'a little bright-eyed creetur' who has warmed his hut, he expresses the same affectionate reverence that made Keats link his glimpses of a stoat or a fieldmouse in the grass with the sight of a man hurrying down a city street. In all these cases, Keats said in a letter in 1819, 'the Creature has a purpose and his eyes are bright with it'; more ambitiously, the man in the street intent on his errand portends 'some birth of new heroism'. David Copperfield nurtures similar 'visionary considerations', but regards them as a reflex of his puffed-up ego, for which he disingenuously apologises. He thinks of himself in boyhood as 'a very honest little creature', though after leaving school he hopes to become a 'magnificent animal', ready to do 'wonderful things'. Yet perhaps because writing makes him an isolated observer, David excludes himself from Keats's continuum of feeling. In the chaise that takes him to his mother's funeral, pained by the high spirits of his fellow passengers, he feels 'cast away among creatures with whom I had no community of nature'. It is the lament or perhaps the boast of a solipsist: *Robinson Crusoe* was one of Dickens's favourite books, although – in a sideways glance at his own imaginative condition – he found it incredible that the castaway's decades of solitude did not induce any 'ghostly fancies' and drive him mad.

David often registers uncomfortable qualms about his treatment of the creatures he designates as characters. Is he assuming an unwarranted power over them, placing himself outside the humanity he shares with them? A taxonomic term which he uses during his apprenticeship at Doctors' Commons conveys his unease. 'We articled clerks,' he sarcastically remarks, were 'germs of the patrician order of proctors.' 'Germ' when added to 'patrician' sounds biological, but the fathers here have done no seeding or breeding; instead David's colleagues have each paid a thousand pounds to qualify for adoption as legal offspring once their training ends. Steerforth, also using professional jargon, regards the beached yokels at Yarmouth as anthropological oddities. 'Let us see the natives in their aboriginal condition,' he says. Rosa Dartle blames Steerforth for his aesthetic connoisseurship of human foibles and says that she has struggled, as David does, against 'the fascinating influence of his delightful art – delightful nature I thought it then'. Another character more indignantly objects to her own exploitation, both inside and outside the novel. The dwarfish hairdresser and manicurist Miss Mowcher, modelled on the chiropodist Mrs Jane Seymour Hill who treated Dickens's wife, is mockingly introduced by Steerforth as 'one of the seven wonders of the world'; she is then anatomised by David, who numbers her chins, measures her 'extremely little arms', adds that she lacked a throat and a waist, and says that her attenuated legs are not worth mentioning, although at least they terminate, 'as human beings generally do, in a pair of feet'. When Mrs Hill read this instalment of the novel she complained to Dickens, who by way of apology set Miss Mowcher to work as a private detective and allowed her to detain Steerforth's embezzling servant Littimer. She goes on to remind David that she 'had no hand, young gentleman, in the making of herself', explains her disability as a genetic inheritance, and tells him 'not to associate bodily defects with mental'. David may take her reproof to heart, but Dickens ignores it: for him, the mind was written on the body.

Again using Steerforth as his alibi, David pleads that both he and Miss Mowcher have been 'hapless instruments' in Steerforth's 'designing hands', even though it is surely the novelist who designs Little Emily's downfall by sending Steerforth to seduce her. Here too, David tries to indemnify himself. Approaching the crisis, he claims that its end is predetermined and says in advance 'It is no worse, because I write of it.' Reluctant to go on narrating, he steels himself to do so: 'It would be no better, if I stopped my most unwilling hand. It is done. Nothing can undo it; nothing can make it otherwise than as it was.' He protests too much, and he is equally shifty when Ham, deserted by

Emily, almost begs to be written out of the story. 'The end of it like,' Ham says, gesturing out to sea. 'What end?' asks David, who despite pretending not to be in charge of the plot sees to it that Ham drowns while nobly attempting to save Steerforth from the storm. Steerforth's death also removes him 'from the scenes of this poor history', which is perhaps a mercy. David knows he must 'bear involuntary witness against [him] at the Judgement Throne'; even so, he is 'not afraid to write that I never had loved Steerforth better than when the ties that bound me to him were broken'. That tenderness coexists with the novelist's willingness to kill the thing he loves.

David's confession about Uriah Heep is even more startling. The thought that Uriah is asleep in the next room weighs on him 'like a waking nightmare'. In his own 'dozing thoughts' he sees Uriah as 'some meaner quality of devil' and muses about running him through with a red-hot poker. 'Haunted' by the idea, he steals in to look at him, but as the unconscious Uriah gurgles and snorts he looks 'so much worse in reality than in my distempered fancy, that afterwards I was attracted to him in very repulsion'. Blake said that the intellectual allure of Satan in *Paradise Lost* showed Milton to be 'of the Devil's party without knowing it'. David's predicament is more disturbing because he admits the attraction of a more squalid, uncharismatic devil, whom he can only pinion with a metaphor not a poker: Uriah, he remarks, sleeps with his mouth 'open like a post-office'. Then in the morning his oily, lanky figure departs 'as if the night was going away in his person'. He has returned to his lair in Dickens's nocturnal imagination.

The writer and his characters are mutually dependent, which is why David is also unable to resist the pleas of Micawber. He warns Traddles not to lend him money, but when Micawber begs for an appointment David agrees to meet him, if only to allow him the opportunity for another gloriously windy verbal performance. To pay back the favour, Micawber does the novelist's work for him by documenting Uriah's crimes, which requires him to become implausibly 'patient and persevering'. This newly conscientious Micawber is finally promoted to the magistracy in New South Wales, from where he sends a letter addressing David as 'THE EMINENT AUTHOR' who is 'familiar to the imaginations of a considerable portion of the civilized world'. Invisibly blushing, David permits Micawber to act as his publicist.

Occasional remarks by David let us look askance at his slippery literary skills. He criticises Peggotty and Micawber for their verbosity or verbiage: she commands a 'militia of words', while he has 'a great parade of them', trotted out in an ostentatious 'show of liveries' on a state occasion. David warns that maintaining 'too large a retinue of words' is risky and adds that 'slaves when they are too numerous rise against their masters'; the stiffly sententious caution preserves his own exclusive right to use more words than might be strictly necessary. Elsewhere, after dismissing a light-fingered servant, he suggests to Dora that the young man's thefts might be the result of a 'contagion in us', since as newlyweds they are negligent in household matters. He speaks in this 'figurative manner' out of delicacy, but Dora reacts badly to the medical metaphor, decides that he equates her with the lying page, and sobs 'You always said he was a story-teller. And now you say the same of me!' David can only protest that 'it's not true', which in a novel is a weak rejoinder. Immediately before this incident, Betsey tells him the long-suppressed tale of her marriage to a man who turned out to be a gambler and a cheat. She concludes by saying 'Now you know the beginning, middle, and end, and all about it . . . This is my grumpy, frumpy story, and we'll keep it to ourselves, Trot!' That, however, is not the end, because the missing husband later reappears, and David has already breached his aunt's confidence by including the episode in his book. Writers of fiction trade in falsehoods, and should never be trusted with secrets.

Apart from mentioning the 'strongest earnestness' of his daily work, David Copperfield avoids discussion of his literary career, which he judges 'will be of interest to no one', and it is Pip in *Great Expectations* who experiences what David calls 'the aspirations, the delights, anxieties, and triumphs' of creativity. Dickens perhaps felt able to let down his guard with Pip because he is not a writer, at least not professionally.

While learning to read, Pip manages to print a smeared and misspelled epistle to Joe, who is sitting beside him at the time. Much later, he writes 'fervently and pathetically' to the Home Secretary begging clemency for Magwitch; although Dickens had fervour and pathos on tap, Pip's efforts do Magwitch little good. He does possess a certain talent for mendacity. When Uncle Pumblechook asks what Miss Havisham is like, Pip says she is very tall and dark even though 'she was nothing of the kind'; aware that Pumblechook has never seen her, he claims that she rides in a black velvet coach and eats from gold plates. A career as a novelist might have followed from these fibs, but he settles for a drearier life as a merchant and renounces all expectations of greatness by saying that his firm was 'not in a grand way of business'.

All the same, Pip comes closer than David to being the hero of Dickens's own life. More than any other character in the novels, he is embedded in literature. Initially he resembles Blake's waifs, especially the 'little boy lost in the lonely fen' from *Songs of Innocence* – except that instead of being led home through the lonely dale to his mother by a kindly God clad 'like his father in white', Pip is waylaid by Magwitch beside the grave of his parents. Wordsworth in his 'Ode: Intimations of Immortality from Recollections of Early Childhood' suggests that we bring with us into the world 'visionary gleams' that are wispy souvenirs of a bright, blessed pre-existence, happier than the shadowy region that David Copperfield imagines when he muses about his non-existent sister. Estella jeers at this Wordsworthian provenance when, as she parts from Pip, she addresses him as 'you visionary boy – or man?' He deserves her dismissive irony, because at this stage in life his visions are of social ascent and financial bounty. In Wordsworth's poem, the celestial radiance gradually dims as we grow up. The change happens more abruptly when Magwitch takes hold of Pip in the churchyard and despoils his innocence by making him an accomplice. Wordsworth has his own mild anticipation of that terrifying scene. As a boy in *The Prelude* he steals a boat, rows out onto a lake, and is startled by 'grim shape' of 'a huge peak, black and huge' that 'upreared its head' to stride after him. The moving mountain is 'like a living thing', but it remains remote, a symbolic father figure rebuking him. Magwitch by contrast is a chthonic deity moulded from the filthy earth that disgorges him, 'soaked in water, and smothered in mud'; nature itself, grappling to keep him underground, seems almost to have crucified him, as he is 'lamed by stones, and cut by flints, and stung by nettles, and torn by briars'.

When Magwitch demands 'You're not a deceiving imp?', Pip denies it. An echo of 'Ode to a Nightingale' argues otherwise. Keats, farewelling the elusive bird, regrets that 'the fancy cannot cheat so well / As she is fam'd to do, deceiving elf!', but Pip's fanciful tendency to deceive himself is his abiding problem. Daydreaming about Estella, he plays at being a 'young Knight of romance', like Wordsworth who as a child transforms his native landscape into 'faëry land, the forest of romance'. More guiltily, he suffers a nervous breakdown after the death of Magwitch and recalls that while ill he 'confounded impossible existences with my own identity'. Romantic poets enjoyed this reprieve from having to be themselves: Keats thought that a poet should have 'no Identity' and 'no self', which enabled him to intuit the sensations of an owl shivering inside its feathers in the winter cold or a snail extending its horns to feel out its surroundings. Dickens was less interested in self-abnegation; instead of empathising with owls or snails he willed into life the 'extraordinary transformations of the human face . . . much dilated in size' that appear to the febrile Pip.

Freud believed that artists are introverts who crave 'honour, power, riches and the love of women', although unlike brawnier men they 'lack the means of achieving these gratifications'. They therefore treat themselves to imaginary rewards, while others must reach an accommodation with their more niggardly circumstances. 'I don't like the Realities,' Dickens admitted in his letter about the old enchanters, 'except when they are unattainable – *then*, I like them of all things.' Pip attains riches without effort, but the fairy gold is polluted when he learns that his patron is Magwitch; the love of his chosen woman is teasingly withheld. Estella is less a person than a muse, a star glimmering in Freud's 'twilight realm of fantasy', and Pip tells her she is 'the embodiment of every graceful fancy that my mind has ever become acquainted with'. He speaks, he says, in an 'ecstasy of unhappiness', after which he tumbles back to earth and plods thirty miles home to London on foot. Although Dickens was a professional fulfiller of wishes, he hesitated about allowing Pip's dreams to come true, and originally ended the novel with a rueful anti-climax. In this first version, Pip returns to London after four years spent working abroad and accidentally meets Estella in Piccadilly. He is accompanied by little Pip, Joe Gargery's child; Estella assumes the boy is Pip's son. She looks careworn, humbled by her time with a callous and arrogant husband who is killed when a horse he mistreats gives him a retaliatory kicking. Pip is pleased to see that she has been hurt, which makes up for the misery she caused him. She apologises for her cruelty, but it is too late for them to think of happiness together. Pressed by the novelist Edward Bulwer-Lytton, Dickens rewrote the conclusion. His calculation was emotional as well as commercial: he had an obligation to look after his characters, like Mr Peggotty who 'forgot nobody' and who first arranges to rehouse the cantankerous Mrs Gummidge before he emigrates to Australia, then decides to take her along. In the amended version of *Great Expectations*, the encounter between Pip and Estella happens in the ruins of Miss Havisham's house, and it is a reunion not an urban coincidence. She expresses remorse, they join hands, and he sees 'no shadow of another parting from her'.

Nevertheless the suppressed ending does cast a shadow, and Pip's optimism contradicts the sad definition of the human lot that Dickens propounded in 1857: man, he said after despatching one of his sons to India, was 'a parting and farewell-taking animal'. Departure is also a euphemism for death in *A Christmas Carol*, where Bob Cratchit calls Tiny Tim's demise as 'this first parting that there was among us' – although here again Dickens corrects the record by asserting in dogmatic capitals that after all Tiny Tim 'did

NOT die'. Enchanters can sometimes be good-humoured frauds, and Dickens was obliged to keep up the morale of his readers by telling such emollient lies.

———————

The reclusive Master Humphrey refuses to disclose his reasons for writing or for collecting the stories he files away in the carved oaken case of the 'old, cheerful, companionable Clock' that stands between the hearth and his bedroom door. 'What wound I sought to heal, what sorrow to forget, originally, matters not now,' he insists. Two confessional narratives by Dickens say more about such authorial wounds and sorrows. 'His Brown-Paper Parcel', published for Christmas in 1862 as part of *Somebody's Luggage*, is the monologue of an artist who effaces and disowns his handiwork; the writer in 'George Silverman's Explanation', which appeared in 1868, suffers deprivations and disappointments that he is unable to fictionalise.

The tattered brown-paper parcel in the story contains chalks and rubbers, the toolkit of 'a young man in the Art line' who writes on London pavements 'in fine round characters', inscribing proverbs, maxims, numbers from one to zero and the alphabet from A to G. Numbers that do not add up into sums and letters that do not make up words are a reminder that for Dickens art was an abstraction from reality, not a replica of it. When David Copperfield learns shorthand, the bizarre signage looks to him like 'an Egyptian Temple'. As if inducted into a heathen cult, he sees the flicks and squiggles in his primer as flies' legs or sky-rockets. But although he finds it ridiculous that 'a thing like the beginning of a cobweb, meant expectation', he gradually comes to marvel at 'the wonderful vagaries that were played by circles' or 'the tremendous effects of a curve in the wrong place': he has found a way of redesigning the world. The creator of the downtrodden gallery in 'His Brown-Paper Parcel' arrives at no such revelation. Moaning that 'such is genius in a commercial country', he leases his work out to imposters who are responsible for 'touching up the down-strokes of the writing', in return for which they pocket tips from passers-by.

Torn between self-effacement and self-declaration, the pavement artist gives in to stammering rage in his written testament and announces 'I – I – I – am the artist', as if adding extra embellishments beneath his signature as Dickens did in his letters. Then he warns anyone who might see his work to watch 'when the candles are burnt down' for a glimpse of 'a neglected young man perseveringly rubbing out the last traces of the pictures, so that nobody can renew the same'; the aim of this erasure is concealment, but all the same he blurts out 'That's me.' Keats differentiated between two kinds of artistic identity, the 'egotistical sublime' of Wordsworth, who wrote an epic about the growth of his own mind, and the 'negative capability' of Shakespeare, the connoisseur of 'uncertainties, mysteries, doubts' who remained unknowable, hidden behind his characters. Despite his meagre talent, the man in the monologue has both temperaments, and their clash leads him to a self-spiting dead end. Dickens understood those mixed motives because he shared them: he was at once a planet sunnily monopolising the horizon and an invisible observer or eavesdropper protected by darkness as he explored the city.

David Copperfield archly refers to the book we are reading as 'this manuscript . . . intended for no eyes but mine'. George Silverman's disclaimers are more heartfelt. He makes two false starts on his memoir and despairs of getting the words to say what he wants, yet he doggedly persists. He resembles Dr Manette in *A Tale of Two Cities*, who in his cell at the Bastille uses flakes of iron, soot, charcoal and his own blood as ink to scratch 'my last recorded words, whether they be ever read by men or not' on the 'melancholy paper' he has scavenged.

Orphaned like David or Pip, George is more profoundly damaged than they are. He spends his impoverished childhood in a cellar; hunger, thirst and cold, together with the pain of being beaten, are the only sensations he knows, and he considers himself to be no better than a mangey dog or a wolf cub. He is rescued, like Pip, by a providential inheritance, then cheated out of it by his godly guardian. A snooty girl who resembles Estella humiliates George when he won't attend her birthday party, although he stays away for fear of passing on a fever. Later he is angrily discharged by the Miss Havisham-like patroness who has awarded him a clerical living. He falls in love with his pupil Adelina Fareway; with no hope of reciprocation, he brings her together with another of his young charges, Granville Wharton, 'fashioning him (do not deride or misconstrue the expression, unknown reader of this writing; for I have suffered!) into a greater resemblance to myself in my solitary one strong aspect'. This is the behaviour of a novelist – grooming the self to graduate from the first to the third person, permitting characters to enjoy experiences that are denied to him. The couple beg George to arrange a happy ending by marrying them, and before the ceremony he stands at the water's edge waiting for the sun to rise 'in his majesty' while he contemplates the 'rosy suffusion of the sky' and 'the ineffable splendour that then burst forth'. Is he preparing to act as God's deputy or abasing himself before a creation that has excluded him? 'I married them,' George says, recognising that he is condemned to live at second hand as novelists do. 'My hand,' he adds, 'was cold when I placed it on their hands clasped together.'

George retires to write in a 'sequestered place' with a view of a graveyard, and in his last sentences, stumbling over stalled repetitions, he numbly grips an implement that he cannot wield as a weapon or flourish as a wand: 'I now pen my explanation. I pen it at my open window. . . . I pen it for the relief of my own mind, not foreseeing whether or no it will ever have a reader.' For Dickens this was an act of mortification: incessantly productive and with devoted readers everywhere, he recognised this blocked, marginalised writer as a kindred spirit, impelled by a need to administer therapy to himself.

13

The So Potent Art

Dickens often mused about a parallel career, a relief from the penitential isolation in which Dr Manette or George Silverman write their hopeless testimonies. In *Little Dorrit* he refers to Shakespeare as both 'author and stage-player': this was the versatility he wanted to emulate. Authors remain out of sight, represented by their silent words, but stage-players come alive before our eyes. Dickens was uneasy about inserting his own experience into his novels; the theatre allowed him to expose more of himself, though still indirectly, and in his letters and essays he adopted the identities of selected characters from Shakespearean drama, sketching a personal and artistic autobiography.

At school Dickens put on plays, and as a young man in London he spent virtually every night at the theatre; in 1832 he was even invited to an acting audition at Covent Garden, which he did not attend because of illness. Cast as the military braggart Bobadil in an amateur performance of Ben Jonson's *Every Man in His Humour* in 1845, he so relished the role that he affected the bombastic persona offstage as well. In *The Frozen Deep* in 1857 he played an explorer who dies in an arctic waste after rescuing a rival in love; having groaned through this character's terminal agony, he reappeared as a frisky elderly bachelor in the 'petite comedy' *Uncle John*, which completed the evening's entertainment. This histrionic flair pointed Dickens towards his public recitals, as he intimates when David Copperfield, having published his first novel, is told that old friends 'read my book as if they heard me speaking its contents'. Yet his solo turns were not enough to satisfy him. He grumbled in 1842 that writing had led him astray, because 'nature intended me for the Lessee of a National Theatre'. The next year, in a letter to Douglas Jerrold, he again pondered this managerial role and mused about an audience rhythmically clamouring for a curtain call from some-one called 'Dick-Ins'. Shortly before his death he told Charles Kent that he still hoped to settle down near a great theatre, 'in the direc-tion of which I should hold supreme authority', with 'the plays as well as the players . . . absolutely under my command'. The role of actor-manager attracted him because, as his emphasis on supreme authority and absolute command proclaimed, it would have placed him in control of actual human beings rather than the so-called 'spectres' in his fiction.

Walter Bagehot complained that Dickens saw man as 'an acting thing' not 'a moral agent'. That, however, is how we often see ourselves, especially when we have to cope with personal crises: Tulkinghorn, on the track of Lady Dedlock's hidden past in *Bleak House*, sees that she 'has been acting a part the whole time' to protect her reputation, and Betsey Trotwood bravely responds to financial ruin by telling David Copperfield 'We must learn to act the play out.' In his own case, Dickens said that acting was the antidote to his 'habit of self-abstraction and withdrawal into fancies', like a healthy bout of outdoor exercise. What he called 'assumption', he explained to Forster, gave him 'the chance of being some one not in the remotest degree like myself'. But in becoming someone else, had he assumed a disguise, or was the alias a secret self? He had, he said, 'many wild reasons' for succumbing to what he pretended was no more than 'exquisite foolery'.

Equally there were good reasons for not doing so. Before he began the reading tours, he worried about 'the public exhibition of oneself', and Forster tried to dissuade him by pointing to Shakespeare's suppos-edly low opinion of acting, 'which, in the jealous self-watchfulness of his noble nature, he feared might hurt his mind'. Forster had no evidence for his presumption about Shakespeare, but the warning was prescient. The frantic travel itinerary of the tours hurt Dickens's body, sabotaging his health, and the reckless vehemence of his later performances unsettled his mind as well.

Dickens introduces *Master Humphrey's Clock* by describing the 'imaginary people whose little world lies within these pages' as they gather around the fireside of the reclusive cripple who is their host; he hopes, 'as authors will', that he can persuade readers to share his solicitude for the 'quiet creatures' and 'gentle spirits' in the chimney corner. Then in a sudden reversal he demolishes the illusion. 'Like one whose vision is disordered', he concedes that he is 'conjuring up bright figures when there is nothing but empty space'.

On stage, that sadly empty space is filled by actors. A fatuous viscount in *Martin Chuzzlewit* confirms this even while he denigrates Shakespeare's characters for literally falling short. Juliet, Desdemona and Lady Macbeth, this opinionated ninny says, 'might as well have no legs at all, for anything the audience know about it'; invoking the armless and legless painter who was so often unkindly cited by Dickens, he says that 'they're all Miss Biffins'. The rakes in the theatre's pit only want to ogle bare flesh, so the viscount calls for an impresario to commission 'plenty of leg pieces'. What, he asks in a dialogue with himself, is 'the legitimate object of the drama'? 'Human nature,' he replies. 'What are legs? Human nature.' He ought to be at a Paris cabaret enjoying the can-can, but there is a wacky logic to his complaint. Shakespeare's speeches supply his people with minds, leaving actors to lend them faces, voices and limbs; for Dickens it was always the body that vouched for a character's true identity.

Making those characters manifest was an eerie process. In his readings, Dickens said he was 'an interpreter of myself'. Although he simply meant that he was acting from his own scripts, the people he portrayed did originate within him. Charles Kent, invited in 1868 to a 'private trial' of some passages from *Oliver Twist* that Dickens was adding to his repertory, watched aghast as Fagin materialised before him. Dickens's chest contracted and his shoulders jerked upwards to make him look like a hungry vulture, his hands became claws, and his 'penthouse eyebrows' were 'the antennae of some deadly reptile'. This grizzled predator, Kent said, was 'the very devil incarnate' – literally incarnate, embodied by Dickens. The connection was all the closer because Fagin is an actor-manager, which Dickens himself wanted to be: before sending Noah Claypole out on a reconnaissance mission he costumes him as a bucolic stranger to the city, and when despatching Nancy to the police station to ask about Oliver he dresses her demurely in a white apron and a straw bonnet from his 'inexhaustible stock'.

Beguiled as Dickens was by the theatre, he also acknowledged its limitations. The enchantment it purveys is intense but ephemeral, as the wide-eyed Kit belatedly realises in *The Old Curiosity Shop* after an outing to Astley's, an amphitheatre like a circus ring that was situated just south of Westminster Bridge. Kit's little brother applauds the show 'till his hands were sore', and a family friend gives vent to her 'ecstasies' by thumping her umbrella on the floor. Dickens joins in with a flurry of exclamations. 'Dear, dear, what a place it looked, that Astley's!' he says. 'Then the play itself!' he continues, enthusing over the clowns, the gymnasts, the dancing chorus and the grimacing villain. But next day Kit wakes up in a drearier reality, aware that 'the inconstant actors in that dazzling vision' will go on reeling through their routines, 'though he would not be there'. Jaques in *As You Like It* calls the world a stage on which we spend seven ages between our first entrance and our final exit. Dickens has his version of the analogy, drastically compressed in time. 'Such is the difference between yesterday and today,' he comments as Kit's rapture fades. 'We are all going to the play, or coming home from it.'

Jaques in his speech about the seven ages says that 'one man in his time plays many parts'. As he sees it, we do so sequentially, advancing or declining from schoolboy to dotard; Dickens's characters are nimbler, not limited to a single self. In *Great Expectations* the church clerk Wopsle acts several parts simultaneously. With a gift for 'pointed imitation', he recites a newspaper report on a murder trial and, like Dickens performing the showdown between Sikes and Nancy, bellows when playing the killer and moans as the victim. In addition he assumes the identity of every witness at the inquest, delivering the coroner's testimony in a voice that suits Timon of Athens and basing the beadle on Coriolanus. He later decides against taking holy orders and instead ventures onstage under the name of Waldengarver. Pip goes to see his Hamlet, but mocks his implausibly curly wig, the pallid legs exposed by his tights, and the way he fussily cleans his fingers with a handkerchief after handling Yorick's skull: the novelist's eye for detail sees through the attitudinising on which the theatre relies. The same contradiction appears in *A Child's History*, where Dickens amplifies an episode from Shakespeare's *Richard III*. As in the play, the king and Buckingham lay a trap for Hastings, pretend to be outraged by his treachery, order his immediate execution, and then spend the evening 'talking over the play they had just acted'. But after the verdict Dickens suddenly moves offstage into the open air. Hastings, he says, is led 'to the green by the Tower chapel' and 'beheaded on a log of wood that happened to be lying on the ground'. The indignity of the log, the casual convenience of its lying there – these details, beneath the attention of drama, give the little scene a raw novelistic truth.

At the end of *The Tempest* Prospero recalls dimming the sun at noon, shaking promontories and raising the dead from their graves with his 'so potent art'. That boast stuck in Dickens's mind. At the pantomime in his essay 'Gaslight Fairies', he smiles indulgently at the theatre's manufactured marvels and is confident that the technicians will have 'so completely settled their so-potent art' that he will not be disappointed by the illusions they devise. He does some quiet boasting of his own in *Little Dorrit*, where he scans the imperial outposts to which the members of the Barnacle clan have fanned out in quest of profit and says that even 'the so-potent art of Prospero himself' could not have summoned them all home to London for a conclave. The novel, however, is not hemmed in by the unities of classical drama, and a goodly number of Barnacles do return for

Fanny Dorrit's marriage to Sparkler. Whose art, in this case, is the more potent?

Prospero's spectacles are stage-managed by his wispy familiar Ariel, who reports that during the tempest he 'flamed amazement' as he darted all over the foundering ship from the cabins below deck to the rigged masts, invisibly multiplying himself to 'burn in many places'. Dickens often set his characters to match Ariel's polymorphous feats, which they do in full view. In *Oliver Twist* the fugitive Sikes dives in and out of a fire, 'now working at the pumps, and now hurrying through the smoke and flame', clambering 'up and down the ladders, upon the roofs of buildings, over floors that trembled with his weight'. Likewise the 'wayward and capricious' Barnaby Rudge, with the raven Grip as his familiar, 'fluttered here and there', calling 'from the topmost branch of some high tree' and using his tall staff to vault 'over ditch or hedge or five-barred gate'. Ariel's athletics recur in *The Chimes*, where the spiders in the belfry cling to 'thread-spun castles in the air' as they 'climb up sailor-like in quick alarm, or drop upon the ground and ply a score of nimble legs'.

Dickens himself was less agile, at least physically. Re-enacting *The Tempest* on the cliffs at Tintagel during a Cornish holiday in 1843, he cast himself as the earthy gnome who is enslaved by Prospero. 'I grovelled and clung to the soil like a Caliban,' he told Forster, while 'you, in the manner of a tricksy spirit and stout Ariel, actually danced up and down before me!' Grovelling did not come naturally to Dickens, and Forster was too plump to be convincingly aerodynamic: each was playing against type, and they both knew which role belonged by right to Dickens. Prospero employs his potent art to punish his enemies, then breaks the staff that serves as his wand and lapses into elderly, penitent impotence. 'This rough magic I here abjure,' he announces as he leaves the island. Dickens eventually uttered his own equivalent of Prospero's downcast farewell, and in a speech at the end of his final public reading in March 1870 he said 'from these garish lights I vanish now for evermore'. But just before vanishing, he reminded the public that he would soon reappear, though not in person, as the first instalment of *The Mystery of Edwin Drood* was about to be published. Unlike Prospero, Dickens never renounced the potency of his verbal spells.

———

Dickens treated Shakespeare with due deference and in 1837 said that he followed him 'at the scarcely-worth-mentioning little distance of a few millions of leagues behind'. He was of course much closer, and keen to catch up or even to dodge ahead. Setting fulsome humility aside, he jostled and even gently mocked the writer whom he viewed – although he was careful not to openly say so – as his only rival.

In 1853 in Paris he saw Ambroise Thomas's opera *Le Songe d'une nuit d'été*, in which Shakespeare, discovered drunk in a tavern, is abducted by order of Elizabeth I; as entranced as Bottom when he spends the night with Titania, the befuddled poet imagines that the monarch is in love with him. Dickens told Forster that the opera was 'nonsense', though he enjoyed hearing the French singers take Shakespeare's name in vain by calling him Willy Am Shay Kes Peer. Encouraged by Dickens, characters in his novels treat Shakespeare with irreverent informality. A drawling aristocrat in *Dombey and Son* salutes 'my friend Shakespeare – man who wasn't for an age but for all time': co-opting Ben Jonson's accolade, he welcomes a mere player into his exclusive class or club. In *Nicholas Nickleby* a self-styled literary gentleman refashions novels for the stage without obtaining the permission of their authors, and when challenged he shrugs that Shakespeare also purloined his plots. 'Bill was an adapter,' he says, adding that 'very well he adapted too – considering.' The ultimate blasphemy is attributed to the air-headed Dora in *David Copperfield*. David reads Shakespeare to her in the hope of enlarging her mind, but the recitations bore her and he suspects that 'she thought Shakespeare a terrible fellow'.

Dickens said that he 'dwelt upon the romantic side of familiar things'; he familiarised romantic things as well, and in doing so he tethered Shakespeare and his characters in contemporary reality. For the title page of his magazine *Household Words* he took a phrase from

Henry V, in which the king predicts that the heroes of Agincourt will become household names. Removed from its context, the epigraph Dickens chose, 'Familiar in his mouth as household words', did not point to tales of military valour; instead it promised that the magazine would cover family matters, of interest to readers in their homes. Needing a Shakespearean tag to christen another periodical in 1859, Dickens remembered Othello telling Desdemona 'the story of my life, / From year to year' and chose to call this new magazine *All the Year Round*, adapting the quotation on the title page to read 'The story of our lives, from year to year'. Othello glorifies himself in his digest of sieges, tense escapes and encounters with cannibals. Dickens opened the phrase out into a statement of his editorial mission: journalism is a synonym for daily life, and he intended to produce a communal diary.

Elsewhere Dickens dealt harshly with Othello's conceited nobility, familiarising him with a vengeance. He first domesticated the tragic hero, then brutally degraded him. In *Sketches by Boz*, the rehearsals for an amateur performance of *Othello* at a house in Clapham cause distress to the furniture: the suburban Moor smothers his Desdemona so energetically that several sofas – genteel substitutes for the marital bed – suffer damage. The scene is restaged without theatrical feigning when Sikes kills Nancy in *Oliver Twist*. Like Desdemona protesting her innocence, Nancy claims to have been true to her abusive pimp and even produces the handkerchief given to her as a token of friendship by Rose Maylie; this is her equivalent to the keepsake that Othello accuses her of passing on to Cassio, and she holds it up as she gasps out a prayer for mercy. Othello insists that his murder is a judicial reckoning and wants to execute Desdemona without shedding her blood, which is why he chooses to smother her. Sikes, less decorous, opens a gash on Nancy's head with his pistol, fells her with a club, and after battering her to death has to cut out the blood-spattered sections of his clothes before he leaves the room.

Allusions to Shakespeare casually slide into Dickens's essays, where the poetry he quotes makes itself at home in his prose. On his visit to a paper mill in Kent he surveys the surrounding landscape and says that there are indeed 'books in the running brooks' – a quotation from *As You Like It*, where the exiled courtiers absorb a pantheistic wisdom from the forest of Arden by harkening to sermons in stones and making brooks their substitute for books. Dickens finds a practical veracity in this play on words: the Kentish streams feed the mill and contribute to its output of paper. Inside, as he watches the pulp being mashed, he hears the grinding mechanism grunt '"Munch, munch, munch!" like the sailor's wife in *Macbeth*, who had chestnuts in her lap'. No witch tries to snatch the treat; the greedy machinery does its mastication unimpeded. With less of an appetite, the Uncommercial Traveller and his companion Bullfinch sample a selection of Shakespeare's plays during a dyspeptic dinner in a seaside town. As they peruse the restaurant menu, Bullfinch begins 'to babble of green geese', which are young birds served without stuffing, more succulent than the green fields about which the dying Falstaff babbles in *Henry V*. Then a waiter confiscates their loaf of bread and disappears with it '"out at the portal," like the ghost in *Hamlet*', though he lacks the excuse of having to return to purgatory when the cock crows. Richard III also haunts the premises. Before his showdown with Richmond, Shakespeare's king nonchalantly treats this decisive battle as a throw of the dice: 'I have set my life upon a cast, / And I will stand the hazard of the die.' The Traveller frets about the fare, but he and his friend are too hungry to look elsewhere. 'We had set our own stomachs on a cast,' he says, 'and they must stand the hazard of the die.' Luckily they risk indigestion not death.

To assume the identity of a character from the plays is a more fraught undertaking – an impersonation but also a self-revelation. Rugged up to sail across the Channel, the Uncommercial Traveller worries when dogs in Dover mistake him for Shakespeare's crookback and 'bark at me in my misshapen wrappers, as if I were Richard the Third'. Others, as Dickens knew, were only too eager to play the villain. *Sketches by Boz* investigates the down-at-heels private theatres where untalented amateurs paid for a chance to perform. The playhouse visited by Boz is presenting *Richard III*, in which all the parts are separately priced: it costs £2 to be Richard for the evening, half that to be Richmond (though he prevails in the battle and wins the crown), and the regalia of the Lord Mayor of London is available to wear for two shillings and sixpence. Boz explains the premium for playing Richard by pointing out that he stabs Henry VI, woos Lady Anne over the corpse of her husband whom he has murdered, and sentences to death anyone who displeases him. Given all these opportunities to strut, shout and brandish a sword, releasing energies and desires that we usually repress, the fee seems cheap.

Crummles in *Nicholas Nickleby* recalls a 'first-tragedy man' who blacked up all over to play Othello: 'that's feeling a part and going into it as if you meant it,' he says, and he adds, perhaps with relief, 'it isn't usual'. Irony apart, Dickens knew how this emotional identification felt. In 1844, describing the dream in which he was visited by a Madonna, he marvelled that 'throughout I was as real, animated, and full of passion as Macready (God bless him!) in the last scene of *Macbeth*'. His friend William Macready was an acclaimed Shakespearean actor, and Dickens again referred to his Macbeth in another letter to Forster in 1856. By then Macready had retired; Dickens had no intention of doing the same, as he attested by remembering the bravado with which Macready used to deliver a line from the play's embattled climax. 'I must, please God, die in harness,' he told Forster – an impromptu paraphrase of Macbeth's fatalistic vow as he buckles on his armour to fight Macduff, and a promise that Dickens kept in his final years of over-exertion. In 1867 Macready repaid Dickens's compliments after seeing him perform the murder from *Oliver Twist*, which he said was the equivalent of 'Two Macbeths!' The strain was indeed doubled because Dickens played both the raving killer and his piteous victim; he did so offstage as well, and in letters he alternated between the opposed personae. Once with case-hardened gruffness he referred to 'a certain Murder that I had to do last night', while on another occasion he simpered sacrificially and explained that he was 'at present nightly murdered by Mr W. Sikes'.

This jocular tone made the duet even more inflammatory. A particularly over-heated performance left him '(like many of my fellow-criminals) in a highly edifying state': was he hinting at sexual arousal? Anticipating such self-betrayals, Forster considered the murder scene to be 'altogether out of the province of reading', inadvisable both morally and medically. But that was why Dickens went ahead: the theatre released him into a more uninhibited, irregular and almost certainly abbreviated life.

In *Nicholas Nickleby*, Mr Curdle, lamenting the decline of the drama when Crummles brings his troupe to town, sighs 'Hamlet! Pooh! ridiculous! Hamlet is gone, perfectly gone!' Not so for Dickens: he brought the character back, usually in the company of his parents, and adopted him as another alter ego. After Wopsle's woeful debut as Hamlet, Pip dreams that he has been thrust onstage to play the role himself 'before twenty thousand people, without knowing twenty words of it'. But he does not need to memorise the lines because he is re-enacting the play as his private psychodrama, with Magwitch cast as the ghost.

Dickens had little sympathy with the soulful meditations that endeared Hamlet to Goethe and Coleridge. When the impoverished Micawber quotes 'the philosophic Dane', he reframes the dilemma posed by Hamlet's thoughts about suicide: he vacillates 'between stipend and no stipend, baker and no baker, existence and non-existence'. Hamlet's eternity, 'the bourne from which no traveller returns', is relocated nearer to home in *Little Dorrit*, where Clennam remembers that as a boy he was shut in a dark closet when he defied his mother's religious bigotry and disregarded a pamphlet that threatened him with perdition. The cupboard was 'the veritable entrance to that bourne to which the tract had found him galloping'. After Dombey's joyless remarriage, the remnants of the wedding breakfast decay in a parody of Hamlet's wish that his flesh would 'thaw and resolve itself into a dew': in the kitchen, among blocks of 'half-thawed ice', the leftovers include some 'pensive jellies, gradually resolving themselves into a lukewarm gummy soup'.

Making light of Hamlet's world-weariness, Dickens concentrated on the snarled conflicts within the Danish royal family, which gave him a pretext for voicing his grudge against his own unfit parents. When Dickens's brother Alfred died, his mother demanded with 'ghastly absurdity' to be dressed in sables 'like a female Hamlet'. Disgusted by her over-acting, he could not forgive her for 'the strife she gets up in my uneasy mind', which turned him into Hamlet sickened by the behaviour of Gertrude. Nicholas Nickleby is embarrassed to find his widowed mother welcoming the advances of the madman next door. Her mourning dress takes on 'a deadly-lively air', and rather than honouring her dead husband the costume has 'slaughterous and killing designs upon the living'. Flirtily advertising her availability, she is more lethal than Gertrude.

The ghost of Hamlet's father prowls through the novels, recast as a villain because he stands in for Dickens's incorrigible father. Ignoring the ghost's purgatorial suffering, Dickens emphasises his baleful effect on his terrified son. In the play, he threatens to tell Hamlet a tale that would make every hair on his head bristle like the quills of a porcupine. Dickens takes this as a challenge and sets about actualising the verbal conceit. During a marital intrigue, Septimus Hicks in *Sketches by Boz* gasps with a horror that outdoes 'Hamlet's, when he sees his father's ghost', and his hair stands on end as if erected by 'an electrifying machine'. For Pancks, the clerk in *Little Dorrit*, those wiry upright locks are not a symptom of fright but a fussily arranged hairdo: listening to Clennam fret about his investments, he tugs the looped and hooked follicles on his head into prongs until he looks 'like a journeyman Hamlet in conversation with his father's spirit'. The jokes are more worrying in *A Christmas Carol*. Before introducing the ghost of Marley, Dickens verifies the old miser's death by consulting the registrar's notice of his burial. He explains that unless we know that Hamlet's father is deceased then the play would begin with the unremarkable sight of a 'middle-aged gentleman rashly turning out after dark' for a stroll 'in a breezy spot', after which he repeats his revisionist opinion about the ghost's purpose: whether the stalking occurs in St Paul's churchyard or on the battlements at Elsinore, the aim of the noctambulant father is 'literally to astonish his son's weak mind'. A first draft of the story went further. 'Perhaps you think

Hamlet's intellects were strong,' says the narrator. 'I doubt it. If you could have such a son tomorrow . . . you would find him a poser' – a problem child, who might be 'creditable . . . to his family' but 'would prove a special incumbrance in his lifetime'. This moment of self-pity, later deleted, is Dickens's most autobiographical comment on *Hamlet*, again diagnosing the damaged son as a victim.

Another phrase of Hamlet's lodged in Dickens's memory. When he admonishes Gertrude by contrasting the portraits of his father and his uncle, he calls the images the 'counterfeit presentment' of the two brothers. In *The Uncommercial Traveller* a widowed mother welcomes her son back to England by pressing him to her bosom; his nose grazes an oval miniature which is 'the counterfeit presentment of his other parent', but at such close quarters the young man, an 'Embodied Failure', is at least spared from having to look his dead father in the eye. In 1856 Dickens used the same phrase when John Edwin Mayall asked him to sit for a daguerreotype. He first replied that he was too busy and had 'a disinclination to multiply my "counterfeit presentments"'. Perhaps he flinched from a family resemblance that he saw in images of his middle-aged face; then, accepting his genetic fate, he consented.

In his appreciation of 'good murderous melodramas' in *Oliver Twist*, Dickens paraphrases Hamlet's disdainful remark about the baked meats from his father's funeral being served up again at his mother's marriage feast. Life, Dickens says, is always shuttling back and forth 'from well-spread boards to death-beds, and from mourning-weeds to holiday garments'. But the passage between tragedy and comedy happens faster in Dickens's novels than in *Hamlet*, and sometimes the two overlap: Traddles in *David Copperfield* expects his wedding to be 'much more like a funeral' because his bride's family can't forgive him for taking her away, and as soon as Edith and Dombey sign the marriage register in the vestry, the church prepares for its next ceremony and 'the sexton tolls a funeral'; there is a ghoul-ish variant when Nicholas Nickleby passes 'a christening party at the largest coffin-maker's' in London. On the riverboat from Pittsburgh to Cincinnati, Dickens remembered *Hamlet* during meals that felt ghoulish. The passengers wolfed their food in unsociable silence like 'melancholy ghosts'; 'a collation of funeral-baked meats', he says in *American Notes*, would have been 'a sparkling festivity' by contrast with these gloomy repasts.

This superimposition of gaiety and grief exactly catches Dickens's outlook on life. Writing to Forster about *Great Expectations*, he referred to the novel's 'grotesque tragic-comic conception', a comment that almost axiomatically fuses tragedy and comedy, with grotesquerie as the outcome of the merger. At Dotheboys Hall in *Nicholas Nickleby*, as Mrs Squeers administers medicine to purge the abused pupils, Dickens points to the 'grotesque features' of the scene – her gigantic wooden spoon, their ill-matched, ill-fitting clothes – and says that 'in a less interested observer than Nicholas' these incongruities 'might have provoked a smile'. Dickens himself is that disinterested observer, and unlike Nicholas he has no compunction about quietly chuckling. When Miss La Creevy is told of Smike's death at the end of the novel, the news provokes more than a smile. She first sobs, then tries to laugh off her distress: 'The laugh and the cry, meeting each other thus abruptly, had a struggle for the mastery', which leads to a hysterical fit.

In *The Stones of Venice* Ruskin defined 'the Symbolical Grotesque' as a kind of allegory and condescendingly called its distortions 'picture writings for children who live in the nursery of Time and Space'. The imperfect human mind, Ruskin argued, is confused by 'the presence of truths which it cannot wholly grasp', and these have to be shown to us in 'a diminishing glass, and that a broken one'. Ruskin's examples come from the torments of Dante's inferno or the apocalyptic upheavals of Michelangelo's Sistine Chapel. He commends the grotesquerie of Shakespeare, presumably thinking of Lear crowned with weeds and Hamlet jesting with a skull, but he does not mention Dickens, who in his opinion had no grasp of this eschatological realm: his Christmases, Ruskin said elsewhere, were all about puddings, with no thought given to 'resurrection from the dead, nor rising of new stars'. Dickens's mind, however, was not so mundane. Resurrection fascinated him, and on his early trips to the theatre in Chatham he was initiated into 'many wondrous secrets of Nature', one of which had to do with reincarnation. In *Macbeth* he noticed that 'the good King Duncan couldn't rest in his grave, but was constantly coming out of it and calling himself somebody else' – a convenience for the under-staffed company in which actors had to play multiple roles but also a parable about minds and bodies, like King Charles's migration into the head of Mr Dick. As for the rising of a new star or planet, that was how Dickens signalled his own advent in his birthday letter, though for him stars were also liable to plummet down from the sky in a sudden apocalypse, as they do when Eugene in *Our Mutual Friend* is banged on the head when gazing at the galaxy. Tragicomedy supplied the grotesquely refracted medium through which Dickens viewed the terrifying, cruelly funny world he created.

Professionally Dickens took the magus Prospero as his model, and in private he saw himself as Hamlet the injured, resentful son. But his most intimate affinity was with Macbeth, the murderer whose 'face . . . is as a book where men / May read strange matters', and his quotations from the play form a running commentary on his motives as a creator.

When it suited him, Dickens treated *Macbeth* with demotic disrespect. Mr Lillyvick, the collector of water rates in *Nicholas Nickleby*, is henpecked by the bossy actress he unwisely marries. 'The plug of life is dry, Sir,' he moans when regretting the match, 'and but the mud is left.' When Macbeth says 'The wine of life is drawn, and the mere lees is left', his formulaic metaphor merely pretends to mourn Duncan's death; Lillyvick's image derives from his occupation, and it makes his despair palpable by ending in drought and mud. In *Dombey and Son*, Miss Tox's neighbours in a shabby mews follow Macbeth's instruction to hang his banners on the castle walls. The battle-flags, however, are replaced by 'the most domestic and confidential garments of coachmen and their wives and families' – an unheraldic and possibly improper display. But such jokes cannot keep the play's morbidity from seeping into ordinary life. Macbeth deflects his wife's curiosity about his plan to kill Banquo by elliptically commenting that 'the crow makes wing to the rooky wood' at dusk. The birds that thicken the twilight are his condensing thoughts, and they reappear in *Edwin Drood*. There the rooks are said to be 'sedate and clerical' because of their black plumage, and as they wing their way 'homeward towards nightfall' they merge with 'divers venerable persons' of rook-like aspect who leave the cathedral after the evening service. One of these avian churchmen is the murderer John Jasper, who with the Dean forms part of an 'artful couple', separated from the flock by a matter 'of some occult importance to the body politic'. The slightest allusion to *Macbeth* carries a taint of complicity, or at least of an internal embarrassment. Macbeth's throttled 'Amen' when he overhears the prayers of Duncan's guards chokes the plumbing in the Inner Temple where, as the Uncommercial Traveller says, 'all the water-pipes . . . seemed to have Macbeth's Amen sticking in their throats'.

The play's supernatural agents pervade society rather than remaining in their own realm. The soothsayers who accost Macbeth acquire professional credentials in *The Battle of Life*, where the lawyers Snitchey and Craggs, teaming up with Doctor Jeddler, resemble 'the three weird prophets on the heath'. Another trio of 'obscene demons' – a charwoman, a laundress and the undertaker's man – help themselves to the dead Scrooge's bed linen and domestic chattels in *A Christmas Carol*. The Uncommercial Traveller comes across 'three weird old women of transcendent ghastliness' cackling as they sew money-bags in a filthy Liverpool slum, and during his visit to a Wapping workhouse he finds that the murky atmosphere in which Macbeth encounters the witches on 'so fair and foul a day' has penetrated indoors. The sick inmates in 'the Foul wards' look inert, even lifeless; then one of them rallies as the Traveller speaks to her, making 'the Foul ward as various as the fair world'. Fair and foul change places or merge, like the opposed moods of Dickens's tragicomic temperament.

At their most suggestive, these citations from *Macbeth* hint at psychological disturbance. Before a fight at school with a young butcher, David Copperfield compares his opponent to the apparition of an armed head that Macbeth sees in the witches' cavern. The butcher concusses David and leaves him feeling 'very queer about the head', and he comments wryly on the 'unprotected heads' of the smaller boys whom the butcher punches; a helmet might have helped, but artists do without such defensive cladding. In an address on technology delivered in Birmingham in 1869, Dickens likened the bodiless head in the play to his own self-willed imagination. One of the witches tells Macbeth that the vision is an 'unknown power' which 'knows thy thought' but 'will not be commanded': she has defined the compulsion that Dickens felt within him.

Lady Macbeth takes Dickens deep into the malaise of 'a mind diseased', and in two extracts from her speeches he hints at his attraction to both madness and criminality. On a visit to the insane asylum of St Luke's in Moorfields, he found the patients dancing around a Christmas tree rather than being scourged to drive out their devils. He pictures earlier internees looking down from 'Wherever in your sightless substances / You wait' and wonders what they might make of this therapeutic revelry. The line comes from Lady Macbeth's appeal to the 'spirits that tend on mortal thoughts' who, as she hopes, will steel her for killing: would those 'murdering ministers' relent after seeing modern medicine at work? Dickens leaves us to guess at his own opinion. In another article from *Household Words* he concludes his tour of a thieves' kitchen in London because night is 'almost at odds with morning, which is which'. This is Lady Macbeth's reply when her husband, anxious for the camouflage of darkness, asks 'What is the night?' She sees dawn as a tug of war between concealment and exposure; Dickens regrets the arrival of daylight because the robbers and ruffians have retired to bed, leaving him with nothing more to write about.

Shakespeare allows Macbeth to murder Duncan offstage. Dickens was less discreet, and in thinking his way through the play he imagined himself in Macbeth's place before, during and after the crime. He began with the dagger that Macbeth fancies he sees before him. 'Thou marshall'st me the way that I was going,' Macbeth says, making the implement take the initiative. In an essay on railways Dickens renders the dagger harmless by using the quotation to introduce a pointsman who patrols the tracks, and in *Little Dorrit* it is daintily bestowed on a young turnkey who dresses up to woo Amy, sporting 'a cane like a little finger-post, surmounted by an ivory hand marshalling him the way that he should go'. More pointedly, in his account of a visit to the dungeons in the papal palace at Avignon, Dickens transfers the weapon to a female guide, a swarthy 'She-Goblin' who 'marshalled us the way that we should go'. The quotation implies that he and the other tourists were being somehow conscripted to visit the Inquisition's torture chamber by this familiar whose flashing black eyes, hag-like forefinger and cackling commentary on the torments prescribed by the inquisitors are evidence that 'the world hadn't conjured down the devil within her'. But Dickens hardly needed to be hustled into the subterranean black museum, having paid for the privilege; he excuses his voyeurism by making the martial guide responsible. And in case we should think Macbeth was prodded to kill Duncan against his will or better judgement, Dickens dismisses his prevarications in *Edwin Drood* when he draws attention to the elegant finesse of a waiter who steadies a swing door with his foot as he leaves the dining room while holding a tray. With 'an angling air', the man's lower extremity briefly lingers after his upper half disappears, 'like Macbeth's leg when accompanying him off the stage with reluctance to the assassination of Duncan'. The angling reluctance is a feint: the waiter shows off a tactical skill, as Macbeth does in his canny rationalisations of his crime.

Having thought himself into the room where the regicide happened, Dickens did not hesitate to picture the residue of gore at the crime scene. In the aftermath, Macbeth with squeamish delicacy describes Duncan's 'silver skin laced with his golden blood'. Dickens had no patience with such poetic laundering and in Rome, taken aback by the multitude of early Christian martyrs, he contemplates a 'panorama of horror and butchery no man could imagine in his sleep' and says he feels the same stupefaction that 'poor old Duncan awoke, in Lady Macbeth, when she marvelled at his having so much blood in him'. During the unseen killings in the play, a storm chorally expresses the outrage of the elements, and Lennox speaks of lamentings heard in the air and horses eating each other. The bad weather that batters Cloisterham on the night of Edwin Drood's disappearance is even more madly extreme. In a reversion to primeval chaos, a 'tangible part of the darkness madly whirls about', tears the hands off the clock in the cathedral tower, then abates at dawn 'like a wounded monster dying'. Shakespeare's Lennox says that where he and his companions slept 'our houses were blown down', but the uproar in the novel rattles latches and bangs shutters 'as if warning the people to get up and fly with it, rather than have the roofs brought down upon their brains'. The Dickensian dwellings do not merely succumb to a gale; they threaten to collapse on the brains of those who shelter there – an apt penalty, because it is there that such fears start into life – and the only way to escape the frenzy is by joining forces with it, riding the air as witches do on their broomsticks.

When the regicide is discovered, Macbeth to general consternation admits that he slaughtered Duncan's guards and explains his impulsive act by asking 'Who can be wise, amaz'd, temperate, and furious, / Loyal, and neutral, in a moment?' In *Barnaby Rudge* Dickens transcribes this rhetorical question, which is another of Macbeth's glib evasions, and uses it to define the shrewish temper of Mrs Varden, who 'not only attained a higher pitch of genius than Macbeth, in respect of her ability to be wise, amazed, temperate and furious, loyal and neutral in an instant, but would sometimes ring the changes backwards and forwards on all possible moods and flights in one short quarter of an hour; performing, as it were, a kind of triple bob major on the peal of instruments in the female belfry, with a skilfulness and rapidity of execution that astonished all who heard her'. Macbeth's wife strikes a single note on a bell as his signal to kill Duncan. That act is here prolonged into a showy display of campanology, as if the goblins from *The Chimes* were doubling as bell-ringers. An incisive pun doubles the meaning of execution: in this case a demonstration of virtuosity by musical performers, in other contexts a killing. As so often when Dickens cites Shakespeare, a competitive ambition makes itself felt. The intricate variations that resound in Mrs Varden's mental belfry tune her to a higher, shriller pitch than Macbeth, who only loses self-control when he sees Banquo's ghost. Perhaps most significantly, the mania by which Macbeth claims he was carried away is said to be evidence of his genius, as if one of Dickens's genies had prompted or perhaps inspired him.

Without naming Shakespeare, the Uncommercial Traveller in his essay on night walks calls him 'the great master who knew everything'. After this genuflection, he immediately enunciates something that Shakespeare did not know. The Traveller is passing another asylum in Southwark at the time, which prompts him to suggest that the sane and insane are indistinguishable after dark, because in our dreams we 'jumble events and personages and times and places' and perform in sensational dramas with kings and queens as our accomplices. Thinking of Macbeth's insomnia, the Traveller finds it odd that Shakespeare, who 'called Sleep the death of each day's life, did not call Dreams the insanity of each day's sanity'. Only Dickens could have answered Shakespeare back in this way, and in rewriting Macbeth's line he issued a manifesto for his own traumatic art.

14

In the Crypt

*O*ur *Mutual Friend* concludes with a 'Postscript, In Lieu of Preface' in which Dickens remembers his experience on the train that derailed on the Stapleton viaduct in June 1865. Merging fiction and reality as he habitually did, he claims that Mr and Mrs Boffin were travelling with him and says that he climbed back into the toppled carriage to extricate them; it was the manuscript of the latest instalment he salvaged, but for Dickens and his readers that too was a matter of life and death. He ascertains that the Boffins are 'soiled, but otherwise unhurt', and is pleased to report on the survival of other characters who were not on the train that day. This is the same protective concern he voices in the coda to *The Pickwick Papers*, where he vows that 'nothing but death will terminate' the fond attachment of Pickwick and Sam Weller. But in *Our Mutual Friend* that confidence becomes more tenuous and more plaintively personal, because the 'terribly destructive accident' at Stapleton threatened another attachment. In the novel's last words, Dickens recognises that he would 'never be much nearer parting company with my readers for ever, than I was then, until there shall be written against my life, the two words with which I have this day closed this book: – THE END'. He appends the date – September 2nd, 1865 – as if imprinting it on his own tombstone, and for four years it did seem as if he had broken off his novel-writing career at that precise moment. 'The closed book', as he puts it in *The Haunted House*, was synonymous with 'the stopped life'.

Then in 1869 Dickens began *The Mystery of Edwin Drood*, which after such a long hiatus reads like an almost posthumous self-appraisal.

He called his novels 'confidential Interviews with myself', and this last work is the most cunning and yet the most candid of these inquisitions. It remained incomplete at his death in 1870, so the mystery of Edwin Drood's disappearance is left unexplained, but the solution would probably not have been a surprise. All indications suggest that Edwin's uncle John Jasper murders him in a fit of sexual jealousy and stows his body in a lime pit in the crypt of the cathedral at Cloisterham, where he conducts the choir. Dickens told Forster that the conclusion was 'to be written in the condemned cell' – a recurring location, previously visited in *Sketches by Boz* during a tour of Newgate, in *Oliver Twist* when Oliver is taken to see Fagin on the night before he is hanged, in *Barnaby Rudge* after the rioters are sentenced, and in *Master Humphrey's Clock* in the course of a story about a child-killer. But written by whom? In effect by Dickens himself, with Jasper as his chosen decoy. The novel is a whodunit in which the novelist is the one who did it.

George Gissing, in a study of Dickens published in 1898, regretted that he had demeaned himself by writing about 'a vulgar deed of blood' that leads to 'a trivial mystery'; Gissing blamed this on the degradation induced by 'his rendering (acting, indeed) of the death of Nancy in *Oliver Twist*'. For Dickens, however, killing was primarily an imaginative scenario, not necessarily requiring bloodshed. 'You have a strong fancy,' says the blind man Stagg when Barnaby Rudge's father describes a vision in which he sees himself committing murder. 'Fancy!' the father exclaims. 'Are you real? Am I?' In *Edwin Drood* we don't see the murder happen and a body is never produced; what we are reading about is Dickens's examination of his own mental workings. He owned the characters he created, fussing over them like Jasper who, Edwin says, would notice 'if I were to make an extra crease in my neckcloth'; he could also coolly eliminate them as Jasper seems intent on doing when he stares at Neville Landless 'as though his eye were at the trigger of a loaded rifle'. In a memorandum scribbled while he was at work on *Bleak House*, Dickens asked himself a question and answered it in short order: 'Jo? Yes. Kill him.' Then, having done so, he went on to grieve over the boy and accuse society of being responsible for the death that he had personally decreed.

Jasper twice studies Edwin as he lies vulnerably asleep, like a character waiting to be created or perhaps to be destroyed. That point of vantage suits Dickens as he toys with his own power: the narrator of *The Haunted House*, an early riser, likes to think of others still in bed, becalmed in a state that is 'anticipative of that mysterious condition to which we are all tending'. Toasting Edwin with drugged wine, Jasper both salutes the young man's freedom and curtails it. 'The world is all before him where to choose,' he says, giving an optimistic inflection to the dejected conclusion of *Paradise Lost*, in which Adam and Eve are left to select the path they will take outside Eden. Jasper adds a synopsis of the future that Edwin – an engineer who intends to take his skills abroad as well as marrying Rosa Bud – expects will be his: he can look forward to 'a life of stirring work and interest, a life of change and excitement, a life of domestic ease and love!' That professionally busy, connubially gratified life is unavailable to Jasper, who complains of being trapped in his 'daily drudging round', and his salute might be the recrimination of an ageing novelist, no longer content to devise adventures and ensure happy endings for characters who will outlive him. He also tellingly cuts short his allusion to Milton: Adam and Eve have been expelled from the garden, so in choosing a place of rest they, like the sleepers in *The Haunted House*, are advancing towards death.

Informed by Grewgious that Edwin before disappearing had quietly broken off his engagement to Rosa, Jasper seems to realise that he has committed murder unnecessarily. He clasps his head, tears at his hair, shrieks and collapses: like Krook dissolving into ash and putrid gas, he is 'nothing but a heap of torn and miry clothes upon the floor', and Grewgious looks down at 'it', a dishevelled bundle that no longer contains a person. After Dickens suffered his stroke at Gad's Hill in June 1870 his own last words were 'On the ground', which is where his family placed him. But Jasper recovers from his swoon, apologises for being a nuisance and eats a hearty meal, while Grewgious – expressing no opinion of what he has seen, in a reaction that is said to be 'highly mystifying' – keeps him under observation. Speculating about the collusion between crime and art but supplying no solution to its puzzle, *The Mystery of Edwin Drood* is an exercise in mystification.

The mystery has its source inside the head, as evidence of a 'wonderful fact' to which Dickens draws attention at the start of *A Tale of Two Cities*. 'Every human creature,' he remarks as he introduces three passengers cooped up in a mail coach, 'is constituted to be that profound secret and mystery to every other' – except, that is, if the other happens to be a novelist, able to pry into thoughts and feelings that we shield from view.

The first paragraph of *Edwin Drood* probes that debarred terrain. It transcribes a disorienting vision without identifying the visionary, and even before going into detail it questions its own veracity. 'An ancient English Cathedral Tower? How can the ancient English Cathedral tower be there! The well-known massive grey square tower of its old Cathedral? How can that be here!' Those opening sentences are meant to bewilder us, although eventually we are given a reason for the incredulous exclamations: the well-known English cathedral town has been somehow uprooted and transposed to the Orient, because the scene contains an iron spike 'set up by the Sultan's orders for the impaling of a horde of Turkish robbers'. Without explaining that intrusion, Dickens allows the place to be taken over by an exotic parade from his beloved *Arabian Nights*, with ten thousand flashing scimitars, thirty thousand dancing girls and an uncountable number of white elephants. But this infidel procession does not dislodge the cathedral, which remains 'where it cannot be'; with the same vexing illogic, there is 'no writhing figure . . . on the grim spike'. Next, in another metamorphosis, the metal instrument of torture dwindles into something harmlessly domestic, 'the rusty spike on the top of a post of an old bedstead that has tumbled all awry'. Without resolving the contradictions between west and east or sanctity and perversity,

Dickens finally calls for 'some vague period of drowsy laughter' as if inviting us to enjoy our mystification: he might be taking a bow after his performance as Rhia Rhama Rhoos.

The hallucination about the cathedral is at last attributed to someone 'whose scattered consciousness has thus fantastically pieced itself together'; we are then allowed to see that the scrambled mind belongs to a figure lying on a filthy bed in an opium den. So far no more than a mess of delusions and cravings, the unidentified being attacks another addict, overcome by an 'unclean spirit of imitation': inside this kaleidoscope of molten images, is mimesis somehow dirty because it matches reality rather than metaphorically remixing it, as Dickens preferred? After a lapse in time, the cathedral reappears 'before the sight of a jaded traveller', having now rid itself of the Sultan's hordes and resumed its Anglican routine. The man on the bed, who has metamorphosed into that jaded traveller, dons the disguise of a surplice and bustles into evensong. At last, when someone refers to him by name, we gather that he is the choirmaster Jasper.

The consciousness that hurriedly pieces itself together is soon scattered again, and it stays that way. Jasper vacillates between heaven and hell: Edwin Drood calls his choir 'celestial', but to Jasper its music sounds 'quite devilish'. The art he practises in the cathedral is about unison, and its 'melodious power' brings him into 'mechanical harmony' with those he conducts, yet the deranging ecstasy induced by the drug dooms him to be 'in moral accordance or interchange with nothing around him'. The old woman who prepares the dose of opium for Jasper refers to him as 'a sweet singer', although his lyrical rhapsodies are not offered up in communal praise as hymns: she remembers him singing himself to sleep like a bird as he puffed the pipe. Watching her succumb to a stupor of her own, Jasper is aesthetically scornful. 'What visions can *she* have?' he asks, assuming that she sees only 'butchers' shops, and public-houses', not cathedrals, elephants and temple dancers. Her opium dream at its most extravagant would probably be of 'much credit' – suitable at best for Micawber or for Dickens's improvident father, and appropriate as well for a novel like George Eliot's *Middlemarch*, which as Henry James said was 'a tragedy based on unpaid butchers' bills'. Jasper's own mental scenography is more poetically refined and sensually liberated. The orgy he imagines could have come from the *Symphonie fantastique* of Berlioz, where the orchestra invisibly illustrates the feverish transports of an artist who, as Jasper says of himself, is 'brain-oppressed' and doses himself with opium to soothe his erotic despair. The symphony's protagonist dizzily gyrates at a ball, unable to fasten on to the woman he desires; frustration leads to a scene of mayhem at a Witches' Sabbath, and there is even a self-condemning March to the Scaffold.

At home in Cloisterham, Jasper lights his pipe again, 'delivers himself to the Spectres it invokes at midnight', and when roused cries 'Who did it?' Although the murder has not yet been committed, it has happened already inside his shuttered head; he is still in 'a delirious state between sleeping and waking', the mental zone where Dickens did his imagining. Comments like this pass on to Jasper the duality that Dickens detected in his own brain in his essay on insomnia in *Household Words*. Deepening that division, in his final years Dickens had taken to living dualistically. Like Jasper moving between Cloisterham and the East End, he was officially resident at Gad's Hill but commuted from there to the obscure addresses in France, Windsor and south London where he kept his mistress Ellen Ternan tucked away, using a pseudonym when he paid her rent. In a milder way he also shared Jasper's addiction. During his second American tour he began dosing himself with laudanum as a painkiller, a sleeping draught, and perhaps as a creative aid. The habit opened wider the disparity between his joviality as a public figure and the private life of the man assailed by what Jasper calls 'a pain – an agony – that sometimes overcomes me'.

At large in the novel, this psychological fragmentation threatens other characters. Grewgious defends himself against it. He is a bachelor, singular and therefore indivisible; being in love, he reasons, must mean that you merge with your beloved, 'living at once a doubled life and a halved life'. The contradictory arithmetic makes him glad to be only an I or a one. Dickens also bifurcates the harmless Miss Twinkleton, who has 'two distinct and separate phases of being'.

Starchy and prudish during school hours, she becomes sprightlier in the evening, partial to gossip and to amorous fancies. Her duality is likened to 'some cases of drunkenness' and 'others of animal magnetism', although no one could be less like a drunkard than Miss Twinkleton, and it was Dickens himself who employed Mesmer's technique when treating Augusta de la Rue. Here Jasper surreptitiously magnetises Edwin's fiancée Rosa Bud during her music lessons, but with no thought of seeking a cure. He is infatuated with the young woman, who recoils from 'his ghostly following of her' and feels that even 'the solid walls of the old convent' where she lives are no protection. The pursuit is ghostly because the enchanter projects his will into the mind of his prey. Accompanying Rosa at the piano, Jasper elicits the music from inside her in a premonition of the relationship between the mesmerist Svengali and the student he turns into an operatic diva in George du Maurier's *Trilby*. 'He followed her lips most attentively, with his eyes as well as hands; carefully and softly hinting the keynote from time to time': eyes do duty for caressing hands, Jasper prompts her by mouthing the sounds she will make in 'a low whisper', and unspoken words invade Rosa's head as she hears him murmur that he desires her. Fighting against this manipulative sorcery, she gives a shriek and stops singing.

As Rosa remembers Jasper's 'self-absorption in his nephew', her odd phrase catches something of Dickens's capacity to inhabit the existence of another person and make it an extension of his own. He admits as much by presenting Jasper as a writer. Chatting in the cathedral close, the Dean remarks that Jasper is 'evidently going to write a book about us'; he assumes it will be an antiquarian study, which prompts Jasper to say that he has 'no intention . . . of turning author or archaeologist'. Cloisterham's pompous mayor is then blamed for any authorial whim Jasper may possess, since it was Sapsea who excited his interest in the alcoholic stonemason Durdles. Proud to be taken for a novelist, Sapsea says 'I regard Durdles as a Character', to which Jasper replies, 'A character, Mr. Sapsea, that with a few skilful touches you turn inside out.' But writers also turn themselves inside out on the page, as Jasper does in a diary which is his outlet for a 'morbid dread

... that I cannot reason with or in any way contend against'. Disrobing after a cathedral service, he hands this journal 'without one spoken word' to Crisparkle, the chosen reader of writing that is supposed to be as inviolably private as George Silverman's desolate memoir. The entry he shows to Crisparkle begins 'My dear boy is murdered', which only Jasper can know for sure, and it concludes with his vow to 'fasten the crime of the murder of my dear dead boy upon the murderer', which he might eventually have done by his confession in the condemned cell. Jasper swears a retributive oath, transcribes it and then, in what might be the angry dialogue of a divided mind, vows to 'devote myself to his destruction'. In 1840, personally unhappy and creatively stalled, Dickens sought Daniel Maclise's opinion about a possible escape from his 'difficulty and darkness'. 'What if I murder myself?' he asked.

Jasper's diary entry is prompted by the discovery of Edwin's watch, fished out of the Cloisterham weir. This leads Dickens to speculate that it was thrown away to prevent identification of his body, which must have been 'artfully disfigured, or concealed, or both': art's purpose is to conceal the truth, as when metaphors disfigure appearances. On Jasper's next visit to the East End, the hag wants him to take the opium 'in a artful form now'. The container in which she artfully mixes the potion is an ink bottle – surely out of place in this dingy, rat-ridden hole, though the container recalls an incriminating pun that we overhear in the nuns' house where Miss Twinkleton educates her young ladies. One of the pupils is in detention for misbehaviour and is suffering, Miss Twinkleton says, under 'an incubus'; this prompts Dickens to comment in an undertone that it ought to be called 'a pen-and-ink-ubus', because her punishment is to write out four of La Fontaine's fables. An incubus is a morally inky male demon, once reputed to impregnate women as they slept. The very word implies sexual possession, because it derives from the Latin verb for lying on something, incubating it like an egg that is being hatched: du Maurier's Trilby feels that the 'dread powerful demon' Svengali 'weighed on her like an incubus', and Miss Twinkleton unknowingly nods at the etymology when she says that her refractory pupil is 'weighed down' by her onerous chore. Dickens's surreptitious pun goes further, associating the incubus with ink, the writer's vital fluid.

Rosa, whose incubus is Jasper, never feels his weight; although she is 'compelled by him', he only once lightly touches her, but his vehemence is visible in his 'working features' and 'convulsive hands', which might be transmitting spells to entrance her. Having begun to suspect him of killing Edwin, she is perturbed by 'her excited memory and imagination' and remains reluctant to articulate 'a fancy that scarcely dared to hint itself'. Here Dickens employs the terms that Coleridge used in *Biographia Literaria* to differentiate between two kinds of creativity – frivolous, artificial Fancy on the one hand, and on the other the more imperative force of Imagination, which fuses opposites like the 'sunny pleasure-dome with caves of ice' in 'Kubla Khan'. Dickens has his own example of Coleridge's 'coadunative' power when the staid cathedral is overrun by 'the changes of colours and the great landscapes and glittering processions' in Jasper's drugged diorama. Rosa, however, is more timid. She feels threatened by her surmises and asks 'Am I so wicked in my thoughts as to conceive a wickedness that others cannot imagine?' Thinking, conceiving, fancying and imagining – these activities, here called wicked, are Dickens's stock in trade. Rosa castigates herself for suspecting Jasper because, as Dickens points out, she knows nothing of 'the criminal intellect', which cannot be reconciled with 'the average intellect of average men' and should be regarded as 'a horrible wonder apart'. Inspector Field, leading Dickens into the thieves' rookery of St Giles's in 1851, makes the same point when he says 'There should be strange dreams here': any crime, no matter how petty, is the acting out of a transgressive fantasy.

Jasper's crime is ultimately an affair of the intellect, and his mind is said to be a wonder. Advancing beyond the timid categories of good and evil, Dickens is marking his own privileged and perilous status as a creator. In *The Strange Case of Dr Jekyll and Mr Hyde*, Stevenson takes a sterner view of such a duality: the respectable Dr Jekyll has 'two natures', one of which is Mr Hyde with his 'greedy gusto' and vicious hedonism, and 'the curse of mankind' is that 'in the

agonised womb of consciousness, these polar twins should be continuously struggling'. This uterine merger is more intimate than Jasper's
'self-absorption' in Edwin. Hyde is said to be 'closer than a wife' to
Jekyll; alternatively they are parent and child, so that 'Jekyll had more
than a father's interest' in his psychic offspring, while Hyde rebels
against the elder who wants to restrain him. According to Jekyll,
Hyde ought to be 'a part instead of a person', and once he escapes
into independence they are both destroyed.

Dickens is more daring: he releases parts of himself from confinement and allows them to do battle. In *Edwin Drood* the stonemason
Durdles happily coexists with the 'hideous small boy' known as
Deputy, who is at once a jeering demon and a censorious hound of
heaven. Durdles pays Deputy to hurl pebbles at him and sing sarcastic
ditties while steering him home on nights when he stumbles through
the town in a drunken haze. Coleridge engaged porters and hackney
coachmen to stop him straying into druggists' shops in quest of laudanum, but Deputy's function is not prevention: he penalises Durdles
after the event, and has no interest in deterring him from future
binges. Further complicating the transaction, the incorrigible Durdles
claims to be Deputy's redeemer. The boy used to be 'a destroyer', a
petty vandal often jailed for his infractions; Durdles has given him
'an enlightened object' by awarding him a halfpenny per pelting.
With 'sodden gravity', he boasts that the arrangement qualifies as an
educational scheme, though he backtracks when Jasper pretends to
be shocked. All the same, Durdles truly is an educator: the last of
Dickens's conductors or psychopomps, he takes Jasper on a nocturnal
tour of the cathedral and inducts him into the mysteries of its crypt.

When Grewgious peeps into the cathedral at dusk, he feels that he is
'looking down the throat of Old Time'. That gullet, damp and sickly,
heaves 'a mouldy sigh' – a subsiding echo of the sound Matthew
Arnold heard in his poem 'Dover Beach' in 1851, where 'the Sea of
Faith' retreats with a 'melancholy, long, withdrawing roar' – and the

distant repetitions of the service are the 'cracked monotonous mutter' of 'a dying voice'. In the 'freer outer air', the landscape basks in a warming sunset, while the cathedral remains dim and sepulchral. Wind expelled by the organ pipes and an outburst from the choir glut the space with a 'sea of music', but the torrent of immaterial sound is deathly: when a single voice tries to resist, 'the sea rose high, and beat its life out, and lashed the roof, and surged among the arches, and pierced the heights of the great tower'. The French impressionists loved to imagine a 'cathédrale engloutie' which, as in Debussy's piano prelude, resonates with chants blurred by water and an organ that exults as the building rises to the surface. Cloisterham, however, is annihilated by a metaphorical deluge, with at least one devotee supposedly drowned. Then as the noise drains away, Dickens cancels this sorcery: 'the sea was dry, and all was still'.

A few days after Dickens's death, Ruskin belittled him in a letter by alluding to Cloisterham and its clerical rooks. Dickens, he said, had 'no understanding of any power of antiquity except a sort of jackdaw sentiment for cathedral towers'. *Edwin Drood*, however, disinters a layered and tragicomically fecund antiquity. In Cloisterham, defunct religion serves as compost, so that salad greens sprout from the remains of abbots, children 'make dirt-pies of nuns and friars', and farmers grind episcopal bones in making bread. Dickens picks his way back through successive occupations by the Romans, Saxons and Normans, and then suggests that the town 'was once possibly known to the Druids by another name'. That drops a clue, calling up scenes Dickens had previously imagined. In *A Child's History of England* he describes the 'strange and terrible' cult of the Druids, enchanters whose priests practised 'mysterious arts' at gatherings 'in dark woods, which they called Sacred Groves'; he adds that these ceremonies included 'the sacrifice of human victims', which might be an echo of Jonas Chuzzlewit going 'down, down, down' into a dell and waiting in its 'innermost recesses' to kill Montague Tigg, among trees that form 'the likeness of an aisle, a cloister, or a ruin open to the sky'. The town's changed name gestures towards Dickens's predilection for onomastic play. Edwin Drood may take his surname from the Druids, making him one of 'the young men who', as the *History* notes, 'came to them as pupils' and identifying him as a victim of their rumoured rites.

Drood also contains rood, an archaic term for Christ's cross. The cruciform layout of Christian churches restages a ritual killing; the religion is a murder story, with its believers as likely victims. At the former convent, unchaste nuns were once 'walled up alive in odd angles and jutting gables', and when Durdles and Jasper are bombarded with pebbles by Deputy and his gang, the incident is facetiously likened to the martyrdom of St Stephen, the patron saint of bricklayers and masons: he was stoned to death after protesting against the crucifixion, so this childish prank mimes a sacrificial slaughter. Jasper, resenting the drudgery of his vocation, sympathises with medieval monks who, as services droned on, amused themselves by 'carving demons out of the stalls and seats and desks' in the cathedral. He has a predecessor in *Dombey and Son*, where Carker looks at his employer with 'the evil slyness of some monkish carving, half human and half brute; or like a leering face on an old water-spout', but Jasper's self-excruciation is crueller: thinking of those effigies, he asks whether he must 'take to carving them out of my heart?' When Notre-Dame catches fire in Victor Hugo's novel, the sculpted monsters on the cathedral's roof sound the alarm. Gargoyles appear to yelp, salamanders puff at the flames, dragons sneeze, and griffins laugh contemptuously at the arsonists. There are no such sentinels at Cloisterham, where hidden devils stage an uprising in the choir stalls.

More than a place of worship, the cathedral is a catacomb of secrets and a portal to the afterlife. Durdles, its 'chartered libertine', knows it best. Remarking on his 'weird life' and 'curious existence', Jasper tells him that 'there is much more mystery and interest in your connection with the Cathedral than in mine'. Tulkinghorn in *Bleak House* is a 'high-priest of noble mysteries', assembling contraband information about his lofty clients; Durdles, who sleeps off his hangovers in the crypt, specialises in mysteries that are more ignoble. He taps his way around the precinct with a hammer to test for the burial places of decaying worthies. As he explains, in his own way he practises an art as arcane as music, communicating with the invisible: Jasper pitches his notes, somehow locating them on staves written in thin air, and the hammer's reverberations tell Durdles whether stone is solid or hollow and can even number the invisible coffins without his needing to see them. Unearthed, the cadavers often bid him welcome because he looks like one of them, 'covered from head to foot with old mortar, lime, and stone-grit'. Even his ailments sound posthumous. The 'dead breath' he inhales in the damp cellarage makes him wheeze, and he suffers from a creaky case of what he calls 'Tombatism'. Holding open the door of the chancel, he seems to have arisen 'as if from the grave', called up by Dickens the necromancer, and he warns Jasper against stumbling into a lime pit, a mound of supposedly carnivorous calcium oxide that 'with a little handy stirring' will quickly consume his boots and his bones.

Jasper, we assume, is researching possible sites for disposing of Edwin's remains, but he is also keen to share the 'strange sights' to which Durdles is privy – visions of putrefaction, unlike the transfiguring mirage of his opium dream. Even before the descent into the crypt, Jasper slides across an existential border, like de Quincey who in his *Confessions of an English Opium-Eater* compares his withdrawal symptoms to 'the torments of a man passing out of one mode of existence into another', as painful as being born or dying. After a confession of his own in a conversation with Edwin, Jasper's 'breathing seems to have stopped'; spared de Quincey's pangs, he becomes 'a breathing man again without the smallest stage of transition between the two extreme states'. During their expedition, Durdles remarks that the resident ghosts tend to lie low because their emergence from hiding would lead to 'a mixing of things'. Yet he encourages Jasper to think about that intermediate state, and asks him whether there might be 'Ghosts of other things, though not of men and women?' Jasper scoffs at the notion by demanding 'What things? Flower-beds and watering-pots? Horses and harness?' When Durdles explains that he means echoes from the beyond, Jasper pretends that this refers to the cries of street traders, but his mockery does not answer the question about matter and spirit. Metaphors are also a mixing of things, and Dickens the animist finds ghosts in mangles and umbrellas, wardrobes and chandeliers.

An actual tomb raider hovers behind the character of Durdles. This is Giovanni Battista Belzoni, a barber's son who set himself up as an archaeologist after performing as a circus strongman at Astley's, where Kit goes to the play in *The Old Curiosity Shop*. Belzoni first travelled to Cairo in 1815 as an engineer, anticipating the plan Edwin Drood discloses to Rosa. His aim was to market a machine to raise the waters of the Nile for the benefit of local agriculture, which would have realised Edwin's ambition to 'wake Egypt up a little'; when that project fell through, he tried his luck as a grave robber and arduously extracted a monumental bust of Ramesses II from a temple at Thebes, then trundled it across the desert on rollers before shipping it to the British Museum. Rosa has heard of Belzoni's travails as he rooted around in the pyramids, from which she believes he was 'dragged out by the legs, half-choked with bats and dust', but Miss Twinkleton's tales of 'tiresome old burying-grounds' bore her, and she ridicules 'Isises, and Ibises, and Cheopses, and Pharaohses'. Dickens more astutely brought Belzoni home from the Valley of the Kings. Clennam in *Little Dorrit* passes a church with no congregation that looks as if it is waiting to be excavated by Belzoni, and in *Sketches by Boz* a stranger at Seven Dials in Covent Garden stands 'Belzoni-like, at the entrance of seven obscure passages', confronting a shady labyrinth like that which baffles and potentially ensnares intruders inside a pyramid. On Planet Dick there are several overlapping underworlds.

Mystery stretches into mysticism thanks to opium, which gave Baudelaire access to an artificial paradise and plunged de Quincey into an 'abyss of divine enjoyment': the cathedral and the East End den offer alternative versions of that supernatural realm, one tepid, the other intoxicating. Jasper tells Rosa that he pursued her through 'Paradises and Hells of visions', and although she recoils from him in disgust, she has her own girlishly sinful taste for Lumps-of-Delight, which as she explains to Edwin are 'a Turkish sweetmeat' – a candied version of the bliss that de Quincey absorbed from opium 'in a solid and liquid shape, both boiled and unboiled, both East India and Turkey'. Even the athletically healthy Canon Crisparkle directly cites one of de Quincey's intoxicated reveries. Fulminating against the philanthropist Honeythunder, Crisparkle says that his followers 'run amuck like so many mad Malays'. This outburst recalls the canon's time on 'the chief Pagan high roads' before he settled into his current 'Christian beat'; it also alludes to an unexpected visit that de Quincey receives in the *Confessions* from a tigerish Malay in a turban. The servant girl who opens the door takes him to be a demon, needing to be exorcised by her master's art. Instead De Quincey feeds him some opium, in return for which his guest 'fastened afterwards upon my dreams, and brought other Malays with him, worse than himself, that ran "a-muck" at me, and led me into a world of troubles'. In Crisparkle's outburst, those marauding savages convert to Christianity and go on making themselves 'an unendurable nuisance' as they proselytise.

Crisparkle's fussy mother has her own debt to the mystagoguery of de Quincey. Women are credited with 'a curious power of divining the characters of men', and this 'fair diviner' will not be dissuaded from her low opinion of Neville Landless, who quarrels with Edwin Drood and is suspected of killing him; she is also of course unaware that Neville's surname is Dickens's illicit nod to Ellen Ternan, whose middle name, derived from her father, was Lawless. Mrs Crisparkle lacks the divining rod that de Quincey calls a 'potent instrument', invested with a 'magical power of evocation' like a conjurer's wand, which may be why she misjudges Neville. De Quincey solemnly declared that 'To unveil or decipher what is hidden – that is, in effect, the meaning of divination', and for him it remained a divine practice, 'even if Mephistopheles should be at the bottom of the affair'. Dickens laughs at what he calls Mrs Crisparkle's inept 'divination', but the novel confirms de Quincey's principle and allows Mephistopheles to take part in the interpretative game.

The best comment on Cloisterham's manifold mysteries is uttered by Deputy, who when arrested frustrates the efforts of the police to 'put me down in the book'. He refuses to give his name, and when asked what his religion is, he pertly replies 'Find out.'

Returning to the riverside where he died and was reborn, Harmon in *Our Mutual Friend* is unsure which way he turned when he set off to resume life as someone else. He travels in a circle, finds himself back 'at the point from which he had begun', and reflects that this is what customarily happens 'in narratives of escape from prison': the track of 'the fugitives in the night always seems to take the shape of the great round world, on which they wander; as if it were a secret law.' Following that secret law, the final paragraphs Dickens added to *Edwin Drood* before his death travel in a grand circle that encloses many of the inescapable motives and motifs that had been with him from the beginning.

As morning sun irradiates the cathedral, sweetens its musty odour and warms the cold tombs, 'changes of glorious light . . . preach the Resurrection and the Life', reaffirming the same covenant that heartens Sydney Carton at the guillotine. A metaphor dispels the remaining darkness as Dickens describes 'flecks of brightness [that] dart into the sternest marble corners of the building, fluttering there like wings'. The sentence that starts with glorious light and ends with the resurrection dilates in the middle to encompass all of awakened nature: the glory shines 'from moving boughs, songs of birds, scents from gardens, woods, and fields – or, rather, from the one great garden of the whole cultivated island in its yielding time'. The reference to the cultivated island and its summer yield of crops belatedly acknowledges an aspect of the country's life that Dickens usually neglected. Fagin, told that Oliver Twist has spent seven days walking to London, asks where he came from. 'Greenland,' quips the Artful Dodger, jeering at the landscape through which Oliver has traipsed. Wordsworth in 'Lines Composed a Few Miles above Tintern Abbey' refers to 'this green earth' and 'this green pastoral landscape', emphasising the simple primacy of the primary colour, but for the Dodger the green world is raw, naive, laughably ingenuous. The unexpected agricultural panorama in *Edwin Drood* makes amends, but not for long.

Although the Sultan's hordes have been expelled from the cathedral, nothing that happens in it on this particular morning looks orthodox. The cleaners who prepare it for the day's first service are irreligiously classed as 'sprites', while the rooks that converge 'from various quarters of the sky' and gather in the tower outnumber the paltry congregation. Dickens surmises that the birds 'enjoy vibration, and . . . know that bell and organ are going to give it them': the Christian observances that bore Jasper are urgently intense for non-human creatures. Does religion, like music or opium, exist to deliver thrilling sensations? Because it is so early, people hover between night and day, dream and reason, unaware that they are in the entranced twilight where Dickens did his writing. Tope the custodian yawns, Crisparkle's 'ministering brethren' are not as fresh and bright as he is, and the choirboys, thanks to another metaphor, send the chronology into reverse. Dickens calls their surplices 'nightgowns', which they struggle into 'at the last moment, like children shirking bed'; then after the service they are as eager 'to get their bedgowns off, as they were but now to get them on'.

Two attendees are more alert. One is the enigmatic Datchery, a new arrival in Cloisterham who is conducting surveillance of Jasper. He is evidently in disguise, with an 'unusually thick and ample' head of white hair; both dramatist and actor, he casts himself as 'a single buffer, of an easy temper, living idly on his means', and goes on playing the role even when alone so that Dickens has no chance to unmask him. In the cathedral, he spies another furtive onlooker – the crone from the East End, who has followed Jasper to Cloisterham. Her malignant air causes Datchery to view her as the Evil One's emissary: she is as hard as the brass eagle on the lectern, whose ferocious glare and sharp beak suggest that it has been 'not at all converted' by the 'sacred books' it supports on its outstretched wings, and her withered ugliness resembles 'the fantastic carvings on the under brackets of the stall seats', hewn and hacked by fidgety monks – a last upsurgence of what the Mudfog expert calls 'carveativeness', which is one of Dickens's most fiendish skills.

In a brief final paragraph Datchery returns to his lodgings, where his landlady has laid the table for him. He pays for his meals on an honour system, adding 'uncouth chalked strokes' to the inside of a cupboard door to match what he has eaten. The total is pleasingly 'illegible except to the scorer', like the drugged mumblings in the opium den which Jasper declares to be 'Unintelligible!' Now he adds 'one thick line . . . extending from the top of the cupboard door to the bottom'. That may seem over-generous, considering that what he has before him is 'a very, neat clean breakfast', but the graphic mark does more than bring his account up to date; given its length and depth, it might be a line drawn under the mystery of Edwin's disappearance, which Datchery perhaps solves when he sees the hag shake both fists at Jasper as he sings a hymn. Shorthand taught Dickens that meaningful signs do not have to be explicitly verbal. Datchery accordingly takes care of the reckoning by cipher and then 'falls to with an appetite'.

With that expectant phrase, the novel ends. For Dickens, unaware that this was his final day of work, it would have been only a temporary interruption. *Edwin Drood* reaches no terminus, and instead an impromptu present tense invites us to accompany Datchery's repast. Dickens was a glutton for experience who, like Oliver Twist, always wanted more. He overcame his early deprivation by celebrating superfluity, as in the gormandising banquet piled up before the Ghost of Christmas Past, who has his choice of turkeys, geese, game, poultry, brawn, sucking-pigs, sausages and oysters, along with chestnuts, apples, oranges and pears, assorted pies, puddings, cakes and bowls of seething hot punch. But behind this voracious glee Dickens always had a wary consciousness of what he called 'the Shadowy World', towards which his phantasmagorical metaphors led him. Here our appetite is not satisfied, because Datchery knows something we do not, and so does Dickens.

Once, questioned by an admirer, Dickens declared his imagination to be an 'unfathomable mystery'. He was holding a wine glass at the time, and said that he could 'fancy it a man' and make it a character by endowing it with 'form and beauty'. Of course he could equally well have dashed the vitreous figure to the floor and shattered it. Visiting the Paris morgue, the Uncommercial Traveller studies the corpse of an old man felled in the street by a lump of stone as it tumbled from an unfinished building. The body carries no means of identification, which means that it is available to be revived, renamed, supplied with a history, then made to die all over again in a novel. The Traveller regards the accidental death as a missed opportunity, and on behalf of an inquisitive crowd he remarks that 'we could have wished he had been killed by human agency – his own, or somebody else's: the latter, preferable'. Dickens might have told a story that presented the random happening as an intentional act, inventing a crime to make the world look orderly; he could have personally committed the crime, as he did when finishing off Paul Dombey or Jo. But on this occasion he decides not to bother. The old man is left to harden into a waxwork, on display among cadavers which for the attendants are 'curiosities', like the antiques collected by Little Nell's grandfather.

With the same detachment, Dickens's birthday invitation in February 1844 describes his eponymous planet arising spontaneously on the horizon, as if it appeared there on its own initiative. He joined the rest of mankind to gaze at it in awe because he felt himself to be the conduit for a force that travelled through him, as irresistible as electricity and as incessant as his flow of words. A solution to the plot of *The Mystery of Edwin Drood* is relatively easy. The other mystery remains unfathomable, and Dickens died without having to solve it.

ACKNOWLEDGEMENTS

My first debt is to Charlotte Merritt, who has been an angel as well as an agent. She restored my confidence at an anxious time and coaxed me, sympathetically but with an acute editorial eye, to properly articulate my thoughts about Dickens. While doing so I was heartened by bulletins from her home, where Charlotte's husband David had begun to read *David Copperfield* to their young son: despite Dickens's own family history, he is everyone's patrimony. After looking over my shoulder as I wrote the proposal, Charlotte then guided it towards my publisher Tomasz Hoskins, who understood at once what I wanted to do. Tomasz's intellectual interests stretch far and wide, but he is a torch-bearer for literature, as I confirmed when we recently met for a drink at The White Horse Tavern in Greenwich Village: he chose the venue because Dylan Thomas, a hero to Tomasz's Welsh father, had been an all too frequent customer there in his final years.

Tomasz handed me on to Octavia Stocker, whom he introduced as 'my brilliant book editor'; she proved to be exactly that, training a very clear mind on my occasionally foggy thinking and showing me how to untie knots in the text. I felt as if I were back at Oxford as a student, eager to earn the approval of my tutor, which I hope I eventually did. It was then my good luck to collaborate again with Richard Mason, who after copy-editing four previous books of mine is an expert on my bad habits. As preparation, Richard undertook to re-read several Dickens novels, so we were able to share our delight in him as we fussed over minutiae. To Charlotte, Tomasz, Octavia and Richard, I am deeply grateful. Throughout the whole process, Sarah Jones expertly and very patiently guided my much-revised text into print.

Four friends made vital contributions along the way. I had an enlivening argument with Carmen Callil about Dickens, whom she saw not as a black magician but as an angry social conscience: she channelled his outrage in her last book *Oh Happy Day*, which takes its subtitle and some of its chapter titles from *Hard Times*, using Dickens's denunciation of the industrial Midlands to frame the early history of Carmen's own Australian family. Towards the end of his life, I asked Richard Hamer – my cherished colleague at Christ Church, Oxford for more than thirty years – to explain the droll transposition of consonants by cockneys like Sam Weller. Richard did so with his usual learned ingenuity and playful wit, even improvising some mock-Dickensian dialogue in which Sam, asked how to spell his surname, replies 'Wiv a wee'. At an early stage, a perceptive remark made in passing by Caroline Dawnay helped me to formulate the central idea of my book and to fix on Dickens as a dark enchanter; in return I prompted Caroline to read *The Pickwick Papers*, which surely counts as fair exchange. As well as showing me her father's copy of *Sam Weller's Pickwick Jest-Book*, Belinda Taylor, quietly acting on instinct, undertook a confidential mission that had better remain our secret, and in doing so she salvaged this project.

The collected edition of Dickens with which I began my re-reading belongs to Jorge Calado, who acquired the set as an Anglophile trophy on a visit to Tunbridge Wells long ago. When society shut down in 2020, that long shelf of books and Jorge himself were all the company I needed for the duration.

SELECT BIBLIOGRAPHY

Sketches by Boz 1836–7
The Posthumous Papers of the Pickwick Club 1836–7
The Mudfog Papers 1837–8
Oliver Twist, or the Parish Boy's Progress 1837–9
The Life and Adventures of Nicholas Nickleby 1838–9
Master Humphrey's Clock 1840–1
The Old Curiosity Shop 1840–1
Barnaby Rudge: A Tale of the Riots of 'Eighty 1840–1
American Notes for General Circulation 1842
A Christmas Carol in Prose 1843
The Life and Adventures of Martin Chuzzlewit 1843–4
*The Chimes: A Goblin Story of Some Bells that Rang an Old Year Out and a
     New Year In* 1844
The Cricket on the Hearth: A Fairy Tale of Home 1845
Pictures from Italy 1846
The Battle of Life: A Love Story 1846
*Dealings with the Firm of Dombey and Son, Wholesale, Retail and for
     Exportation* 1846–8
The Life of Our Lord 1846–9
The Haunted Man and the Ghost's Bargain 1848
*The Personal History, Adventures, Experience & Observation of David
     Copperfield The Younger Of Blunderstone Rookery* 1849–50
Bleak House 1852–3
A Child's History of England 1852–4
Hard Times: For These Times 1854
Little Dorrit 1855–7
A Tale of Two Cities 1859
Great Expectations 1860–1

The Uncommercial Traveller 1860–1
Our Mutual Friend 1864–5
The Mystery of Edwin Drood 1870

Selected Journalism 1850–1870 edited by David Pascoe
The Selected Letters of Charles Dickens edited by Jenny Hartley

John Forster *The Life of Charles Dickens* 1872–4

INDEX